The
Heart of the
Declaration

THE LEWIS WALPOLE SERIES IN
EIGHTEENTH-CENTURY CULTURE AND HISTORY

The Lewis Walpole Series, published by Yale University Press with the aid of the Annie Burr Lewis Fund, is dedicated to the culture and history of the long eighteenth century (from the Glorious Revolution to the accession of Queen Victoria). It welcomes work in a variety of fields, including literature and history, the visual arts, political philosophy, music, legal history, and the history of science. In addition to original scholarly work, the series publishes new editions and translations of writing from the period, as well as reprints of major books that are currently unavailable. Though the majority of books in the series will probably concentrate on Great Britain and the Continent, the range of our geographical interests is as wide as Horace Walpole's.

The
Heart of the
Declaration

*The Founders' Case for
an Activist Government*

STEVE PINCUS

Yale UNIVERSITY PRESS
New Haven and London

Published with assistance from the Annie Burr Lewis Fund.
Published with assistance from the Kingsley Trust Association
Publication Fund established by the Scroll and Key Society of Yale
College.
Published with assistance from the foundation established in
memory of Amasa Stone Mather of the Class of 1907, Yale College.

Yale University Press books may be purchased in quantity for
educational, business, or promotional use. For information, please
e-mail sales.press@yale.edu (U.S. office) or sales@yaleup.co.uk
(U.K. office).

Set in Minion type by IDS Infotech, Ltd.
Printed in the United States of America.

Library of Congress Control Number: 2016932676
ISBN 978-0-300-21618-9 (hardcover : alk. paper)

A catalogue record for this book is available from the British
Library.

This paper meets the requirements of ANSI/NISO Z39.48-1992
(Permanence of Paper).

10 9 8 7 6 5 4 3 2 1

Contents

Acknowledgments

This book, more than most, is a coterie production. It is the result of many years of discussions with Yale and Chicago undergraduate and graduate students, innumerable conversations with friends and colleagues, and many a family dinner. While I put the ideas on paper, many people were responsible for the interesting thoughts that are in this book. The boring ones are all my own.

I would like to thank the many people who have discussed these issues, read draft chapters, or simply stimulated me to rethink assumptions and correct mistakes. This book took shape, by accident, very quickly. The initial stimulus came from an invitation by Doug Bradburn, founding director of the Fred W. Smith National Library for the Study of George Washington, to present a public lecture on the British influences on George Washington. This book is the working out of the ideas I presented boldly at Mount Vernon. I benefited much from the criticism I received at that event. At the same time, I held fellowships from the John Simon Guggenheim Memorial Foundation and from the Dorothy and Lewis B. Cullman Center for Scholars and Writers. It was in the latter remarkable setting that

I conducted most of the research for this project and also had the privilege of testing my ideas formally and informally with a fantastic group of journalists, novelists, and academics. To all of them, and especially to the director Jean Strouse, I am more grateful than they could possibly know.

Chris Rogers at Yale University Press and Wendy Strothman both played key roles in persuading me that this was a project worth pursuing.

I have benefited from discussions with many, many scholars in the past several years. I had the opportunity to present some of my ideas in seminars, lectures, and workshops at the American Historical Association, New York University, Binghamton University, Cambridge University, Dundee University, the Huntington Library, the Institute of Historical Research in London, the London School of Economics, the McNeil Center at the University of Pennsylvania, NYU Law School, Ohio State University, Rutgers University, the University of Texas at Arlington, and the Center for Historical Enquiry and the Social Sciences at Yale. At each of these events I received suggestions and criticism that made me rethink or recalibrate the claims advanced here.

I am especially grateful to those who read draft chapters and offered pointed criticism. David Blight, John Brooke, Christian Burset, Alejandra Dubcovsky, Joanne Freeman, Bruce Gordon, Don Herzog, Alan Houston, Dan Hulsebosch, Jim Livesey, Peter Mancall, Paul Mapp, Renaud Morieux, Isaac Nakhimovsky, Bill Novak, Jim Oakes, Claire Priest, Ed Rugemer, and Mark Somos all provided comments that, I hope, made the manuscript better. Chris Rogers, Alyssa Reichardt, and Justin du Rivage read every word several times over and offered suggestions that often transformed chapters. Catherine Arnold provided a thorough and vital final reading of the prose. My wife read every turgid word and made suggestions to make the prose less so. To them I am exceedingly grateful. Conversations with John Brewer, Don Herzog, Jim Livesey, Frank Trentmann, and James Vaughn all helped shape my thinking in fundamental ways.

While he never read a word of this book manuscript, my graduate supervisor, Wallace MacCaffrey, shaped this book in important ways. His gentle and persistent prodding to ask big questions was always in the back of my mind. His humane and sympathetic guidance will always serve as a model. He is missed.

My greatest thanks goes to my family. They put up with many archival forays and trips to Charleston, London, and Paris, among many other places. They also cheered me up when some of the intellectual puzzles seemed too difficult to crack. David, now eleven, kept pointing out things about my story that I did not know. Andy persistently and usefully asked when the book would be done. Our newest family member, Avalanche, kept up my spirits in the race to the finish line. My greatest debt is owed to Sue, who was vital in too many ways to count.

The
Heart of the
Declaration

Introduction

On July 9, 1776, George Washington read to his troops, assembled in what is now the Washington Heights section of Manhattan, a document that would radically alter the course of history. Washington had received a copy of the freshly drafted Declaration of Independence from John Hancock, the president of the Continental Congress, while nervously preparing to defend New York City against General William Howe's redcoats, who had disembarked on Staten Island. The Declaration that Washington received was a remarkable and sophisticated promise to create a modern state. More than two centuries later, this document is still read annually at Fourth of July celebrations and reprinted in local newspapers. Throughout the subsequent centuries, mayors, members of Congress, political pundits, and presidential candidates from every political party continue to cite and refer to it. This is not surprising: the Declaration was a modern document, and the problems America's Founders grappled with remain of vital consequence today.

The political crisis that ultimately led a set of Americans to separate themselves from the British Empire was the product of the alarming growth of Britain's national debt during the Seven Years' War (1757–63), a massive and expensive global conflict that was fought in theaters from the Ohio Valley to Bengal, continental Europe, Africa, and the West Indies. In its aftermath one group of politicians, led by Britain's Prime Minister George Grenville, tried to pay down the debt with cost-saving austerity measures and by compelling Britain's colonies to pay a share of the burgeoning British tax burden. Grenville's political opponents, self-proclaimed members of the Patriot Party on both sides of the Atlantic, argued instead that the best way to reduce the debt was to encourage economic development in all of the colonies. Experience had taught them that consumption of British manufactured goods in the colonies kept the imperial economy growing at a rapid pace. North American consumers were understood by Patriots to be the most dynamic piece of Britain's now global economy.

Politicians, pundits, and political essayists on both sides of the Atlantic debated how best to respond to the debt crisis. Government debt was *the* most widely discussed and hotly debated political issue of the 1760s and 1770s, just as it had been throughout the eighteenth century in Europe. In the British Empire since the 1730s, this debate had focused on issues that still engage us today: the economic effects of immigration; the political, economic, and legal status of the African diaspora; and the best ways for the government to support economic growth. My contention, then, is that the Declaration of Independence is—and should remain—"American Scripture" precisely because its authors were the first to seek to address these quintessential issues of the modern era.[1]

As soon as he received the newly penned and freshly printed Declaration of Independence from Hancock, Washington had it "proclaimed before all the army under my immediate command" and was pleased to report that "the measure had their most hearty assent." His troops were enthusiastic, Washington implied, because the Declaration promised to "secure us that freedom and those privileges which have been and are refused us, contrary to the voice of nature and the British constitution."[2] To contemporary readers this seems a shocking, almost heretical admission. Washington was commanding American troops in a war against British troops in order to defend the *British* constitution. How could this be? What did Washington mean by giving voice to this paradox?

The American commander in chief was a sophisticated, though not necessarily original, reader of the Declaration. Washington, like many Patriots in Britain, North America, and the West Indies, was in fact fighting on behalf of the Patriot interpretation of the British constitution. The Patriots believed that the constitution had been debased by a series of inept and possibly corrupt British politicians ever since King George III's accession to the throne in October 1760. For Washington and his contemporaries, the British "constitution" was a capacious term. It did not mean a written document with formal legal standing. Instead, Washington referred to what he took to be the British way of governing, grounded in the principles set forth in England's Revolution of 1688–89. By constitution, then, Washington and his contemporaries referred to a government's policies and the institutions that supported them, rather than a formal set of written laws. The great British statesman Edmund Burke referred to the British method of regulating colonial commerce in exchange for capital to support colonial development as "the inevitable constitution" of America. In a text that was "continually in the hands of the members of our congress," the Swiss republican theorist Emmerich de Vattel insisted that a "constitution is in fact nothing more, than the establishment of the order in which a nation proposes to labor in common" to promote the general welfare. The British method of governing asserted not only the primacy of the rule of law. It also entailed a commitment to government support for economic development, development that would benefit the widest possible range of English or—after the Anglo-Scottish Union of 1707—British subjects. It was this dual commitment to rights and governmental activism to which Washington referred when he evoked "that freedom *and* those privileges" granted by the British constitution. Washington, like countless fellow Patriots, believed that before 1760 the British imperial state had not been a malevolent force or even a necessary evil. In July 1774 the Fairfax County Committee, chaired by George Washington, declared that "the experience of more than a century" proved the "utility" of the British imperial constitution, resulting in the "mutual and uninterrupted harmony and goodwill between the inhabitants of Great Britain and her colonies." In that "long" pre-1760 period, Britons on both sides of the Atlantic "considered themselves as one and the same people."[3] In the view of the Patriots like Washington, the post-1688 British state, though imperfect in many ways, had been a uniquely benevolent force throughout the British Empire.

George Washington's understanding of America's founding document as a call for an energetic government stands in stark contrast with the majority of interpretations of the Declaration. Whereas Washington complained that the British imperial state since 1760 had done too little to promote the welfare and happiness of colonial North Americans, twentieth- and twenty-first-century commentators criticize the British for having done too much. Whereas scholars, pundits, and politicians now agree on little else about the American Revolution, most concur that the authors of the Declaration celebrated limited government. One leading progressive historian, for example, interpreted America's Declaration as the manifesto of "a revolt against the centralized coercive power of Great Britain and the colonial aristocracy." The political philosopher Hannah Arendt, who understood more than most that the American Revolution was itself a successful project of state formation, also read the Declaration as a document that fundamentally "abolished the authority and power of crown and Parliament." In contrast to the French Revolution, she believed, social questions rarely arose in America's founding. The authors of the Declaration were committed to a concept of negative liberty, according to one leading legal scholar, by which they meant "freedom from a number of social and political evils, including arbitrary government power." America's Founders, chimes in one leading historian of the American Revolution, especially those who penned the Declaration, "tended to see society as beneficial and government as malevolent." Another eminent historian agrees in this regard: the American revolutionaries drew on a legal tradition that was committed to "limited government." The Declaration, insists yet another scholar, "gives voice to a political philosophy of extremely limited government." The Declaration put into words a long-held commitment by British Americans to independence, agrees another expert in early American history, because they "cast a suspicious eye on even their own colonial governments, which many of them considered remote and unrepresentative."[4] Countless commentators and politicians have drawn on this scholarly tradition in their insistence that the Declaration of Independence enshrined the American commitment to small government.

In fact, Washington understood the meaning of America's founding document far better than we do today. He was immersed in the culture of Anglo-American political argument in which the Framers of the Declaration also participated.[5] What, then, was the nature of this political discussion? What were the contours of the imperial state that George Washington and his fellow North Americans celebrated in the 1770s? Only by answering these questions will it be possible to comprehend fully the document the North American Patriots drafted in June and July 1776. Only by understanding what the Patriots understood to have been the benefits of the imperial government that was replaced in 1760s will it be possible to comprehend the kind of state they hoped to construct in and after 1776. Interpreting America's founding document requires understanding the policies pursued by the eighteenth-century British imperial government.

For more than a century politicians, pamphleteers, and political essayists had wrestled with the consequences of the fundamentally new kind of state created by Britain's revolutionaries of 1688–89. England's revolution had created a different sort of government: a powerful one capable of defeating the world's greatest power (France) in a series of wars fought on an increasingly global scale; but a state that was at the same time responsive to the needs and desires of its subjects. Britain's revolutionaries of 1688–89, uniquely in Europe in the seventeenth and eighteenth centuries, had created an energetic *and* participatory state.[6]

    Britons could create a new kind of imperial state in the seventeenth and eighteenth centuries because they lived in a quickly changing commercial society. English society was radically transformed over the course of the seventeenth century. At a time when most of Europe was suffering through a long and sustained recession, England became more economically diverse, more committed to manufacturing, and more urban. By 1700, the manufacturing and commercial sectors of England were responsible for fully one third of the national product. The English developed new manufactures throughout the length and breadth of the country, including new lighter cloths, metalware, ceramics, and shipbuilding. All of these new industries immediately catered not only to domestic markets but also to a new and growing set of colonial consumers. In many ways, as recent work by economists has shown, burgeoning Atlantic markets helped to drive England's economic transformation. New industries gave rise to new towns. Manchester, Halifax, and Leeds quickly became important centers for the production of the lighter cloths. Sheffield, Birmingham, and other towns in the Midlands produced metalwares. Shipbuilding was centered in London, Portsmouth, and Harwich. Liverpool emerged alongside Bristol and Whitehaven as a great port for Atlantic trading. Not only did the English economy grow and diversify; it also became more refined. Thatched villages were replaced with ones filled with brick houses and glass windows. More and more towns and cities paved their streets. Towns now had new amenities like lending libraries, coffeehouses, and a variety of shops. At the same time, newer and better roads and turnpikes, stagecoaches, and postal services connected towns and villages in new and denser networks. By the late seventeenth century England had properly become a trading nation.[7]

British North Americans in the eighteenth century understood the commercial issues facing the British imperial polity because they, too, lived in a commercial society. In the eighteenth century, British North America was similarly and quickly becoming a commercial society. As for Britain in the seventeenth and eighteenth centuries, foreign trade drove economic growth in the British North American economy. That trade, however, generated growth that was twice as fast as in Britain itself. Wages were well known to be higher throughout North America than they were in Britain at the same time. All of this was particularly true after 1745. While British North America remained primarily agricultural in the eighteenth century, agricultural production was increasingly geared toward producing goods consumed outside the household. British North America was emphatically a commercial society. South Carolinians sold slave-produced rice—Carolina gold—to West Indian and European markets for massive profits. From the 1740s the combination of British bounties and declining market prices for rice drove many Carolinians to produce indigo for export as well. Landowners in Maryland, Virginia, and North Carolina had their slaves harvesting tobacco for European markets for much of the eighteenth century. Though there, too, market pressures led farmers, including George Washington himself, to diversify their crops, generating the "wheat boom" of the middle of the eighteenth century.[8] New Englanders produced grains and a variety of animal meats for the market.

What was even more remarkable than colonial production was the massive growth in colonial consumption of British manufactured goods. By the middle of the eighteenth century there was, in the view of Benjamin Franklin, "a vast demand" for British manufactured goods—furniture, cloth, metals of all sorts—that was so great and increasing so quickly that it would in the foreseeable future outstrip even Britain's prodigious capacity to supply the North American colonies.[9] In fact, exports from Britain to North America more than quintupled between 1720 and 1770. North America, especially the mainland colonies, had become in this period Britain's most important trading partner. All of this production and consumption, of course, necessitated the presence of merchants who became an increasingly prominent element in North American society. Just as in England in the seventeenth century, burgeoning trade made it possible for North American towns—Boston, Philadelphia, New York, Charleston—to become increasingly refined places in the eighteenth century. Libraries, theaters, racecourses, clubs and associations, coffeehouses, and shops abounded.

North America's spectacular economic dynamism generated commensurately remarkable population growth. Benjamin Franklin estimated in 1751 that "our people must at least be doubled every twenty-five years." The Newport minister Ezra Stiles confirmed Franklin's theory with reams of surveys, while Edward Wigglesworth of Harvard concurred based on statistical calculations. More threateningly, Franklin concluded that within a century "the greatest number of Englishmen will be on this side the water." Modern calculations confirm British America's spectacular growth rate. While it was still dwarfed by the population of Spanish America on the eve of the revolution, the British American population was growing faster both through natural increase and through higher rates of immigration. British North America was by the 1770s a diverse, dynamic, and complex society. Just as in Britain there was significant regional variation. But from New England to Georgia the vast majority of British North Americans were part of a modern and increasingly global commercial economy.[10]

Britain and its empire, of which British North America was a part, were connected after the Revolution of 1688–89 by an increasingly active and powerful imperial government.[11] England's economic growth had made possible, though not at all inevitable, the creation of a powerful state. Whig politicians had long been agitating for a state based on different economic principles from the ones adopted by the Restoration monarchs Charles II and James II. Whereas Charles II, James II, and their

Tory supporters had believed that land was the basis of property, Whigs, including their great ideologist, John Locke, argued that human labor created wealth. The Whigs, like many in modern America and Europe, therefore believed that the government should promote the manufacturing sector, where human labor could add value to raw materials by producing cloth, metalwares, or ceramics. The Tories, for their part, sought to relieve tax burdens from the landed sector. It was only in the wake of the Revolution of 1688–89 that Whig politicians found it possible to create a state that could simultaneously help finance war against the world's greatest power, France, and help stimulate the development of the manufacturing sector. The post-revolutionary regime created the Bank of England (1694) to lend money both to the government and to the manufacturing sector, the board of trade (1696) to coordinate commercial and imperial policy, and an expanding bureaucracy to collect taxes efficiently and fairly.

As a consequence of the revolution itself and the expanding capacities of the government, Parliament and British society at large began to devote an increasing amount of time and energy to discussing social, economic, and imperial issues. Indeed, imperial issues that reached Parliament often generated the most controversy, the hottest debates, and the most press commentary precisely because so much money was at stake. While Parliament, like many modern states, expended more money on the military than on any other item, the British state in the eighteenth century was far more than a military machine. "The period since the Revolution [of 1688–89] is distinguished by principles of a very different nature," the Scottish political economist Sir John Sinclair said of the British state at the end of the eighteenth century. "The State has assumed the appearance of a great corporation: it extends its views beyond the immediate events, and pressing exigencies of the moment. . . . It borrows money to cultivate, defend, or to acquire distant possessions, in hopes that it will be amply repaid by the advantages they may be brought to yield. . . . In short it proposes to itself a plan of perpetual accumulation and aggrandizement, which according as it is well or ill conducted, must either end in the possession of an extensive and powerful empire, or in total ruin." Analysis of the British treasury reports reveals that the British state was able, at the same time that it erected a powerful military, to spend significantly and consistently on economic development. This set the British state apart from its European rivals. One historian of the British state of the eighteenth century found that in Britain "current military expenditure accounted for between 61 per cent and 74 per cent of public spending during the major wars of the period." This "outlay," though large, this scholar concludes, "probably represents a much smaller percentage of national resources than in many other states." Indeed, no other European state spent less than 80 percent of its revenue on the military, and most spent a far higher percentage than that.[12] The British Parliament, it turns out, spent far more heavily than the nation's European rivals in the eighteenth century on developing social and economic infrastructure in its colonies, and in Scotland and Ireland. The British in the eighteenth century were unique in their commitment to energetic government.

All of this parliamentary expenditure after the Revolution of 1688–89 generated a great deal of political discussion in society at large. Beginning around 1680, British publishers produced a dizzying array of pamphlets, essays, and position papers discussing and debating the best way to improve Britain's economy. It was "about the year 1680," recalled Daniel Defoe—who was a successful journalist and political pamphleteer long before he became a novelist—that "began the art and mystery of projecting to creep into the world." "The projecting age," as Defoe called it, generated a widespread public discussion of schemes "of public advantage, as they tend to the improvement of trade, the employment of the poor, and the circulation and increase of the public stock of the kingdom." One of England's most successful early financial journalists, John Houghton, concurred in 1680 that "trade is a subject that hath not only taken up the thoughts and time of private men, but also of late years especially hath been one of the main concerns of the greatest princes." "Trade and negotiation has infected the whole kingdom," concluded one memorandum that circulated at King James II's court in 1685; "by this means the very genius of the people is altered."[13] After the Revolution of 1688–89, this newly important discussion of political economy exploded, permeating sermons, infiltrating all of the newspapers, and dominating discussions both in the fashionable coffeehouses and in the increasingly significant House of Commons.

Party political dispute in late-seventeenth- and eighteenth-century Britain, not unlike party politics today, was as much about political economy as it was about religion and political rights. Thousands of Britons now had access to political economic information. Daniel Defoe's *Review* and Charles Povey's *General Remark on Trade* reached thousands of readers each in the first decade of the eighteenth century. Their circulation numbers were almost certainly dwarfed by the wildly popular competitors the *Mercator*—a joint production of the Tory Charles Davenant and the Whig Defoe—and Henry Martin's *British Merchant*. Joseph Addison estimated that he and his *Spectator*, a journal that included sophisticated discussions of political economy among the various topics it covered, had "three score thousand disciples in London and Westminster" alone.

Charles Davenant thought his numerous tracts on political economy were "an entertainment for the country gentlemen, for whose service they were written." The young James Brydges, a future government specialist on finance, held discussions about trade and the East Indies in London chocolate houses. At Lambeth Palace, with Thomas Tenison, the archbishop of Canterbury, he chatted about "the plantations and new discoveries that might be made."[14]

Given the intensity of party conflict, it was hardly surprising that debates over political economy and empire were quickly politicized. Economic issues in the seventeenth- and eighteenth-century British Empire, much like these same issues in the twenty-first century, generated intense partisan disputes. There was no agreement on supposed mercantilist principles. Fierce debates in quick succession in the later 1690s over the creation of the board of trade, the Scottish scheme to establish a colony at Darien in the West Indies, the renewal of the East India Company charter, and ultimately over whether to go to war to prevent the French from taking over the wealth of Spanish America helped to map imperial issues onto party politics. "As of late many controversies have arisen in the English nation," observed a Virginian in 1701, "so 'tis observable that the two great topics of trade and plantations have had their parts in the dispute." Trade to the Indies, the value of joint-stock companies, and the national economic interest have "become the general subject of conversation; every man with the greatest freedom, bestows his censure upon these things," thought the economic writer and economic guru for the Patriots Henry Martin. Addison was convinced that the dispute over whether Britain could make peace without the Spanish West Indies "has fixed all men in their proper parties."[15]

The Revolution of 1688–89 had indeed transformed the nature of politics in Britain. Parliament, which had previously been summoned at the whim of the monarch, now became a regular institution that met every year. Before 1688 Parliaments had passed very little legislation. After the Revolution, Parliament devoted much more time to discussing, passing, and rejecting legislation—the vast majority of it dealing with social and economic issues. Unsurprisingly, the rapid expansion of the volume and importance of parliamentary activity provided ample opportunity for regular and sustained partisan debate. "The heats and animosities grow everyday higher in England," the imperial and martial administrator William Blathwayt wrote in the early eighteenth century: "parties very much animated against one another." The British were "a nation so divided into parties," wrote the politically enigmatic former paymaster of the queen's forces James Brydges in 1714, "that no one is allowed any good quality by the opposite side." Party divisions cut deeply into British society. Party politics was not a game played only by a rarefied metropolitan elite. "A country fellow distinguishes himself as much in the church-yard, as a citizen does upon the 'change,'" noted Joseph Addison in the *Spectator*. "If an Englishman considers the great ferment into which our political world is thrown at present, and how intensely it is heated in all its parts," the influential journalist suggested in 1711, "he cannot suppose it will cool again in less than three hundred years." These divisions were so profound, so ubiquitous, that Addison worried that in them he could "discover the seeds of a civil war."[16]

The British establishment Whig politician Sir Robert Walpole (1676–1745) was able to create single-party rule in Parliament in the 1720s and 1730s, but he was not able to end partisan debate. Indeed, from the 1720s political economy and imperial issues became the central arena of ideological contestation. "We have lately had none of these party divisions amongst us with which this nation used formerly to be per-plexed," observed Daniel Finch, 8th earl of Winchilsea, in the late 1730s, "nothing like a division has for many years appeared amongst us *but* what was occasioned by some ministerial measure which was thought ruinous to trade or inconsistent with the honor of the nation." Winchilsea knew whereof he spoke. The issues that divided Britons in the 1720s and 1730s, the issues that dominated the press, were no longer primarily about religion or the royal prerogative, as they had been in the seventeenth century, but about commerce and taxation. In that sense they were remarkably modern debates. Parliament and the British press constantly debated the size of the national debt and rate of economic growth. Questions of the Irish and colonial monetary supply, the rate and means to tax Scotland, whether or not to tax the English directly through land taxes on the rich or indirectly by means of excise (or sales) taxes on the poor and middle classes excited the most bitter partisan squabbles. Increasingly these debates pitted establishment Whigs—followers of Prime Minister Walpole—against their self-described Patriot opponents. Walpole believed that the best means to promote British prosperity was to free wealthy *English* landowners from the crushing burden of property taxes. His Patriot opponents, by contrast, sought to promote prosperity through state investment in the most dynamic elements of the economy, the manufacturing sector in Britain and the overseas colonies. In the later 1730s the two most popular newspapers, *Common Sense* and *The Craftsman,* were run by prominent Patriot politicians and regularly serialized in the new weekly news magazines, the *London Magazine* and the *Gentleman's Magazine.* While the intensity of partisan conflict in eighteenth-century Britain ebbed and flowed, it never came to an end. Beginning with the accession of George III in 1760, party animosities reached new

levels of intensity. John Wilkes, himself one of the most ideologically committed Patriot politicians, observed rather uncontroversially in 1775 that "party rage unhappily divides us."[17]

The Whig Party, the self-described party of the Revolution
of 1688, had divided into competing groupings in the 1720s and
1730s. Establishment Whigs, or supporters of Walpole, found
themselves facing off against Patriot Whigs on the floor of the
House of Commons, in company committee rooms, in Britain's
increasingly ubiquitous coffeehouses, in the partisan press, and
throughout the empire. Ideological differences distinguished
the Patriots from their establishment Whig opponents. Just as
in the modern United States, and in most advanced industrial
democracies, these parties involved networks of individuals
who shared many but not all of the same beliefs. Just as in today's
politics, there were individuals who embraced large parts of the
Patriot political platform but dissented from other parts. Nevertheless eighteenth-century commentators easily perceived the
coherence and political importance of these groupings inside
Parliament and out of doors, in the towns and in the country-
side, and in England and throughout the colonies.[18]

These British partisan debates about political economy
had a profound impact on the North American political
imagination. British debates about economic matters quickly
became British American talking points in coffeehouses, taverns,
and town meetings. At the same period that the provincial press
emerged in England, Scotland, and Ireland—in the 1720s—a
robust colonial press emerged in North America and the West
Indies. And just as in the British Isles, the new journalists in
North America took their cues, and many of their articles, from
the wildly popular Patriot newspapers. Beginning in the early
eighteenth century, North American newspapers made available
the best essays from the radical Whig and Patriot newspapers,

from Joseph Addison's *Spectator* to John Trenchard and Thomas Gordon's *Cato's Letters,* to *Common Sense* and *The Craftsman* in the 1730s and 1740s; from *The Monitor* and *The North Britain* to the *London Evening Post* in the 1750s, 1760s, and 1770s. Many North Americans eagerly bought, collected, and bound their own copies of the essay magazines. Already by the 1730s, Americans as diverse as the Virginia planter William Byrd and Abigail Franks, a member of a New York Jewish merchant family, made sure they were kept up to date with the latest and most fashionable Patriot publications.[19] While the American press in the 1760s and 1770s increasingly published local news and political essays written in North America, these additions supplemented rather than displaced British news and British political commentary. So, even as tensions between the British government and the North American colonies accelerated in the 1760s and 1770s, newspaper readers from Savannah to Boston were kept abreast of the latest developments in the imperial Parliament, in London politics, and in social and economic discontent in the British Midlands. North American colonists were eager participants in a British imperial political culture. British Americans happily spent their hard-earned money purchasing journals detailing "metropolitan" political debates because they knew them to be their own.

Colonial Americans overwhelmingly read and collected the partisan publications of the British Patriot opposition. Almost half a century ago scholars called attention to the significance of British "opposition thought" of the seventeenth and eighteenth centuries that was "devoured by the colonists." That contribution above all highlighted the importance of "English radical whigs" and deployed "the social scientists' concept of ideology." While these scholars emphasized the "political" aspects of the radical or Patriot Whig program, and their

indebtedness to the seventeenth-century writings of John
Milton, Algernon Sidney, and James Harrington, among others,
we now know that in the century-plus spanning the execution
of Charles I (1649) and the accession of George III (1760), the
Patriots developed a sophisticated political economic and imperial ideology as well. Patriot Whigs not only looked backward
to the great English struggles of the seventeenth century, they
looked forward to the new problems generated by the emergence
of powerful states. It is no longer possible to assert, as some
scholars have, that "opposition poets and polemicists alike . . .
set classical models and morality against the spreading commercialization" of imperial society.[20] Radical or Patriot Whigs
on both sides of the Atlantic embraced commercial society, the
Bank of England, the manufacturing sector, and well-designed
trading companies. Patriot essayists, poets, and politicians celebrated the imperial state, not only because it protected British
liberties but also because its actions promoted British happiness.

By suggesting that political economic thinking mattered,
and mattered decisively, in the coming of the American Revolution, I am not calling for a revival of the economically deter-
minist arguments made popular by the progressive-era historian
Charles Beard. Beard's early-twentieth-century determinism
rested on the conflict between "the interests of real and personal
property"—between the vast majority of North Americans who
held property in land and the powerful minority whose wealth
was based in money and manufacturing.[21] While not denying
that social and economic differences mattered, the case I am
advancing rests on *ideological* differences that defined
partisanship on both sides of the Atlantic. By "ideology" I mean
a worldview shared by broad swaths of people from all social
classes. Ideologies were shaped, not determined, by social and
economic realities. These ideologies were prisms through which

people understood new information about government activities, economic performance, and foreign affairs. Ideological
convictions led different groups of people to interpret the same
piece of information in radically different ways. In the same
way, twenty-first-century Americans might, depending on their
ideological convictions, understand the soaring cost of medical
care either as the result of insufficient government involvement
in the health care sector or as the consequence of too much
government regulation.

North American Patriots responded to the critical events
of the 1760s and 1770s from a particular ideological standpoint.
The authors of the Declaration defended a government devoted to promoting economic growth; they believed in the
possibility of limitless prosperity achieved through the creative
interplay of production and consumption. Government, they
were convinced, needed to support the numerical increase and
the buying power of consumers to guarantee future prosperity.
Their opponents in the British ministry and elsewhere argued
instead that production was all that was important. They were
therefore happy to tax colonists, constrain their trade, and
limit migration in the belief that taxing colonial production
and limiting expenditures on the colonies were the best means
to pay down the national debt. These were conflicting interpretations of economics, to be sure. But these were above all ideologies, belief patterns that may well have been influenced by
economic interests but were by no means determined by them.
Just as relatively less affluent voters in the American South today
often vote for Republican candidates for ideological rather than
narrowly economically self-interested reasons, and relatively
more affluent voters in the Northeast of the United States tend
to return Democratic candidates, so North Americans and
Britons developed their political preferences through a complex

matrix involving cultural and economic reasoning.[22] Ideas mattered decisively. And many of the most important and hotly contested ideas in the eighteenth-century Anglo-American political world were about how the economy functioned and what the proper role of the state was in making the economy.

Patriots, from all social classes, on both sides of the Atlantic, shared a commitment to a common set of economic principles. They believed that Patriot Whig politicians, pursuing their political economic commitments, had transformed Britain into Europe's most powerful and prosperous polity. Patriots believed that it was Britain's willingness to borrow money and invest in the manufacturing sector and colonial infrastructure that resulted in the duke of Marlborough's great victories in the War of Spanish Succession (1701–13). Four decades later they credited the government activism of William Pitt's Patriot ministry with the great victories of 1759 in the Seven Years' War (also known as the French and Indian War), which seemed to bring with them the prospect of unending prosperity. They believed that a British imperial state organized along Patriot lines—that is, an energetic government committed to supporting both producers and consumers—could help generate virtually limitless growth.

The vast majority of British North Americans well into the 1770s believed that the British government under Patriot leadership had promoted both liberty and prosperity throughout the Empire. They understood themselves to be British Americans sharing interests, culture, and tastes with their brethren in the British Isles. "We have every influence of interest and affection to attach us to one another, and make us wish to preserve the union indissoluble," observed the Virginian Patriot Arthur Lee in 1775 of the relationship between Britons and British North Americans. "The same laws, the same religion, the same constitution, the same feelings, sentiments and habits, are a common blessing and a common cause." Lee's views on this if on little else followed those of the New York lawyer and moderate member of the Continental Congress, James Duane, who also highlighted "the ties of friendship and common interest, the similarity of our government, laws, and manners," that united Britain and British North America. In 1775, the Newport minister and future president of Yale College, Ezra Stiles, shared Lee's commitment to the British Empire. "It is my most ardent prayer to the Most High," he wrote to the British Patriot historian Catherine Macaulay, "that the union between Great Britain and these colonies may never be dissolved: and that we may always boast and glory in having Great Britain the head of the whole British Empire." The American historian Mercy Otis Warren, a sister of one revolutionary and the wife of another, hoped to see "the beautiful fabric" of the British constitution "repaired and reestablished on so firm a basis that it will not be in the power of the venal and narrow hearted on either side of the Atlantic again to break down its barriers and threaten its total dissolution." "It is the ardent wish of the warmest advocates of liberty," agreed the Virginian George Washington in 1774, "that peace and tranquility upon constitutional grounds may be restored" between Britain and America. "I am sure," reflected the Pennsylvania member of Congress Robert Morris, "that America in general never set out with any view or desire of establishing an independent Empire." This cultural and ideological affinity convinced the Pennsylvania Patriot Benjamin Rush, who had himself studied medicine in Edinburgh, that "not one man in a thousand contemplated or wished for independence of our country in 1774."[23]

Why, then, did British Americans feel compelled to declare independence in July 1776? Why did George Washington believe that he could defend the liberties and privileges guaranteed by the British constitution only by taking up arms against the British army? These questions can be answered only by remembering that colonial North Americans were Britons engaged in the fiercely partisan debates about the future of the British Empire. Until the very last moment, North Americans and their British political allies wanted not separation but imperial reform.

The Declaration of Independence, I am suggesting, was an alternative means to achieve the political reforms the Patriots on both sides of the Atlantic had long desired. It is therefore essential to recover the content and specificity of the Patriot political program for state-driven economic development. Where others have interpreted the Declaration by placing it in the context of the cut and thrust of "American politics" between April 1775 and July 1776, or in terms of a broad set of European ideas, or in the context of rhetorical strategies, I insist that the Declaration also be understood in terms of a broad imperial debate that began to take shape early in the eighteenth century. That debate centered fundamentally on the aims and purpose of government.[24] This book traces the emergence and development of Patriot politics. The Patriots wanted to restore an imperial constitution, a way of governing the empire, developed in the wake of the Revolution of 1688, an imperial constitution that had promoted the social and economic development of the colonies. This Patriot imperial constitution had been rejected by a set of British politicians who had come to power after the accession of George III in 1760. Instead of pursuing the Patriot policies of promoting colonial economic development, of subsidizing immigration to North America, of developing North American infrastructure, of helping British Americans to penetrate Spanish American markets—policies the authors of the Declaration lauded—these opponents of the Patriots sought to balance the books by cost savings and shifting some of the tax burden onto the humbler North American colonists and onto their newly gained South Asian territories. They pursued a strategy of austerity and extraction rather than a policy of government-driven economic stimulus. Both in North America and in Britain, Patriots called for a new government and a new set of policies. They wanted both new men and new measures. When the North Americans, against their fondest wishes, became convinced that their British political allies could not deliver imperial reform, they took matters into their own hands. The authors of The Declaration of Independence made no anti-imperial or antigovernment statement. Instead, Thomas Jefferson, John Adams, Benjamin Franklin, Roger Sherman, John Jay, and their fellow members of the Second Continental Congress proclaimed their commitment to a Patriot government that would promote American development. The Declaration marked not the end of empire but the beginning of a new and energetic government in North America.

I

Mount Vernon

Patriot Estate

Every year, more than one million tourists visit George Washington's beautifully maintained and gracious estate, Mount Vernon, on the banks of the Potomac River in northern Virginia. Tourists come, no doubt, to visit the wonderful collections, the eighteenth-century gardens, and the re-created slave cabin. But above all they come to visit what the American postal service dubbed in 1956 "an American shrine." Americans and foreigners alike flock to see the home of an American Founder, the man who, first as commander in chief of the revolutionary army and then as the country's first president, did so much to bring the United States of America into being.

Few of these visitors, however, stop to ponder why it was that Washington's beloved estate is called Mount Vernon. Why did George Washington's eldest half-brother rename the Little Huntington Creek Plantation?

"On his return" in 1741 from the siege of Cartagena, in the country we now call Colombia, Lawrence Washington, noted his admiring younger brother George, "called his patrimonial Mansion, Mount Vernon, in honor of the Admiral of that name with whom he had contracted a particular intimacy." That Lawrence Washington renamed his family's property after the British naval war hero Admiral Edward Vernon was all the more surprising in that Lawrence did so after having participated in a humiliating British defeat. Lawrence had been one of more than three thousand North American volunteers who joined more than six thousand British regulars in an unsuccessful amphibious assault that was part of the War of Jenkins' Ear. Not only did the British forces fail to conquer the city of Cartagena, more than half of the Americans and 80 percent of the British perished (mostly from disease) in the attempt.[1] Lawrence Washington did not rename his family's property to celebrate a great military achievement.

Why, then, did Lawrence Washington see fit to call his home Mount Vernon? The answer is that Edward Vernon was much more than a naval hero; he was a Patriot hero. Britons on both sides of the Atlantic celebrated Vernon as a leader who gave voice to, and stood for, a new kind of imperial politics. Vernon was merely the most prominent of a new group of Patriot politicians who believed that they could and would create a new kind of state, one that would improve the well-being, the happiness, of the full range of its subjects.

Edward Vernon, together with Lawrence Washington and their Patriot allies, used a wide variety of media to enunciate a radical political program that they believed would put into practice the principles of England's Glorious Revolution of 1688–89. The Patriots assumed that economic growth depended on the creative interplay between consumption and production. The British needed to play an active and decisive role in supporting economic prosperity, the Patriots argued. The government, they believed, needed to develop markets for British manufactured goods and colonial agricultural products. Patriots also insisted that the state needed to support a growing British consumer base in the colonies. In the first instance this meant state support for the poor, who would then have the wherewithal to purchase both food and manufactured goods. The Patriots' second core proposal was to subsidize immigration to the colonies. New immigrant workers, they maintained, would quickly augment the consumer base. Finally, the Patriots argued against slavery. Slaves were necessarily bad consumers, and slave societies encouraged unhealthy concentrations of wealth that did little to promote mass consumption.

Admiral Edward Vernon had become an overnight celebrity in 1740, the year that Lawrence Washington made his acquaintance. As soon as news reached Britain and North America that Vernon had taken the Spanish town of Porto Bello in modern Panama with only six ships, Vernon became "the adoration of all the kingdom." British and American consumers rushed to purchase and display commemorative plates, cups, medals, and maps. Both houses of Parliament congratulated the victorious admiral. City dwellers throughout the empire illuminated their houses in celebration. The corporations of both London and Dublin made him an honorary freeman of their respective cities. Newspapers celebrated his exploits. Balladeers serenaded his triumphs. The great British novelist Henry Fielding even composed a heroic poem, *The Vernon-iad*, in his honor. The young bluestocking Elizabeth Robinson wished that Vernon be "made a peer when he returns: Baron something and Viscount Porto Bello will sound very well."[2]

Britons on both sides of the Atlantic, in prose and in verse, celebrated Edward Vernon as a great Patriot. At his death in

1757, the *London Evening Post* reminded its readers that Vernon had been "an Honest Patriot, who loved his country dearer than his life." This was no new attribution. As soon as poets learned of the great victory at Porto Bello, they urged Britons to "drink success to this great work / And all the Patriot crew." Vernon, insisted another rhymester, was "for honor loved, for Patriot esteemed." One author chose to commemorate Vernon's birthday in 1740 by publishing a treatise on Patriotism, in which he explained that Vernon deserved "that honest name" because he preferred "the good of that state, of which he is a member, to any consideration whatsoever." It was no coincidence that James Thomson's great Patriot anthem "Rule Britannia," celebrating British naval triumphs, was first performed at the prince of Wales's country house of Cliveden in August 1740, at the height of Vernon mania.[3]

To be a Patriot in the eighteenth century was much more than to be a lover of one's country. As early as the 1720s, the political opponents of Britain's long-serving prime minister, Sir Robert Walpole, had appropriated the term as a political label. They constantly referred to themselves as the Patriot Party, with Edward Vernon as one of their most prominent spokesmen. By the middle of that decade, one of Walpole's leading economic advisers disdainfully referred to the now identifiable group in Parliament as "our Pretended Patriots."[4]

What, then, were the political beliefs of the Patriots? Why were they so bitterly critical of Walpole? Why did Lawrence Washington and thousands of Britons on both sides of the Atlantic find Vernon and the Patriots so worthy of admiration?

The Patriots believed that Walpole had squandered Britain's economic and geopolitical advantages. After the duke of Marlborough's great victories in the War of the Spanish Succession had humbled France, the Patriots insisted that Britain should have enjoyed a period of unprecedented prosperity. Instead, Walpole, fixated on the enormity of the British national debt, had sought to save pennies and balance the budget. "For almost 20 years France has been making a very good use of our blunders," the Patriot John Lord Carteret complained pointedly; "by so doing they have greatly increased their trade and of late increased their dominions." The French "have wisely been doing what we ought to have done," the flamboyant Boy Patriot George Lord Lyttelton agreed. While Walpole had been saving money, France's leading minister, André-Hercule Cardinal Fleury, had spent liberally to reconstruct the French economy and expand the French colonial empire. This point was made repeatedly in the great Patriot newspapers on both sides of the Atlantic. The editors of the wildly popular Patriot newspaper *The Craftsman* pointed out that Cardinal Fleury "hath omitted no means of increasing" French "riches, power and dominions." France's "treasures are no longer wasted in wild and expensive projects to alarm her neighbors, they are laid out in mending highways, and in repairing fortifications, cutting canals, promoting commerce, and making France the wonder and delight of all the strangers who visit the country," reported the editors of the equally popular journal *Common Sense.* In a later essay, the editors of the same journal insisted "the French court is never at rest in improving and encouraging trade." John Peter Zenger reached similar conclusions in the pages of his Patriot newspaper, the *New York Weekly Journal.* Cardinal Fleury made sure to set "some hours aside 3 days in a week particularly to attend and examine proposals made to him for the benefit of trade." "France appears to me the most thriving nation in Europe," he wrote, "the great measures taken by the minister at head of her affairs" having laid "a solid foundation of power and greatness."[5]

The Patriots praised Fleury and castigated Walpole's policies in part because they had very different economic assumptions from the leading minister's. Robert Walpole and his followers narrowly interpreted the principles established in the Revolution of 1688. They believed that John Locke, the great Whig political thinker, had shown that labor created property, and therefore any productive workforce, whether free or unfree, would generate economic prosperity. Maximizing labor productivity and producing goods at the lowest possible cost, Walpole and his supporters believed, was the key to British imperial prosperity. Given these views, it was hardly surprising that they privileged the British Sugar Islands—Jamaica, Barbados, and Antigua in particular. "It is universally allowed," insisted the author of a government-sponsored tract, "that our sugar colonies are of the greatest consequence and advantage to the trade and navigation of Great-Britain." They were, this pamphleteer maintained in a telling comparison, the "equal to the mines of the Spanish West-Indies." Again and again, pro-government polemicists pointed out that the Sugar Islands were far more important to Britain than the northern colonies, whose "chief use and benefit" lay in supplying the British Sugar Colonies "with provisions and necessaries for planting." Of course, the massive riches generated in the British West Indies were completely dependent on slave labor. "The labor of negroes is the principal foundation of our riches from the plantations," Sir Robert Walpole's economic adviser William Wood put it succinctly. Another of Walpole's economic confidants, the Quaker Joshua Gee, similarly pointed out that "our plantations are supported by the labor of slaves, and our profit either more or less, according to the numbers there employed." "Planting sugar and tobacco"—"the great causes of the increases of the riches of the kingdom," Gee noted—"could not be supported" without African slaves.[6]

Robert Walpole and his supporters placed a high value on importing slave-produced sugars from the West Indies to Britain. They also knew war to be a hugely expensive enterprise. For both these reasons they sought to avoid war at all costs. Because Britain was a trading nation, the Lord Chancellor Philip Yorke, 1st earl of Hardwicke, argued in the House of Lords, "We ought to be more cautious of entering into a war than many others." "As war must always interrupt our trade," he elaborated, "we ought to be extremely cautious of engaging in war." War "is both a dangerous and a destructive expedient to any nation, especially a trading and industrious nation," asserted the leading minister's brother, Horace Walpole, who derived his expertise from his period as the surveyor and auditor general of America, "it is the bane of trade, and the parent of idleness."[7]

Washington's hero Edward Vernon opposed Sir Robert Walpole's policies and dissented from his economic principles. Vernon was the second son of the English revolutionary hero and postrevolutionary Secretary of State James Vernon. Edward had served honorably in the navy in the War of Spanish Succession (1701–13) and the subsequent War of the Quadruple Alliance (1718–20). Though he inherited his father's radical Whig principles and was returned for his father's parliamentary seat of Penryn in Cornwall, he felt himself unable to support the prime minister. From soon after his election until the minister's fall in 1741, Vernon was "in opposition to all Walpole's measures." "In all the measures of the Ministry he had no share," one pamphleteer said of Vernon, "he opposed as steadily those schemes which tended, in his opinion, to rivet chains upon the nation, as he firmly supported every motion, which contributed to ease the subject or make us happier."[8]

Vernon and his Patriot allies opposed the imperial policies of Sir Robert Walpole, which drew on a vastly different set of political economic principles. While Vernon and the Patriots shared Walpole's commitment to the Revolution principles of 1688, they interpreted these ideals in fundamentally different ways. They followed Locke in believing that human labor created property. They believed, however, that economic prosperity was created not through production alone, but by means of the dynamic interaction of human production and human consumption. In the view of the Patriots, then, high wages were a positive benefit rather than a drag on the economy. "It is an undoubted truth, that in the multitude of inhabitants consists the welfare, riches and power of any people," Hugh Jones of Virginia intoned in typically Patriot fashion. The larger the free population, "the greater consumption will be made of such things as tend to the public good." "Natural commodities, however valuable," argued the Patriot Lord Mayor of London Sir John Barnard, who more than anyone else articulated the precepts of Patriot political economy, "are never of any great service to a country, because they maintain no great number of subjects, nor enrich many individuals." Sugar and tobacco, however valuable they might be to the planters, did not create new consumers. Whereas Walpole and his supporters described the Sugar Islands as Britain's equivalent of the Spanish American mines, Barnard pointed out that though "the gold and silver of the Spanish and Portuguese settlements of America are commodities of great value; but as they are produced by the labor of slaves, and enrich only the King and a few Lords, they have rather diminished than increased the power and the riches of both these kingdoms." The problem with mineral extraction and the cultivation of sugar, tobacco, or rice is that "they maintain no great number of industrious subjects in which the power of a country subsists."[9] Economies based on slave labor did not create subjects whose desires to consume could drive economic growth or whose civic activities would protect or develop the colonies.

The Patriots' focus on consumption led them to several conclusions. First, they denounced regressive taxation that severely restricted the purchasing power of the lower and middling classes throughout the empire. To maximize consumption, the Patriots maintained, a country's wealth needed to be evenly distributed. "The wealth which is in the hands of the great and the few goes out for luxury and lessens the public stock," argued the editors of *Common Sense,* the journal that more than any other came to define the Patriot cause, whereas "that share which is in the hands of the industrious and the many, is employed in manufactures and all kinds of commerce and of consequence increases the stock." "It is certain that as the wealth of the nation runs into few hands," they summarized, "arts, manufactures, and commerce will in proportion decline." This led Patriot politicians to denounce the Walpole government's taxation schemes that aimed to protect producers at the expense of consumers. Patriots bitterly opposed Sir Robert Walpole's proposals to lower the land tax by imposing new excise (or sales) taxes on essential consumer goods. The New Yorker Cadwallader Colden, who in his early career was a great advocate for Patriot policies, advised the state "to take off all burden from the laborers or manufacturers of a country ... because whilst labor and industry are encouraged, the country people thrive, grow rich, and are enabled to pay the merchant for what they buy." The Patriots did not want to lower or eliminate taxes, they simply wanted progressive taxation schemes that would generate revenue from the wealthiest subjects rather than regressive ones that would hit the middle and humbler classes the hardest. "It is a scandal to any free government," argued the editors of *The Craftsman,* that "whilst the poorer sort of people are obliged to pay heavy duties for all the necessaries and conveniencies of life, the rich should not lay in proportion for indulging themselves in pride, vanity and riot." Implementing the "long desired tax on luxury," they insisted, "would either raise a very great sum or reduce that destructive vice." Washington's hero Vernon thus opposed a proposed salt duty in 1732 on the grounds that "the Bill is only to ease the rich at the expense of the poor." "The only way to retrieve our manufacture," agreed the Patriot founder of Georgia James Oglethorpe in the same debate, "is to reduce the price of labor by easing the poor of those heavy taxes which oblige them to insist on high wages." Vernon's fellow Patriot Samuel Sandys had earlier spoken against the duty on soap and candles, two widely consumed products in the eighteenth century, because these taxes were "a burden too grievous and heavy on the poor." The following year Vernon joined a wide range of Patriots and others in denouncing Robert Walpole's plan to levy a new excise tax on tobacco and wine "with great warmth."[10]

The Patriots likewise rejected the Walpole government's prioritization of sugar production. Free labor in the colonies played a vital role in creating consumer demand for British manufactured goods. It was colonial demand for British goods that kept the imperial economy humming. "The great exports we make to and from" the colonies, Sir John Barnard insisted, "have hitherto maintained our trade and manufactures." The former lieutenant governor of Pennsylvania turned Patriot journalist Sir William Keith made the same point. When he came to catalogue "the principal benefits arising to Great Britain from the trade of the colonies," the first three items he listed were colonial consumption of the "woolen manufactures exported from Britain," the colonists' robust taste for British-produced "linen and calicoes," and their burgeoning desire for "luxury" items such as silks, "haberdashery, household furniture and trinkets of all sorts."[11]

The rapidly growing British American colonies generated essential demand for British manufactured goods at a time when imperial competitors increasingly shut British products out of European markets. Exports to "Portugal and the British plantations" had become, according to the authors of the Patriot journal *The Craftsman*, "the most beneficial if not the only branches of trade which give a balance to Great Britain." "Of all the branches of our commerce that to our colonies is the most valuable," wrote the Patriot George Lyttelton in an essay reprinted in *Gentleman's Magazine;* "it is by that alone we are enabled now to carry on the rest." The reason was that, unlike European markets that could be shut to British manufacturers by trade restrictions, colonial markets were "most secure." John Campbell, the 2nd duke of Argyll, one of Sir Robert Walpole's bitterest critics, noted that "the balance of our trade in almost all other places in the world, except our own settlements, is against us." "Our trade to America is of the utmost consequence to this kingdom," chimed in the long-time Patriot Samuel Sandys, and because the Walpoleians were so obsessed with colonial production rather than colonial consumption, he was "sure that [trade] has neither been secure nor encouraged for almost these 20 years past."[12]

Third, the Patriot emphasis on colonial consumption rather than colonial production led them to doubt the wisdom of slave-based economies. Long before the heyday of abolitionism, Patriots on both sides of the Atlantic developed a wide-ranging critique of slavery and the slave trade. In widely disseminated pamphlets and newspaper essays, in parliamentary speeches and private letters, the Patriots married moral arguments against chattel slavery to economic ones. Slaves were denied moral agency on every level, including the right to purchase goods. Predictably, the Patriot Sir John Barnard "wished none of the plantations found it necessary to have any" slaves. The Virginia tobacco planter William Byrd, who had established deep ties to a range of British Patriots during his sojourn in London, hoped that the "British Parliament" would "put an end to this unchristian traffic of making merchandize of our fellow creatures." One contributor to the *Gentleman's Magazine* insisted on the injustice of slavery because "all mankind are brought into this world with natural right to liberty," pointing out the cruelty and inhumanity of the "shocking" treatment of slaves "in the West Indies." Not only could slaves never be free and active consumers, the institution of slavery ineluctably led to precisely the extreme concentrations of wealth that was inimical to a vibrant consumer society. "The use of negroes," wrote Harman Verelst in his capacity as secretary to the trustees of the new province of Georgia, would inevitably lead to the consolidation of economic power "into the hands of a few." Another Georgia advocate agreed that with slavery "all the small properties would be swallowed up, as they have been in other places, by the more wealthy planters." Instituting slavery, the Patriots believed, also skewed colonial economic priorities. Colonists increasingly diverted money and energy toward the prevention of slave rebellions and away from colonial development. The cruelty and oppression of slavery, many noted, brought with it the endemic possibility of slave rebellions. These inevitably would "cost our Mother Country many a fair million."[13] Patriots increasingly came to believe that, on balance, slave-based economies were detrimental to imperial prosperity.

Finally, the Patriots had a radically different perception of the importance of Britain's West Indian possessions. Whereas the supporters of Walpole valued the West Indies for slave-generated sugar production, the Patriots prized Jamaica and the other West Indian possessions as ideal staging points to send British manufactured goods into Spanish America. Jamaica's prosperity had long depended on the trade "opened with the Spaniards," recalled the islander James Knight, because thereby "great quantities of the manufactures of Great Britain were yearly vended, and the reputation of the riches brought in by these means occasioned the island to be well supplied with all kinds of materials." All of the West Indies' sugar exports "to England and the rest of the world besides New Spain [do] not furnish them with a tenth part of their subsistence," opined another observer, because the chief basis of their wealth was exporting British manufactured goods to the Spanish American colonies. Spanish America depended on exports of clothing and metalware from Britain and foodstuffs from British America. Because it was "impossible for the Spanish settlements to subsist for want of the necessaries of life were they not supplied by our plantations," the Patriot parliamentary leader William Pulteney explained to his fellows in the Commons, "the Spanish governors" themselves often "send to our settlements for provisions," which they purchased "either with the current coin of Spain or with the goods of the produce of their settlements in America." "Such is the genius of the Spaniards in America," agreed John Lord Carteret in the Lords, "so much are they overrun with luxury, ease and pride, supported by a great affluence of money, that they cannot apply themselves to the ordinary arts of life, as other people do, and for that reason they must purchase conveniencies and necessaries with money, or they must want them."[14]

Because Spain officially prohibited other states from trading with their colonies, the vast majority of British exports to Spanish America were in fact illicit. The Patriot Sir William Keith, for example, confessed to the existence "of a clandestine correspondence in trade with the subjects of New Spain, whose wants and necessities greatly encouraged the same." The British, he conceded, "had a very considerable share" in the wildly profitable "illicit trade" to Spanish America. Without that "contraband trade" to British America supplying the "current coin," he concluded, based on his years of observation in Pennsylvania, "all manner of traffic in those parts must inevitably stagnate and cease." Because the Spanish could not "satisfy the desires of the inhabitants of their American colonies" a great and profitable "illicit trade" had in fact developed in the "American seas," observed another Scottish Patriot, Hugh Hume Campbell Lord Polwarth.[15] In the 1720s and 1730s, the Spanish unleashed a swarm of semiprivate vessels called *guarda costas* into the Caribbean to put an end to this illicit trade.

Lawrence Washington's political mentor, Edward Vernon, insisted that all British Patriots had an interest in supporting this illicit trade. He famously denounced Sir Robert Walpole's refusal to allow Vice Admiral Francis Hosier, with his massive fleet of twenty ships of the line, to take Porto Bello in 1726. Vernon announced in the House of Commons that victory could easily have been achieved with "six ships of war." Vernon's oft-repeated lament that Walpole's pacific policies meant "that we cannot exert ourselves in a hostile manner to protect our merchants" was part of a larger critique of the imperial priorities of Britain's leading minister. Walpole pursued pacific policies because he valued West Indian sugar exports more highly than colonial consumption of British manufactured goods. Because of that assessment peace was always to be preferred to conflict in the Caribbean. The Patriots, by contrast, prioritized colonial consumption. The Patriots therefore followed Vernon in maintaining that war might be necessary to protect the most valuable parts of British imperial commerce. The "depredations of the Spaniards"—their seizing British merchant ships in the Caribbean—needed to be stopped, argued the authors of a petition from the merchants of Glasgow, primarily because "the American colonies (particularly the West India islands) are the principle [*sic*] mercat for the manufactures of this country, whereby thousands of His Majesty's subjects are employed and maintained." The London Patriot Micaiah Perry believed that "these unjust and violent proceedings of the Spaniards have rendered the American trade so unsafe and precarious" that "the revenue arising to the Crown therefrom must be very much diminished if not entirely lost." In such circumstances war had become necessary to protect British trade. "When trade is at stake it is your last retrenchment," argued the Patriot rising star and future Patriot minister William Pitt, "you must defend it or perish." "Our trade is at present in the most imminent danger," agreed the Patriot Alderman Robert Willimot of London, "undone" by the ministry's refusal to "resent any injury done to our trade." "A just and well conducted war," Willimot argued by contrast, "can never bring our trade into any danger." "The miseries" of Britain's current peace were worse "than the most dismal effects of war," maintained William Pulteney; therefore "the last will be found a safe, an easy and a glorious expedient."[16]

In the 1730s, Edward Vernon and many of his Patriot friends put their imperial economic ideas into practice with the founding of the new British province of Georgia. James Vernon, Edward Vernon's older brother, joined with James Oglethorpe and John Perceval (1st earl of Egmont beginning in 1733) to become leaders of the trustees to establish the new colony on the southern frontier of British America. James Vernon, like his brother, had an impeccable Patriot Whig pedigree. He had been educated in the Netherlands, where he imbibed the new enlightenment thinking and also observed the wealth generated in a high-wage economy. Upon his return to Britain, James Vernon was elected to Parliament for Cricklade in Wiltshire on "the Whig interest" with the support of the local manufacturers. In his brief parliamentary career he championed measures to support immigration into Britain. He was prevented from being seated on the board of trade by the intervention of the Tory leading minister, Robert Harley. His deep ties to the Patriots deepened when the future Patriot parliamentary leader William Pulteney introduced Vernon to Arethusa Boyle, who would soon become his wife. In 1729 Vernon's friend the philanthropist and clergyman Dr. Thomas Bray introduced him to James Oglethorpe. Oglethorpe was himself deeply engaged in a parliamentary committee investigating prison reform in "the service of the public and relief of their fellow creatures." On that parliamentary committee Oglethorpe met Egmont and a number of other future Georgia trustees.[17] Together this group of Patriots initiated a remarkable colonial experiment—an experiment based on principles that would resonate deeply in America's Declaration of Independence three and a half decades later.

Georgia was a state enterprise that melded the economic ideas of the Patriots with the philanthropic fervor of Dr. Bray and the parliamentary prison reformers. Georgia was not a private enterprise initiated during a period of imperial salutary neglect. While the Georgia project had its origins in the world of private charity, Vernon, Oglethorpe, and Egmont soon realized that their vision required massive government support. They realized that without it, Georgia would founder, just as Virginia had done before state intervention saved the province a century earlier. Within a year of the founding, Georgia's trustees had determined that financial aid from the British imperial government was essential to start up projects aimed at promoting prosperity. The trustees did all they could to muster parliamentary support for their project. They printed books that they "dispersed to all the members of both Houses," they lobbied individual MPs, and they appealed to their friends in prominent institutions from the Bank of England to the Freemasons to contribute to the enterprise. In May, the Patriot elder statesman Sir Joseph Jekyll presented the petition on behalf of parliamentary grant for Georgia. He was ably seconded by the Patriot London alderman Sir John Barnard. In early June, George II gave his royal assent to a grant of £10,000 "for establishing the colony of Georgia in America." By 1740 the British government had astoundingly devoted more than £100,000 toward the establishment of the new colony—this in an era in which the overall state expenditure was less than £6 million per year.[18]

What, then, were the aims of this state enterprise that was awarded a royal patent in June 1732? What was the nature of this new province that loomed so large in the Patriot imagination?

Georgia was the embodiment of Patriot economic principles. From the beginning James Vernon, the Georgia trustees, and their Patriot supporters sought to create a colony that would generate new consumers as well as producers. Joseph Jekyll pleaded with Parliament for state support for "relieving several indigent persons here by transplanting where they will prove useful for the Mother Country." James Oglethorpe wanted "a suitable quantity of acres whereon to place those persons, who now are at liberty to starve about the streets or lie an encumbrance to their friends." The result, he thought, would be a new colony that through their consumption and production of some vital raw materials would "promote our manufactures."[19]

The Georgia trustees sought to create a consumer-driven economy in three ways. First, they wanted to turn the British underclass into active participants in the economy. Vernon,

Oglethorpe, and Egmont initially imagined a small-scale enterprise "to settle a hundred miserable wretches" in Georgia. But their ambitions grew. With the prospect of state support the trustees were able to promote their aim "to relieve such British subjects as are by misfortunes rendered incapable of supporting themselves and families here" on the principle that "every person preserved from perishing by want is a subject gained." Georgia was founded on the principles of the redistribution of wealth and greater income equality. Their business, announced one contemporary newspaper, was "to convey the benevolences of the rich to the support of the poor."[20]

In their lavishly illustrated and industriously disseminated pamphlet advertising their design, *Some Account of the Trustees for Establishing the Colony of Georgia in America,* the group's secretary, Benjamin Martyn, highlighted the Roman inspiration for their design. The Romans, he informed his readers, had hit upon a brilliant "expedient" to lessen poverty in the heartland by "planting" the poor "in colonies on the frontiers of their Empire," thereby giving a "new strength to the whole." So valuable was this enterprise, Martyn pointed out, that the Romans resolved to finance the endeavor from "the public treasury." In this manner the Trustees proposed to "relieve such unfortunate persons as cannot subsist here" by defraying "the charge of their passage to Georgia" and giving them "necessaries, cattle, land, and subsistence until such time as they can build their houses, and clear some of their lands." The trustees aimed, James Oglethorpe elaborated, for new settlers to be "carried gratis into a land of liberty and plenty, where they immediately find themselves in possession of a competent estate." "One of the first principles" of Georgia, Oglethorpe reminded the trustees in 1739, was "agrarian equality."[21] The state would provide the start-up costs to begin the new egalitarian enterprise.

By providing housing and a means of livelihood, the government would be creating a whole range of new consumers. The project would create more disposable income in Britain by lessening the "poor tax by relieving great numbers of unfortunate people." But more important, the new inhabitants of Georgia would become voracious consumers of British manufactured goods. This would be made possible by creating a diverse economy based on the production of valuable, but less labor intensive, goods. The inhabitants of the new colony would be set to work "in raising silk, wine and [olive] oil." Because of the high wages in North America and the constant demand for the proposed colonial products, the new colonists would "earn 30 or £40 a year by their labor on those rich commodities" and they would purchase manufactured goods "where they are made by men who work for 15 or £20 a year." "Numbers of manufacturers here [in Britain] will be employed for supplying them with clothes, working tools, and other necessaries," predicted Benjamin Martyn.[22] In short, the trustees imagined that by providing for the start-up costs of the new inhabitants of Georgia, they would create thousands of new consumers of British manufactured goods. This mushrooming consumer demand would, in turn, improve the welfare of workers back home.

The trustees were also keen to populate the new colony with immigrants. Subsidized immigration was central to the Patriot economic program. Not only did immigrants represent an additional labor force, they also increased the consumer base. When James Vernon learned of the persecution of Protestants in the Archbishopric of Salzburg in Germany in 1732, he immediately proposed that the trustees "make a comfortable settlement for as many as accepted of it in the new colony of Georgia." Georgia, the trustees announced in their official description of the project, will provide "a refuge to the distressed Salzburgers and other persecuted Protestants," thereby increasing "the power of Britain" by "the addition of so many religious and industrious subjects." This was no mere ideal. Immigrants flocked to Georgia in droves. Many of them were persecuted Protestants. Others were Catholics who brought desired skills in silk, wine, and olive oil production. Salzburgers, Swiss, Italians, Irish, and Highland Scots all came in substantial numbers to the new province, founding towns like New Ebenezer and New Inverness.[23]

The trustees of Georgia also outlawed slavery. The Patriot supporters of Georgia adduced the full range of moral, economic, and political arguments against enslaving fellow humans. They were urged by their supporters to "prohibit within their jurisdiction the abominable and destructive custom of slavery," with the prediction that "if they go upon the glorious maxims of liberty and virtue, their province, in the age of man, by being the asylum of the unfortunate, will be more advantageous to Britain than the conquest of a kingdom." The trustees heeded this call and outlawed the use of chattel slavery in their colony because, as James Oglethorpe later recalled, it was "against the Gospel and fundamental law of England." They added that slaves were no great economic boon. The cost of a Negro slave, they claimed, was about the same as the cost of paying for a white male immigrant and setting him up with tools and "other necessaries." The immigrant, unlike the slave, would be an active consumer and also be able to serve in the province's militia. The Georgia trustees thought that slavery inevitably fostered exactly the kind of oligarchical society that the Patriots believed was inimical to economic growth. "The use of negroes," wrote Harman Verelst in his capacity as secretary to the trustees, "will rather destroy" Georgia because it will inevitably lead to the consolidation of economic power "into the hands of a few than help it to become useful to the Mother Country." Another Georgia advocate agreed that with slavery "all the small properties would be swallowed up, as they have been in other places, by the more wealthy planters." The Georgia trustees were convinced that slavery fostered severe income inequality even among the white population. Many Patriots shared this view. When a Georgia faction with close ties to Carolina slave traders proposed that Georgians be allowed to keep slaves, the town of New Inverness petitioned the trustees, setting "forth the inconvenience of having negroes." They argued that slaves represented a net economic disadvantage, that they represented a potential fifth column in time of war, and that it was "shocking to human nature that any race of mankind and their posterity should be sentenced to perpetual slavery." "I wish," wrote the Patriot planter William Byrd II of Virginia to his old friend John Perceval 1st earl of Egmont, that Virginia "could be blessed with the same prohibitions" against slavery and rum that prevailed in Georgia. Jonathan Belcher, the Patriot governor of Massachusetts and bitter enemy of Martin Bladen, who led Walpole's board of trade, similarly lauded Georgia's prohibition against slavery, noting, "I was always in that way of thinking that no part of mankind was made to be slaves to their fellow creatures."[24]

In the late 1730s Patriots feared that the revived Bourbon alliance between France and Spain threatened the very existence of their consumer-based empire. They worried that Spanish attacks on shipping in the Caribbean would make it impossible for West Indians to export Britain's manufactured goods to Spanish American consumers. They were certain that a combined Franco-Spanish offensive from St. Augustine and the French bases in Louisiana would cripple the new consumer colony of Georgia. James Oglethorpe worried that the French and Spanish in concert sought "to root the English out of America." Above all, the Patriots were convinced that Britain's Prime Minister Sir Robert Walpole would do little to prevent the Spanish attacks on British merchant shipping in the Caribbean and would even go so far as to surrender Georgia to Spain to maintain the peace. Walpole was so desperate to avoid war, they were certain, that he would accede to Spanish diplomatic assertions that Georgia was illegally situated on Spanish territory and that British trade in the Caribbean violated international agreements.[25]

To counter these possibilities the Patriots organized a broad-based propaganda campaign that ultimately, in the spring of 1739, forced Walpole to take a stance in defense of Georgia and of British shipping in the Caribbean. In October 1739, the Patriots compelled Britain's leading minister to accede to the necessity of declaring war against Spain. With war inevitable, the British administration saw the necessity of recalling the experienced Caribbean naval commander Edward Vernon, overcoming their "prejudices" against him for his "unguarded conduct" in Parliament.[26] It was as vice admiral of the Blue, with six men-of-war, that Vernon achieved his great victory, at Porto Bello in November 1739, setting off a great wave of Patriot enthusiasm on both sides of the Atlantic.

North Americans greeted Admiral Vernon's great victory with unbridled enthusiasm. They saw both the Declaration of War against Spain and Vernon's opening salvo as great triumphs for the Patriot imperial program.

On both sides of the Atlantic, Patriots called for a great expedition against the Spanish West Indies—Cuba being the most popular target—that would allow the British to seize control over the Caribbean waterways, pry open Spanish

American markets for British exports, and prevent any Franco-Spanish attack upon Georgia. "Let us attack" Spain "in the West Indies with such a force as cannot be defeated," the Patriot leader William Pulteney chimed in from the Commons, "and let us put it out of the power of any ministry to give up the conquests we shall make: we shall then put the trade and navigation of this nation beyond all future violation." "A harbor, a settlement, a colony can alone conclude our disputes, assert and preserve the rights of Great Britain, and protect the trade even of Spain," argued Hugh Hume Campbell Lord Polwarth; "these the people expect, these they demand, and to these they have a right."[27]

Cuba quickly emerged as the preferred Patriot acquisition. "No part of the world is at this day of greater consequence to our nation than the port of the Havana and the island of Cuba," Alexander Spotswood, the Patriot former lieutenant governor of Virginia and future leader of the American expeditionary force of 1739–40, explained. "By taking Havana," he elaborated, "we seize the key of all the treasure of the Spanish dominion in America." When the British controlled Havana, their "shipping may at length come to engross the portage of the wealth of Mexico and Peru." To achieve this great aim, Spotswood recommended raising "a body of at least eight or ten thousand volunteers both from the continent of North America and our islands in the West Indies." Havana was "the gate from the Indies which whoever possesses shall be able to give terms to all the Spanish trade in that part of the world," wrote Governor William Dummer of Massachusetts, elder brother of the radical Whig and Patriot Jeremiah, in advising an attack on the Cuban port. This American idea quickly became Patriot dogma. "Great Britain has it in her power to make a prosperous war against Spain," the great Patriot veteran of Marlborough's wars John

Dalrymple the 2nd earl of Stair insisted. The key was the "taking the Havana," which he believed could "be done by raising troops in our colonies in America, headed by a very few regular troops sent from Britain." So important was Havana commercially that taking "Havana only," he believed, "*decide la guerre.*" Havana was "the key to the gulf of Florida," chimed in another Patriot-leaning political commentator.[28]

The Patriot-inclined North American press also agitated for the conquest of Cuba so as to pry open the commerce of Spanish America. "By taking Cuba you put a bridle in their mouths," the editors of the *Boston Weekly Post-Boy* wrote of the Spanish, "you tame then, you humble them, and make the Spaniards who are left to inhabit the continent, the instruments of your wealth and grandeur." Benjamin Franklin's *Pennsylvania Gazette* predicted that after Admiral Vernon's heroic capture of Porto Bello he would "sail for Cuba on a design to attempt the Havana." In 1738 the New York printer and defender of freedom of the press John Peter Zenger reprinted *The Craftsman*'s call for an attack on Havana in the pages of his *New York Weekly Journal.* Two years later Zenger pointed his readers to a geographical description of Cuba because there was reason to believe that the British should soon "be masters of it." Readers of the *New York Weekly Journal* would have been in no doubt that the great expeditionary force was "designed against the Havana" to give the British "the sovereignty of the sea in the Mexican gulf."[29]

North Americans enthusiastically embraced the Patriot military strategy. It was no doubt the well-advertised and widely discussed prospect of taking Cuba that led thousands of North Americans, including Lawrence Washington of Virginia, to enlist eagerly as volunteers in the proposed expedition. Almost immediately the colonial governor Sir William Gooch enlisted four hundred men in Virginia, with great hopes "to increase the number by the time they are called for." All sides in the bitter partisan squabbles in Massachusetts commented on the "eagerness which appears in the people here to serve in the expedition against the Spanish West Indies." In New York City there was a "lively" interest in the expedition. The *Boston Weekly Post-Boy* asserted, with some reason, that "a considerable body of men will be raised on this occasion, even in Pennsylvania." The Connecticut Assembly passed an act "to encourage the raising five hundred men to proceed upon the intended expedition." More than eighty enlisted in less than a week in Newport, Rhode Island.[30]

Up and down the eastern seaboard and throughout the West Indies, Britons eagerly volunteered to serve in the great West Indian expedition. Most, no doubt, believed that they were enlisting to achieve the great Patriot goal of capturing Havana and opening the lucrative Spanish American markets for British commerce. By the summer of 1740 the adjutant-general of the West Indian expedition, William Blakeney, had succeeded in raising about thirty-five hundred men. Indeed, so enthusiastic were the colonists that Blakeney could report that "we shall be able to raise a great many more men than what was expected before I left England." By September he could inform Newcastle that had the British been more ambitious, and supplied the expedition with more clothing and more arms, he could have raised a significantly larger force in North America.[31]

Lawrence Washington was one among thousands of North Americans who, in the late 1730s and 1740s, eagerly and enthusiastically embraced the Patriot cause. Washington outcompeted many leading Virginians to become one of the four leaders of the Virginia companies sent on the expedition. It was in this capacity as one of the American commissioned officers that Lawrence came to know and admire Vernon.[32] That the great expedition of 1740–41 was a complete military failure, that the expeditionary force attacked Cartagena before the few survivors mounted a desultory assault on Cuba, did not diminish the ideological significance of the moment. Lawrence Washington named his estate after Admiral Edward Vernon despite the miserable disaster at Cartagena because he had embraced his vision of energetic government. Edward Vernon, along with his brother James and the Georgia trustees, insisted that the state had a vital role to play in promoting prosperity. They wanted a state that would promote the creative interplay between production and consumption by promoting a more equal society, a society where the poor and middle classes would have the wherewithal to purchase consumer goods and thereby encourage the manufacturing sector. Vernon and the Patriots strongly believed that state-sponsored and -supported immigration would augment the consumer base. And they believed that an immoral slave-based society was inimical to economic development. Slaves would never be prolific consumers, and slavery promoted income inequality, even among the free population. Vernon and the Patriots were certain that the government needed to do all it could to open Spanish American markets for North American foodstuffs and British manufactured goods. It was this ideology that Lawrence Washington and thousands of other North Americans embraced. It was this ideology that Lawrence Washington inscribed on the American landscape by naming his estate Mount Vernon.

I I

Patriots and the Imperial Crisis of the 1760s

Admiral Edward Vernon was a hero for thousands of Patriots in North America, the West Indies, and the British Isles. But the British Admiralty Board that took shape in the 1740s saw him in an entirely different light. That board, under the leadership of John Russell, 4th duke of Bedford, summoned Vernon in April 1746 to explain why two pamphlets had recently appeared in print containing the board's correspondence with Vernon. Vernon had in fact published the letters as part of his complaints against the Admiralty Board's plans to reform the British navy. Vernon was furious that he and senior officers like him were being treated in "a contemptuous manner." He therefore refused to answer the board's queries and was summarily dismissed for "telling tales out of school." Vernon and his admirers knew as well as his detractors that the pamphlets were a mere pretext for dismissing this decorated hero, who had the previous year played a key role in putting down the great Jacobite Rebellion led by Bonnie Prince Charlie against British authority. The board had long "raked into, scrutinized and weighed in the balance" every action taken by the Patriot hero.[1]

Why was the British Admiralty Board so eager to rid itself of a wildly popular and decorated hero? Why in the midst of a war with France fought on a global scale were the British interested in dismissing one of their most experienced naval officers? The answer is that beginning in 1745 the Admiralty Board had initiated a series of naval reforms that would simultaneously transform the British navy into the greatest European fighting force on the sea and make it into a powerful political weapon for an emerging group of British politicians led by the duke of Bedford and John Montagu, 4th earl of Sandwich. The leading spokesman for the naval reformers in the House of Commons was a young addition to the Admiralty Board, George Grenville.

Bedford, Sandwich, and Grenville believed that the key to naval success lay in establishing discipline and hierarchy. In their view this was also the key to successful imperial governance. They wanted both a more centrally organized navy and a more uniformly governed empire. From 1744 Bedford and Sandwich worked together to professionalize the navy. They insisted that the Admiralty Board, rather than the naval officers, had the final authority in all decisions. They insisted on a rigidly enforced chain of command. They instituted the first naval uniforms. They instituted new methods of training to regularize naval maneuvers. They expanded the role of courts martial in order to widen the scope and the authority of their discipline. Within two decades these reforms transformed the British navy into one of the world's greatest fighting machines.

But these reforms also provoked widespread Patriot opposition. The Patriots wanted an effective navy. But they did not want a hierarchically organized force that could be deployed by a centralizing ministry with little political oversight. Patriot newspapers, the *London Evening Post, Old England,* and *The Remembrancer,* led the assault on the naval reforms. They regularly argued for the importance of popular political oversight. One of their greatest spokesmen was Admiral Edward Vernon.[2]

Despite his public dismissal by the Admiralty Board in 1746, Vernon remained a Patriot hero. When he died, in 1757, he was remembered in the Patriot press on both sides of the Atlantic as an "Honest Patriot" who had through "his great and good actions for his country's interest" raised "Britannia's drooping fame."[3] In 1763 an elegant monument to Vernon, designed by the famous sculptor Michael Rysbrack, was placed in the north transept of Westminster Abbey. The inscription emphasized his Patriot credentials: "The friend of man, the lover of his country, the father of the poor." Ironically, the monument was erected the same year that his political nemesis, George Grenville, became Britain's leading minister.

George III appointed George Grenville first lord of the treasury and chancellor of the exchequer in 1763 at a great moment of British imperial triumph. The British had just concluded the Seven Years' War (1757–63), in which the British army and navy had successfully expelled the French from Canada and Bengal and seized the Caribbean sugar-producing islands of Guadeloupe and Martinique, as well as Cuba and Florida from France's Spanish allies. The war had been glorious. But it had also been expensive. Britain and its imperial rivals emerged from the war with unprecedented levels of sovereign debt. The British national debt in 1763 was more than £120 million—one and a half times the gross domestic product, according to one admittedly loose estimate.[4]

Grenville adopted a radically different approach to addressing Britain's burgeoning debt than had his predecessors. Whereas successive Whig and Patriot Whig ministries had sought to deal with the massive debt by spending more on colonial development than any of Britain's imperial rivals in order to encourage colonial growth, Grenville chose to lower the debt by cutting spending and extracting revenue from the colonies by a combination of administrative reforms and new legislation. Just as Grenville had worked with Bedford and Sandwich to implement a set of naval reforms based on French precedents, so he turned to French models in adopting widespread imperial and fiscal reforms. Indeed both the French and Spanish governments pursued similar policies, leading to what Ezra Stiles, with his expansive vision, called "struggles for liberty and revolution AD 1765 and 1766" around the world.[5] In every case imperial states provoked reactions in both colonies and in Europe by adopting economic policies of austerity and colonial extraction.

In Anglo-American scholarship and popular memory the events of the 1760s have come to be known as the Stamp Act Crisis, after the 1765 British parliamentary act that levied a new tax on stamps in the colonies. Most have interpreted the crisis as the beginning of a struggle over rights and sovereignty within the British Empire.[6] In part it was that. But what connected discontent in British India with riots in Britain, what connected uprisings in Quito and Madrid, Paris and Saint Domingue (modern Haiti), was less a consistent transimperial constitutional theory than a commonly experienced economic hardship resulting from ministerial policies designed to pay down sovereign debt. Ministerial attempts to cut government spending and raise more revenue spawned popular anger in the Spanish, French, and British Empires.

What was unusual, what marks the British imperial experience as exceptional at this moment of transatlantic crisis, was that the British ministers who came to power after 1760 inverted the political economic commitments of their imperial state. They rejected the Patriot political economic principles that had been developed in the 1720s and 1730s, tested in Georgia, and implemented successfully by William Pitt's ministry in the 1750s. Ministers in France and Spain reacted to defeat in the Seven Years' War by developing and accelerating reform programs aimed at minimizing costs and increasing the revenue collected from their colonies. In Britain, by contrast, the ministers who came to power after the fall of William Pitt's Patriot ministry in 1761, John Stuart, 3rd earl of Bute, and above all George Grenville, reversed the political economic strategy of the British Empire and looked back to the success of the early-eighteenth-century French imperial program.[7] George III's new ministers embraced a new imperial program that sought to cut government spending and raise revenue from under-represented populations in Scotland and Ireland, the manufacturing districts of England, India, the West Indies, and North America as well.

Ideological disagreement more than personal animosity and political rivalry characterized a new age of partisanship that began in the 1760s. From the moment George Grenville took over as first lord of the treasury in March 1763, he made it clear that he intended to pursue a coherent ideological program—an ideological program based on economic principles entirely different from those of his Patriot brother-in-law William Pitt.

George Grenville came into office certain that whatever territorial gains the British had secured in the late 1750s and early 1760s were far outweighed by the fiscal and social consequences "of the late ruinous war." The war, he proclaimed to anyone who cared to listen, had required "boundless expense," most of which he implied was pointless. Grenville promised he would restore British finances by reversing the late disastrous policies. His strategy involved, he later explained to his friend and political ally the duke of Bedford, "maintaining the peace abroad with the utmost vigilance," establishing "a settled, moderate and frugal government at home to heal the grievous wounds which contrary principles have inflicted upon us," "availing ourselves of every resource to save if possible our sinking public credit," and "the asserting and establishing the lawful authority of the King and Parliament of Great Britain over every part of our dominions in every part of the world."[8] Grenville determined to implement his "system," his commitment to peace, frugality, fiscal recovery, and imperial extraction. His enemies and his supporters alike were all convinced that George III's new prime minister had resolved on a new political orientation for Britain and its empire. The newly reformed board of trade, reported the South Carolina agent Charles Garth in 1764, now had a "great plan to establish throughout America one uniform system of government and policy."[9]

Grenville, his old friends, and his new political associates based their system on the belief that the British Empire had long pursued misguided policies. Just as Grenville and his associates on the Admiralty Board in the 1740s had lamented the British navy's failure to adopt French techniques, so he and many of the same associates castigated William Pitt, the duke of Newcastle, and the late Henry Pelham for failing to adopt French methods of imperial governance.

Again and again George Grenville and members of his inner circle compared British colonial policy to that of its European neighbors and found it wanting. Britain's politicians had failed to grasp that imperial powers created colonies in order to gain revenues from them. Britain's unwillingness to tax its colonies and eagerness to subsidize their development, George Grenville told Thomas Whately, one of the secretaries of the treasury, was a "new and extraordinary doctrine hitherto unheard of in the colonies of any European power."[10]

Despite Britain's remarkable victories in the Seven Years' War, Grenville and his inner circle were convinced that French fiscal and imperial policy was far more rational than that pursued by Britain. Charles Jenkinson, Thomas Whately's fellow secretary of the treasury, was a committed Francophile. He eagerly sought out and transcribed French financial treatises. He admired John Law's early-eighteenth-century system that had sought to restore French finances by rationalizing collection and extracting wealth from the French colonies. He vacationed with the French ambassador to Britain. And he copied and translated approvingly the late marquis de Montcalm's assessment of British imperial policy. "As to the English colonies," Montcalm had written, "they are never taxed." "An enormous fault this in the policy of the Mother Country," Montcalm concluded; "she should have taxed them from the foundation." "If the increase of territory [does] not increase the public revenue," argued Grenville's fellow former Admiralty Board member John Montagu, 4th earl of Sandwich, in the House of Lords, "we should give it up again in order to save the expense of defending it. Does not France when she adds Alsace or any other conquered province add to her revenue by laying duties or taxes on such provinces?"[11] Grenville and his associates knew that for France and its empire the answer to this question was always yes.

The Grenvillians believed passionately that Britons, rather than celebrating their victories in the Seven Years' War, should be asking themselves why a much less developed French Empire had come so close to eviscerating the British in North

America and in South Asia. From their perspective superior
French imperial policy had brought the French to the brink of
hegemony despite demographic and geopolitical disadvan-
tages. In making these claims, the Grenvillians were continuing
a line of political analysis they had developed when they were
coming of political age. Britons had pointed repeatedly to
France's remarkable recovery after the War of Spanish Succession (1701–13) and Cardinal Fleury's masterful efforts to guide
French fiscal, commercial, and imperial recovery. The Grenvillians wanted to make sure that Britain would not squander the
fruits of war in the 1760s as they had half a century earlier. It
was for that reason that one contemporary correctly noted that
George Grenville "had two notable precedents for his project;
M. Choiseul, the minister of France, and M. [Esquilache], the
minister of Spain, had just formed the like projects for the good
of their respective colonies."[12]

George Grenville and his colleagues energetically sought
to reverse British imperial policy. They sought to implement a
French system based on austerity and colonial extraction.
Whereas their predecessors had avoided taxing the colonies and
tried to provide them with necessary start-up costs when possible, they demanded that the colonies pay their fair share.
Whereas their predecessors had failed to enforce the Navigation
Acts when restrictions and regulations seemed outmoded or
inefficient, the Grenvillians ramped up enforcement to the
letter of the law. Whereas their predecessors had welcomed
exporting British manufactured goods to Spanish America as
a commercial boon, the Grenvillians feared that such interaction
might lead to colonial independence. Whereas British governments in the first half of the eighteenth century had resisted
stationing an army in America despite the dangers of French
encirclement, Grenville's administration believed that only an

army could guarantee stability. Whereas previous British governments had allowed colonial governments to emit paper
currency, the Grenvillians feared that local assemblies would
only do so irresponsibly, leading to credit crises and potential
claims of autonomy. In short, George Grenville and his political allies demanded that Britain adopt a coherent colonial
system, a system geared to extracting as much revenue as possible from Britain's colonies, a colonial system modeled on that
of other European imperial powers.

George Grenville's political analysis, like that of his predecessor Bute, began with the formidable size of the national
debt, generated by the "ruinous measures" of William Pitt's
wartime government. George Grenville and his supporters were
quick to point out that this great national blight, this immense
national debt, was generated in an imperial war fought on
behalf of the Americans.[13]

George Grenville and his ministers advanced a multifaceted
program of cutting government spending and augmenting revenues outside England. Grenville designed these measures to pay
down the enormous national debt. The famous Stamp Act levied
on British Americans was only the final prong in a wide-ranging
system. Grenville and the members of his treasury began with
frugality and enforcement of existing rules. The Grenville ministry made every effort to instill this new ethos of austerity and
fiscal efficiency throughout Britain and the empire. Robert Melvill reported from Grenada in the West Indies that he and his
fellow colonial governors understood well that at the moment
"public economy seems in every sense to be the highest duty which
a public officer can pursue." "Economy is the word" in England,
the New York merchant John Watts put it succinctly.[14]

With respect to colonial America and the West Indies,
public economy and efficiency meant above all replacing the

previous lax attitudes toward trade with Spanish and French American colonies with strict enforcement of legislative prohibitions. From top to bottom members of Grenville's administration worked tirelessly to gather information, tighten regulations, and ultimately pass new legislation to prevent illicit colonial trade with Britain's imperial rivals.[15]

The problem of currency was very much on the minds of the Grenvillians. They deplored paper currencies precisely because they were speculative: they were bets that future economic growth would justify current debts. This, after all, had been the principle upon which the Whig Bank of England had been established in 1694. This was the principle that had made possible the phenomenal borrowing that created the massive British national debt. Unsurprisingly, the Grenvillians had little sympathy with colonials adopting fiscal policies modeled on the political economy of those who had created Britain's debt crisis. While they applauded the Currency Act of 1751 for its intention to limit New England paper currency, they believed that its remit was too limited. Throughout the 1750s and 1760s colonial assemblies had printed paper currency under the pressure of wartime demands. Allowing the colonies "to issue paper—bills of credit, which are often calculated to enrich particular persons although at the same time they destroy public credit," Henry McCulloh warned, "may likewise lay the foundation of a kind of independency." "The extravagant increase of paper money in some colonies," agreed Thomas Whately, "had ruined the credit of those where it was so multiplied, had embarrassed their dealings with the neighboring provinces, and was destructive to the British merchants who traded to America." Provoked by Virginia's experiments in paper currency and inspired by yet another memorandum from Henry McCulloh, "the Board of Trade have voluntarily taken up this matter," reported Charles Garth in early 1764. They saw a new Currency Act "as part of their great plan to establish throughout America one uniform system of government and policy."[16] The resulting act, passed in April 1764, banned the use of paper in all public and private transactions in the colonies south of New England, thus complementing the Act of 1751.[17] It also forbade the colonies to emit any new paper currency as legal tender. While the new legislation was building on the precedent set in 1751, this act, unlike its predecessor, was moving toward a French-style uniform policy for all of the colonies. As in the rest of the Grenvillian program, Wills Hill, earl of Hillsborough, president of the Board of Trade, wanted to make certain that customs revenues returning to Britain would not be in inflated colonial currency. He wanted to make sure that colonial customs would make a larger dent in the national debt.

Pontiac's Rebellion and ongoing tensions with Indians on the colonial frontiers gave Grenvillians reason to promulgate two other elements of their plan for imperial consolidation and generating, French-style, a colonial revenue. In a memorandum now lodged among the papers of Grenville's secretary of the treasury, Charles Jenkinson, Richard Grosvenor, Lord Grosvenor argued that it was the perfect time to impose a standing army on America. "The Americans are as fond of a standing army as the bigoted Protestants of Ireland and for similar reasons," he maintained. "They have both an internal enemy by whom they are always under apprehensions of being massacred, and their fear of that shuts out every suspicion of danger from a standing army." Such an army, he believed, was "necessary for securing the dependence of the colonies on Great Britain." The Connecticut radical and Susquehanna Company speculator Eliphalet Dyer was not wrong to suspect that the Grenville ministry had "determined to fix upon us a large number of regular troops under pretense for our defense but rather designed as a rod and check over us."[18]

Similarly Richard Grosvenor argued along with the superintendents for Indian affairs Sir William Johnson and John Stuart that it was vital to limit colonial expansion onto Indian lands and to regulate commercial relations with native peoples. He was a strong supporter of the Proclamation Line of 1763 that limited the westward expansion of colonial North Americans. But Grosvenor, and one must assume that Jenkinson and Grenville shared these sentiments, saw the proclamation line as also providing "an immediate and effective check" on the migration "of our common people" to North America in search of cheap land. By protecting Indian lands, Grosvenor reasoned, colonists would also fear for their own safety against violent raids as they had done before the French were removed from the continent. Limiting the demographic growth of the colonies and retaining a powerful enemy nearby the Proclamation Line would help "secure their dependence" on the mother country.[19]

The Stamp Act was the final element in the Grenvillian strategy for imperial reform in North America. Once again Grenville's aims followed the political economic principles for empire established in France. Once again he sought to establish a policy for the entire empire that would help to pay down the enormous national debt. Two of Grenville's chief advisers, Thomas Whately and Henry McCulloh, played a significant role in crafting the Stamp Act in 1764 and 1765. McCulloh had long advocated imposing stamp duties on the colonists. Whately argued in Grenvillian terms that "this mode of taxation is the easiest, the most equal and the most certain that can be chosen." Stamp duties, in other words, were a tax that could be applied to all of the colonies equally and would provide a guaranteed revenue for the empire. What went unsaid, but was undoubtedly part of the larger Grenvillian political economic program, was that by laying a tax on "obtaining land grants, securing and publicizing property rights (such as title deeds and mortgages in land and slaves), obtaining and enforcing credit agreements, and advertising in newspapers" the duties would, much like the Proclamation Line and the Currency Act, place a limit on the unfettered growth of the colonial economy.[20] The Grenvillian strategy, it must be emphasized, was an attempt to pay down Britain's ballooning debt that followed the pattern set by the leading ministers of France and Spain.

Between 1763 and 1765 George Grenville and his hardworking group of associates in and out of government fundamentally transformed the political economic precepts underpinning the British Empire. He and his political allies had followed what they believed to be "the true principles of commerce," the principles of commerce followed by the French and the Spanish, in erecting a formidable new set of imperial institutions. Grenville and his governing clique successfully implemented a policy that significantly decreased government spending while also increasing the tax burden on Scotland and Britain's overseas colonies. "No period of our history," bragged Thomas Whately, "can within the same compass boast of so many measures, with regard to the colonies, founded upon knowledge, formed with judgment, and executed with vigor, as have distinguished the beginning of His Majesty's reign."[21]

George Grenville thought of his economic strategy in imperial terms. Not only did he implement his political economic precepts in a broad series of reforms in Britain, North America, and the West Indies, but he also saw to it that his vision took root in India. Britain's new acquisitions in India were far richer and thought to be an order of magnitude more valuable than the North American colonies. Because Grenville and his supporters imagined that this eastern empire could play a key role in paying down the British war debt, they took an active part in the East India Company struggle between the commercialist director Laurence Sulivan and Robert Clive, the victor at the Battle of Plassey in June 1757, which had effectively driven the French out of Bengal.[22] Where Sulivan hoped to promote the commercial development of Britain's hard-won new provinces, Clive from the first believed his great victory would allow for the extraction of vast wealth that could be deployed to pay down the national debt.

The British political classes and the British press focused their attention in early 1764 on "the debates among the proprietors of the East India stock." While the Patriots Isaac Barré and William Petty 2nd earl of Shelburne threw their support behind Sulivan, Grenville marshaled all of his resources in support of Clive. Grenville personally lobbied company directors, worked through Charles Jenkinson to secure the election of other directors friendly to Clive, and exerted immense pressure to ensure that the victor of Plassey would be named a knight of the Bath.[23] Grenville was naturally ecstatic when Sulivan's group was defeated in the company and Clive set off back to India with the full support of the company in June 1764. Just at the moment when Grenville was beginning to implement his new political economic policies in North America, a year before he secured the passage of the Stamp Act, Britain's prime minister succeeded in putting his anti-Patriot imperial ideology to work in South Asia.

Grenville trusted Clive and Clive relied on Grenville because they had a shared imperial vision. Just as Henry McCulloh and Charles Jenkinson had expressed great admiration for French fiscal and colonial policy in their plans for North America, so Robert Clive had long studied and admired the administration of the French governor of Pondicherry, Joseph François Dupleix. It was Dupleix, Clive wrote admiringly, who "was the first who discovered the superiority of European [military] discipline, and from hence was led into the idea of acquiring a territorial sovereignty in India." Dupleix "disdained the narrow limits he might at first prescribe to himself" and aimed eventually at "the extirpation of all other European nations" and "the reduction of the whole Mogul Empire . . . to make it a dependent state on the crown of France." Whereas the commercialist Laurence Sulivan and his supporters castigated Dupleix for transforming a trading enterprise into an imperial endeavor, Clive concluded that the only French error was a failure to cultivate Indian allies. Had the French done so, "We had not now been laying schemes for driving the French entirely out of India." Indeed, the earl of Sandwich assumed that Clive would soon bring to fruition Dupleix's great imperial ambition. "I take for granted," he wrote, "you are long before this in possession of the capital of the Nabob of Bengal, if not of the Great Mogul" because "you must of course have the whole affairs of the East under your direction."[24]

Just as Grenville followed the advice of Jeffrey Amherst, Richard Grosvenor, and Thomas Gage in establishing a standing army in North America, so Clive advised militarizing Bengal. As early as 1759 Clive had suggested to William Pitt "the expediency of sending out and keeping up constantly such a force, as will enable [the East India Company] to embrace the first opportunity of aggrandizing themselves." Clive returned to this theme after he had successfully evicted Sulivan and his supporters from the leadership of the East India Company. He insisted that a further "four or at least three thousand Europeans" be sent to Bengal to ensure "that due obedience and subordination which is consistent with the true interest of this service."[25]

Above all Clive shared with the Grenvillians the view that the purpose of colonies was to generate revenue for England. Clive taxed Bengal in exactly the same manner that Grenville sought to raise revenue in North America and the West Indies. In Bengal Clive perceived huge possibilities for procuring wealth to pay down Britain's national debt. Gaining control over the provinces of Bengal, Bihar, and Orissa, Clive promised William Pitt in 1759, would generate "an income of two millions sterling yearly." This was potentially "an immense source of wealth to the kingdom and might in time be appropriated in part as a fund towards diminishing the heavy load of debt under which we at present labor." While the Patriot William Pitt did not share Clive's political economic outlook, Grenville and the members of his ministry did. So it was in 1765, not 1759, that Robert Clive and the East India Company assumed the *diwani*, "the super-intendency of all the lands and the collection of all the revenues of the provinces of Bengal, Bihar, and Orissa." Clive had fundamentally transformed British "circumstances." No longer would the company confine its "whole attention to commerce." Instead it had "become the sovereign of a rich and potent kingdom." The revenue the company could extract from these three provinces "will defray all the expense of the investment, furnish the whole of the China treasure [allowing trade to the East], answer the demands of all your settlements in India, and leave a considerable balance in your Treasury."[26]

George Grenville and his political allies transformed the British Empire in North America, the West Indies, and India. They did so because they adhered to a different political economic vision from that of their Patriot predecessors. While many scholars who have focused narrowly on North America rather than the whole British Empire have missed the coherence and power of that ideology, contemporaries did not. Ezra Stiles, for example, anxiously followed Grenville's Indian strategy from his vantage point in Newport, Rhode Island. He dutifully noted Robert Clive's assumption of the diwani, he marveled at the vast riches that the East India Company would be able to extract from hard-won provinces, and he worried whether Britain would ever be able to fully incorporate its fabulously wealthy and populous new possessions into its empire. But above all he noted the similarity of Britain's extractive aims. "Hitherto the East India Company have carried into India a million sterling annually," he noted, while foreseeing that in the future the company could import precious and valuable cloths from Bengal without having to send out any silver to exchange. The British East India Company was in a position simply to extract revenue from its new Indian provinces. This transformation in the imperial relationship in the East reminded Stiles of one thing: the Stamp Act.[27] By thinking beyond North America, Stiles understood well what many scholars have missed: Grenville had a coherent and global vision for the British Empire. In India, North America, and the West Indies Grenville and his associates sought to reverse what they believed to have been decades of misguided imperial economic policies. While the Patriots had spent lavishly from the British treasury on promoting colonial development, Grenville wanted to tax the colonies to pay down the British national debt.

Like Esquilache in Spain and Choiseul in France, George Grenville and his political allies responded to the imperial fiscal crisis of the 1760s with a wide-ranging program of reform. Unlike in France and Spain, however, their imperial policy was based on a political economic ideology that reversed the strategies of their Patriot predecessors. Grenville's system, revolutionary though it was in a British context, was not based on a unique or innovative set of political economic ideas. Rather,

Grenville deviated from his predecessors, and starkly from the program of his brother-in-law the Patriot William Pitt, in his adoption of a continental imperial blueprint. For the first time since the Tory ministry of 1710–14, a British prime minister responded to a massive augmentation of the national debt with a policy of austerity and increased taxation of the politically underrepresented. Grenville chose to tax those—largely outside of England—who were unlikely to threaten his parliamentary majority. Grenville and his political allies put into place a Bourbon-style imperial political economic program that sought to make the colonies pay for imperial governance.

Ministerial anxiety to pay down the ballooning national debts in the Spanish, French, and British Empires produced similar results. In the colonies and in Europe the policies of retrenchment and seeking new modes to raise revenue generated extensive and often violent popular responses. Discontent in North America in the 1760s was part of a large transimperial pattern.

Popular uprisings shook Europe's great imperial powers throughout the 1760s. France, Britain, and Spain had all expended vast resources, sacrificed thousands of lives, and placed incredible burdens on their respective institutions of governance in the Seven Years' War. The great imperial conflict of the mid-eighteenth century—a conflict fought in Asia, Africa, North America, the West Indies, and Europe—had left a legacy of social and economic devastation. Even before the Treaty of Paris, signed in February 1763, ended the conflict, each of the great imperial powers began recalibrating its policies to adjust to new geopolitical and fiscal realities.[28] The new peacetime policies adopted in each of the imperial regimes—a variety of burdensome taxes, more efficient revenue collection, and increased military presence in the colonies—provoked wide-spread and violent discontent.

In the immediate aftermath of Spain's humiliating defeat in the Seven Years' War, the leading Spanish ministers, Jerónimo Grimaldi and Leopoldo de Gregorio, marquis de Esquilache, together devised new methods, characterized as "widespread modernization," for extracting resources from Spain and Spanish America. In Europe they were "bent upon nothing but saving." In America they imposed new colonial taxes, tightened up controls on contraband trade, reformed the system of customs collection, and reorganized the army—reforms not altogether dissimilar to those proposed almost simultaneously in Britain.[29]

Spanish colonial reforms provoked a firestorm of protest. When the Conde de Ricla implemented a series of military and fiscal reforms on the recently reacquired island of Cuba he provoked "a mutiny amongst their troops on account of a diminution of their pay" and "great disturbances at the Havana" as a result of some "new duties on tobacco." Convinced that New Spain, modern Mexico, "was at present in a most flourishing condition, rather better peopled than Old Spain," the marquis de Esquilache sent Juan de Villalba y Angulo and José de Gálvez to transform the military and fiscal organization in Mexico. Initially, as in Cuba, the troops protested diminution in pay and "committed some disorders." In Puebla, where Gálvez began his fiscal reforms, there was "a great insurrection" in which "the regular troops were thrice repulsed and obliged to take refuge in the mountains, whilst the populace destroyed three customs houses which had been lately erected." While violent resistance in New Spain was quelled, fiscal reforms initiated by the Viceroy Pedro Messía de la Cerda in New Granada provoked even more dramatic, larger, and far more long-lasting protests in Quito. The viceroy of New Granada was implementing an empire-wide plan of eliminating tax evasion, raising revenues, and simultaneously strengthening imperial defenses. In May and June 1765 a remarkable coalition of "the natives of Spain" and "a number of Indians" "joined the Creoles" in rebelling against new "heavy taxes" imposed by the Viceroy's representative Juan Díaz de Herrera. The rebels, numbering "one hundred and twenty thousand men" in one account, succeeded in driving out the royal authorities and establishing temporarily an independent government.[30]

Spanish American protesters, just like their North American counterparts, responded to imperial reforms by voicing their political economic grievances and suggesting constitutional reforms that would alleviate their concerns. The discontented in Havana demanded greater freedom of trade, diminution of import taxes on their products and export levies on Spanish products, the repeal of new colonial taxes, and a permanent Cuban representative at the Spanish court. In Quito, now in Ecuador, the city council complained that the fiscal reforms had drained specie from the local economy and "exacerbated the poverty of the province." The council also demanded that it be consulted directly in all fiscal matters. In the Quito uprising, the creole elites insisted on their constitutional rights so that they might give voice to their economic complaints.[31]

Spanish fiscal and administrative reform provoked spectacular resistance in Europe as well as in the New World. The far-reaching changes initiated by the Spanish state after 1763 provided the context and cause for a remarkable popular insurrection known as the *motín de Esquilache,* named after the marquis de Esquilache, Charles III's minister of war and finance. In March 1766 the Spanish capital erupted in violence. There was, the British ambassador the earl of Rochford reported, "a dreadful insurrection of the people, calling out for Esquilache's head." Within hours thousands of Madrileños had seized control of the city, driven out almost 1,500 of the king's Spanish and Walloon guards, and ultimately forced the king to dismiss his leading minister. This was no tame affair. Not only did the crowd break the windows of the houses of Esquilache and his fellow minister Grimaldi, the protestors also killed several of the Walloon guards in a series of street skirmishes. They then dragged the guards' dead bodies "about the streets, put their eyes out, plucked out their tongues and burned their bodies." On Tuesday, 25 March, no one could stir out of the house "without being insulted and running the greatest risk of one's life." Soon several other Spanish municipalities rose in arms against the reformist government. In the end Charles III was able to regain control of his capital city only by occupying it with fifteen thousand to twenty thousand regular troops. Few were in any doubt of the broader context of the rebellion. George Henry Lennox reported from Paris that his information and that gathered from the French court agreed that the Madrileños had taken up arms "on account of some taxes." Significantly, many in Madrid understood the Spanish state's new fiscal policies as having French origins; among their oft-repeated slogans was *Long Live England and Death to France*.[32]

Attempts to cut spending and raise more taxes in France and the French Atlantic similarly provoked a spirit of resistance. Even before the final French defeat in the Seven Years' War, Frenchmen initiated a robust debate over imperial reform. As British victories piled up from 1759 onward, a group in France, "*les anglophiles*," began to argue for comprehensive commercial and financial reform modeled on the British Patriot Party's commitment to colonial development. The Mirabeau brothers, Victor Riqueti, comte de Mirabeau, and

Chevalier Jean-Antoine-Charles-Elzéar Riqueti, governor of Guadeloupe—drew up numerous memoranda, and Victor published the celebrated *Friend of Man* (1758), calling for colonial reform. The Mirabeaus denounced the notion that colonies existed to serve the commerce of the metropole, condemned chattel slavery, and proposed a significant relaxation of the colonial trade restrictions imposed by the *Exclusif*, which required French colonies to trade directly and exclusively with the mother country. Despite the range of proposals for radical domestic and colonial reform advanced by a range of well-connected French thinkers and administrators that called, among other ideas, for promoting colonial development, these plans were never fully adopted. Instead, Louis XV's leading minister, Étienne-François, duc de Choiseul, initiated a series of fiscal, military, naval, administrative and political reforms designed to pay down France's enormous war debt and rejuvenate the French Empire.[33]

French response to these reforms in both the Atlantic and Europe was more restrained than in Quito or Madrid. Nevertheless, international observers sensed a profound spirit of resistance and rebellion. Despite the radically restricted nature of the French colonial empire in the aftermath of the Seven Years' War, Choiseul's reforms still provoked unrest. In Saint Domingue the reformist Charles-Hector Comte d'Estaing provoked an "insurrection" in 1765. The islanders responded violently to "very considerable" new taxes and a demand that all the merchants "take up arms and form themselves in a kind of militia." Similarly, in Martinique the reforms and new taxation scheme initiated by the intendant Pierre Paul Le Mercier de la Rivière provoked outrage among the planters and led to his recall in 1764.[34]

In France itself, Choiseul's reforms were greeted with "that spirit of innovation and liberty which of late has been so universally diffused in France." Because the prestige of the crown and clergy had been decimated by defeat in the Seven Years' War, the philosopher David Hume noted, "all public bodies are apt to become troublesome" in France. Hume was right. When Choiseul's government sought to initiate a new set of taxes, most important to retain the wartime *vingtième*, a flat 5 percent tax on income, and to streamline repayment of the national debt, "almost all the Parlements of France took fire at once." "Without previous concert," noted the editors of the *Annual Register*, but "animated by a participation of the same spirit, they all resolved on the most strenuous opposition; and they determined to take this opportunity, not only to frustrate the edicts, but of setting up their authority at so high a point as to prevent all abuse of the same kind in future." Parlement after Parlement, from Paris to Bordeaux, from Rennes to Grenoble and beyond, protested against fiscal reform and new methods of peacetime taxation. Historians agree that this level of domestic conflict over taxation schemes had not been seen in France for more than a century.[35]

These new ministerial measures aimed at aggressively paying down the national debt and cutting back on spending intended to promote economic development prompted a response in the British Empire similar to the pattern set in Spain and France. There was nothing exceptional about the North American Stamp Act riots. Patriots on both sides of the Atlantic greeted the Grenvillian British imperial program with a storm of discontent. On both sides of the Atlantic a wide variety of people, from politicians and wealthy merchants to humble laborers and farmers, reacted forcefully and often violently against the final prong of the Grenvillian program, the Stamp Act. They did so because instead of leading to a postwar recovery, George Grenville's political economy of austerity and extraction led to unprecedented economic hardship. According to the Bristol merchant Richard Champion, the economic reforms undertaken "under the administration of Mr. George Grenville" before the passage of the Stamp Act had struck "very fatal blows . . . at the commerce of the Empire."[36]

North Americans and West Indians reacted to George Grenville's new policies of austerity and extraction with fury and disbelief. While Grenville's policies had some prominent and outspoken American supporters, public opinion turned overwhelmingly and decisively against the prime minister's innovative policies. "The flame is spread through all the continent," lamented the Virginia Governor Francis Fauquier, "and one colony supports another in their disobedience to superior powers."[37]

While the stories of colonial violence against George Grenville's Stamp Act distributors and their friends from Massachusetts to Maryland, from Connecticut and Rhode Island to New Jersey and Pennsylvania, from New York to South Carolina have been well chronicled by historians, there was significant opposition to the Stamp Act even in provinces where the stamps were actually distributed. Only the presence of overwhelming military force compelled the distribution of stamped paper in Nova Scotia, Georgia, and Jamaica.[38]

Popular outrage in the colonies paralleled and often mimicked resistance to the Grenville ministry's cost-saving measures adopted in the British Isles. These "events" in North America, thought the Massachusetts Patriot Samuel Adams in a telling comparison, were "much like some that we hear of in the quiet cities of London and Westminster." "All America is in commotion," agreed the editor of the New Haven–based *Connecticut Gazette*, "and the people very exactly copy the example set them by their brethren at home [in Britain]."[39]

The combination of new taxes on manufacturers and cider producers and a tightening of collection procedures provoked an unprecedented series of protests against George Grenville's government in England itself. Those who gathered in favor of "John Wilkes and Liberty" in 1763—a wide range of people upset with a peace that had made it too easy for France to recover economically and did too little to promote the expansion of British commerce—were socially and ideologically similar to those who protested on both sides of the Atlantic throughout the decade. The first wave of protests in Britain came from the workers in textiles who were most badly and directly hurt by the revival of French economic competition after the war. In the spring of 1763 John Russell 4th Duke of Bedford, one of George Grenville's leading political allies, "was insulted by a body of weavers and even received a slight wound in the face" as he left the House of Lords. The following day "there was a great riot at Bedford House." In January 1765 "some thousands of weavers went in a body" to Parliament complaining that the state had done nothing to prevent rising unemployment among manufacturers. In May "a large body of weavers marched in procession from Spitalfields," the center of London cloth production, "on account of the decayed state of the silk manufactories in this metropolis occasioned by the importation of foreign silks." Once again they threatened Grenville's staunch political ally the Duke of Bedford, who felt "obliged to keep garrison" in Bedford House with one hundred infantry and thirty-six cavalry. Within days the silk weavers, significantly involving large numbers of recent immigrants, had been joined in their protests, the readers of the *Providence Gazette Extraordinary* were told, by "near 40,000 weavers, glove makers, and other manufacturers." All of this, this newspaper noted, was "occasioned as 'tis thought by some late regulations." The

Patriot MP George Cooke, a bitter critic of George Grenville's colonial policy, would later argue that the Stamp Act protests in America were akin to "the late Spitalfields riot."[40]

People from a wide variety of geographical and social milieus throughout the British Empire protested, often violently, against the new economic and fiscal policies adopted by George Grenville and his political allies. Patriots on both sides of the Atlantic identified Grenvillian economic policy as the prime cause of discontent. Benjamin Franklin told a parliamentary committee that "a concurrence of causes" explained colonial unhappiness: "the restraints lately laid on their trade by which the bringing of foreign gold and silver into the colonies was prevented; the prohibition of making paper money among themselves; and then demanding a new and heavy tax by stamps; taking away at the same time trial by juries, and refusing to receive and hear their humble petitions." In the House of Commons, the Patriot Secretary of State Henry Seymour Conway blamed "the Sugar Act," which had the effect of significantly increasing the price of sugar from the French islands in continental North America, and "the dollar trade with Spain being stopped." "The grand causes of the complaints of the provinces," explained the New York lawyer William Smith Jr., "are the Stamp Duties, a monopoly of trade in favor of the islands to the prejudice of the continent, and an enlargement of the Admiralty jurisdiction in derogation of trial by juries." The accumulated consequence of these policies was to bring the colonial economy to a grinding halt. From Massachusetts to Jamaica, from New York to South Carolina, Grenville's policies increased the cost of ordinary consumer goods, limited colonial exports to French and Spanish colonies, and at the same time deprived the colonies of coin and paper money. The wealthy and poor alike were driven to desperation. It was this cumulative effect of Grenvillian political economy, rather than the consequence of the Stamp Act alone, that led Great Britain to lose "the affection of all the colonists."[41]

Grenville's policies caused widespread misery in Britain itself. Daniel Mildred, who exported nearly £100,000 per year of manufactured goods to New York and Philadelphia, sent "none" in 1765–66. Josiah Bunry's Leicester stocking exports had declined by two-thirds since the passage of the Stamp Act because North Americans no longer had the wherewithal to purchase his products. Capel Hanbury's exports of woolen and iron manufactured goods to Virginia and Maryland were "suspended" by 1766. The value of the loss to British merchants was almost unfathomable. According to the London merchant and MP Barlow Trecothick, before the implementation of the Grenvillian program, British merchants exported almost three million pounds of manufactured goods to North America annually. By early 1766 that vast commerce had "almost wholly stopped."[42]

In addition to rioting against Grenvillian budget cutting and attempts to restrict the colonial trade, Britons conducted a mass petitioning campaign to demand a return to Patriot policies. Convinced that Grenville's colonial policies were destroying their own livelihoods and those of thousands of British workers, the London merchants initially met to organize their own petition in early 1765. By the end of the year they "wrote to the manufacturing boroughs" across the length and breadth of England, "representing the distressed state of the friends in America, and the great decay in consequence thereof to the trade and commerce of Great Britain and her colonies." Petitions poured into Parliament from merchants and manufacturers in Bristol, Liverpool, Halifax, Leeds, Lancaster, Manchester, Leicester, Bradford, Birmingham, Coventry,

Macclesfield, Wolverhampton, Stourbridge, Dudley, Minehead, Glasgow, Chippenham, Melksham, and of course London denouncing the consequences of Grenville's new extractive policies. Twenty-five significant trading centers, in all, presented petitions to Parliament protesting against Grenville's measures. The Bristol merchant Richard Champion explained to his brother-in-law the South Carolina stamp distributor Caleb Lloyd that popular pressure in Britain itself made repeal of the Stamp Act inevitable. "Petitions came from every trading and manufacturing town which had the least connection with the American commerce" demanding repeal, Champion explained; "out of doors the whole kingdom seem to be united on the same sentiment."[43]

In fact, the disastrous economic consequences of Grenville's imperial system led British colonial merchants to work hand in hand with their American counterparts to reverse these policies. Many American merchants worked with their British correspondents to coordinate an assault on Grenville's extractive political economy. Consumers and producers on both sides of the Atlantic realized that Grenville's political economy radically diminished their bottom line. The decision by many North Americans to sign nonimportation agreements was the colonial strand of a transatlantic Patriot political strategy.[44] Patriots on both sides of the Atlantic worked together to force the Grenvillian ministry to reverse course.

Reform-minded ministers in the French, Spanish, and British Empires, then, embarked on an ambitious series of fiscal adjustments in the 1760s. In every case these imperial ministers sought to rationalize and accelerate imperial recovery from the cost and devastation of the Seven Years' War. In every case these reforms, which involved cutting government spending and raising taxes on the disenfranchised, provoked violent and articulate protests both in the New World and in Europe. Set in this context, the Stamp Act riots were hardly a unique or unusual phenomenon. They were part and parcel of a debate about the political economy of empire that spanned Europe and the Americas.

British and American Patriots, unlike their brethren in the Spanish and French Empires, succeeded in advancing an alternative imperial vision to that advanced by Grenville and his political allies. Whereas the Spanish and French critics of Esquilache and Choiseul worked locally to roll back the most onerous aspects of the new policies, British Patriots coordinated activities on an imperial scale and succeeded in implementing, albeit briefly, an alternative imperial strategy that called for government activism in promoting economic growth. In the place of Grenvillian cost cutting, the Patriots called for an energetic state that would support colonial economic and demographic development as part of a strategy to pay down the debt.

Four Patriot commentators articulated this political economy with particular clarity: John Huske and Samuel Garbett in Britain and John Dickinson and William Bollan in North America. John Huske, MP for the port city of Maldon in Essex and formerly a Boston merchant, had turned against his former friends in the Grenville administration in 1764 because of his adamant opposition to their political economic strategy. He had made such a name for himself as an expert on American questions that he was apparently asked to draw up an alternative imperial strategy by leading parliamentary opponents of Grenville. Like other Patriots on both sides of the Atlantic, Huske began his analysis with a bitter denunciation of Grenvillian policies. "Great Britain ever since the late peace, hath contrary to sound policy and the truest commercial principles, taken such measures for destroying the paper currency of the continent of America; for the obstructing the obtaining any other currency by all the colonies; for preventing the superfluous produce of the American continent and British goods from all our colonies from being exported to foreign colonies," Huske fumed, "that many in North America have been deprived of the means of paying the enormous taxes they were subject to in consequence of the late war in particular, of carrying on their trade, and making good their engagements with one another, of making remittances to Great Britain for what they owed, and of demanding from her such goods as they required for the usual course of their trade and business." The consequence "was such a scene of distress and bankruptcy" in America "as is not to be described." Grenville's colonial policies were just as destructive for the Mother Country. "The export of Great Britain to her colonies [was] reduced" in Huske's estimation "more than one fourth per annum," and was ongoing. For Huske the most important fact to be grasped in analyzing the colonial trade was the exponential growth in colonial demand. The remarkable demographic surge of British America made it the most dynamic consumer market for Britain's manufactured goods. Instead of adopting a policy of austerity and extraction, Britain should, Huske insisted in his report to Grenville's Patriot opponents, provide an economic stimulus to the colonies.[45]

The Birmingham industrialist and future abolitionist Samuel Garbett also outlined a colonial growth strategy in a memorandum he submitted to the Patriot politician William Petty 2nd earl of Shelburne. "The greatest commercial object of this nation," Garbett argued, "is to maintain a medium to enable the Americans to purchase the manufactures of Great Britain." He thought the imperial state should try to rationalize land

policy in America in the hopes that it would encourage migration, that "population may go on" and generate even more
consumers. Above all, he believed that a policy of colonial
extraction was counterproductive. "Every means of taxing
America is playing with edge-tools," he argued, "and however
easy the Americans may appear or really be, under any mode of
taxation," American consumption of British manufactured
goods would be diminished. An extractive policy "will injudi-
ciously increase the revenue; for every shilling obtained to the
revenue will, as trade is now circumstanced with America, stop
the circulation of many shillings in our manufactures and
thereby prevent an annual clear gain to our country by lessening
our manufactures."[46]

British Americans advanced nearly identical arguments
in favor of an imperial political economy of growth rather than
the Grenvillian policy of extraction. The former agent for
Massachusetts, the Episcopalian William Bollan, argued powerfully that the recent "sudden changes of British policy" had
"plunged" British America "into a state of distress, difficulty
and danger." Bollan knew that the protectionist policies "of
other princes and states" meant that British exports to Europe
were declining. The dynamism of consumer demand in British
America before Grenville's reforms, by contrast, had "exceeded
all these diminutions" and provided a growing market for British manufactures. Bollan thought that the whole tendency of
Grenville's extractive policies ran exactly counter to the interests
of Britain as a manufacturing nation. "In a country dependent
on commerce," Bollan maintained, "the primary object of political consideration" had to be "the increase and exports of its
manufactures, the benefits whereof are diffused through all
parts." Grenville's "revenue project," by contrast, "would by its
natural operations certainly have caused so great a diminution

in the exports of British commodities that for every penny collected in the colonies by way of revenue, this kingdom would very soon have lost sixpence, and probably in a short time considerably more." Patriot governments had previously helped stimulate the colonial economies by assisting "in providing for them such profitable employment as might enable them to pay for large quantities of British manufactures." Bollan concluded that "cherishing and regulating" was "far preferable to the impoverishing system" employed by the Grenvillians.[47]

The Quaker John Dickinson, born in Maryland and a prominent politician in both Pennsylvania and Delaware, offered a similar defense of a consumption-based growth policy. Dickinson argued that Great Britain's "prosperity depends on her commerce; her commerce on her manufactures; her manufactures on the markets for them; and the most constant and advantageous markets are afforded by the colonies, as in all others the rest of Europe interferes with her." By consuming British manufactures in large quantities, British Americans "pay a heavier tax to Great Britain, than if they were consumed at home," Dickinson reasoned. Grenville's policies ran exactly counter to those political economic principles. By the Grenville administration's actions "we are prohibited by new and stricter restraints laid on our trade from procuring these [foreign] coins as we used to do; and from instituting among ourselves bills of credit in the place of such portions of them as are required in our internal traffic; and in this exhaustive condition, our languishing country is to strive to take up and to totter under the additional burden of the Stamp Act." The consequences of the Stamp Act would be nothing short of disastrous for the British economy as well. "Our demand will be much less for British manufactures, as the amount of the sums raised by the tax," Dickinson argued.[48]

The Patriots were certain that a dynamic colonial consumer market would generate far more revenue for the treasury both at present and in the future than extractive taxation. They argued that a developmental strategy for the empire would better solve the fiscal crisis than an extractive one. "The colonies," the Maryland lawyer Daniel Dulany pointed out, "in proportion to their consumption of British manufactures, pay also the high duties of customs and excise with which the manufacturers are charged, in the consequential price set upon their consumptions." James Otis calculated that "the neat revenue that has accrued by means of 'our American colonies' alone would amount to five times the sum the crown ever expended for their settlement, protection, and defense from the reign of Queen Elizabeth to this day." This was because "the coarsest coat of the meanest American peasant in reality contributes towards every branch of our gracious and much adored sovereign's revenue." The American "consumer ultimately pays the tax," and already America, Otis exaggerated slightly, "consumes one half the manufactures of Britain." "Taxes and duties are laid in England upon the goods that are imported here," Thomas Cushing and Samuel Adams pointed out; "consequently the consumers here pay a proportionable part towards the defraying the charges of the government there."[49] These Patriots were not opposed to taxation. They merely thought it was wiser to directly tax relatively wealthy British producers than more modest colonial consumers. The Patriots believed stimulating colonial consumption rather than extracting revenue directly from the colonies was the most effective fiscal policy.

This articulate and sophisticated Patriot political economic vision for the British Empire was widely embraced on both sides of the Atlantic, where a number of prominent Patriots made clear their support for a political economy based on colonial growth and consumption rather than one based on austerity and extraction.

In Britain, the collapse of the Grenville administration in the summer of 1765 unleashed a chorus of ideological critique among Patriot MPs. Sir William Meredith, who had been one of the few to stand up to speak against the Stamp Act in February 1765, explained the following year that "our advantage from America arises from their buying our manufactures." Any political economic system that lessened that consumption was necessarily a system inconsistent with the interests of the British Empire. As secretary of state in the new Rockingham ministry, the Patriot Henry Seymour Conway detailed the re- markable increase of British manufacturing exports until the advent of the Grenville ministry and then suggested that the Grenvillian system had reversed that growth. Conway's argu- ments, one observer recalled, "were founded entirely on the state of our manufactures and the decay of trade." But no one was more eloquent, no one had a greater impact on both sides of the Atlantic Ocean, than the Great Commoner and leading Patriot spokesman, William Pitt. In early January 1766 Pitt returned to the House of Commons after a long absence. When he rose to speak, everyone anxiously awaited his views on the American crisis. Pitt did not disappoint. "In a long speech" Pitt quickly "silenced" all the arguments of the "Old Ministry" in favor of their extractive policies. "Every capital measure they have taken has been entirely wrong," Pitt said of the actions of his brother-in-law George Grenville's ministry. He insisted that "it was the interest of Great Britain to extend [American] commerce and open every market for your produce." If the Americans resisted Grenvillian political economy, Pitt replied that "I rejoice that America has resisted," for "three millions of people so dead to all the feelings of liberty, as voluntarily to submit to be slaves, would have been fit instruments to make slaves of the rest."[50]

In North America, too, many prominent Patriots argued in favor of an imperial policy that would stimulate growth as against one of extraction and austerity. Colonial assemblies and merchant groups from Rhode Island to South Carolina, from New York to Virginia made clear their attachment to a political economy of consumption-driven growth. The Boston maltster and former tax collector Samuel Adams argued (along with his former employer Thomas Cushing) that "Great Britain can make her colonies useful to her by no more effectual means than encouraging their trade." They argued that it was "certainly" much "more for the interest of Great Britain to encourage the trade of the colonies, by which means their riches flow spontaneously into their lap, than to exact revenues from them at the expense of their trade." "I wish that Trade Policy . . . was better understood and exercised by the Mother Country with regard to the colonies," Samuel Adams later wrote; "by restrictions and duties she has even now endangered the loss of their usefulness to her, whereas, by relinquishing these duties, and giving them indulgencies, they might even make the French colonies in America tributary to her in the way of trade and repay her an hundred fold."[51] Samuel Adams and many other Patriots were convinced that by subsidizing colonial development, rather than by restricting trade in the North American provinces, Britain would be in a position to gain commercial hegemony throughout the Americas.

George Washington, echoing the views of Edward and James Vernon and the Patriots of the 1730s and 1740s so admired by his brother Lawrence, also announced his preference for an imperial economy driven by colonial consumption of British manufactured goods. "Certain it is," Washington wrote in

September 1765, "our whole substance does already in a manner flow to Great Britain and that whatsoever contributes to lessen our importations must be hurtful to their manufactures." The net effect of Grenvillian political economy had been to decrease the ability of Americans to consume British manufactured goods; "Where then is the utility of these restrictions?" Washington asked. The future president hoped that Grenville's political economy would be replaced by a "commercial system" in which the colonies were "put on a more enlarged and extensive footing than it is, because I am well satisfied that it would ultimately redound to the advantages of the Mother Country." Colonial profits from trade "would center in Great Britain, as certain as the needle will settle at the poles."[52]

Imperial Patriots advanced a powerful alternative political economy of Empire. Grenville's policies provoked both resistance and critique. But that resistance was not limited to the periphery, nor was it restricted to constitutional or anticolonial polemic. Instead, Patriots responded to Grenville's French-style political economy with an elaboration of the distinctive British political economy of empire. They did not respond to Grenville's extractive policies with calls for independence; rather, they demanded a renewed commitment to a political economy of imperial growth.

William Pitt and his Patriot supporters in England and America desperately wanted to restore the energetic imperial government of the 1750s. They wanted the British ministry to pursue policies that promoted colonial development, through opening trade to Spanish and French America, through encouraging immigrants, and through bounties that would subsidize a more diversified economy. Contrary to the assumptions of many historians, the British Empire before the 1760s was no weak reed.

The eighteenth-century empire was never characterized by "colonial autonomy and localized agency." The British imperial state was not distant from the material or imaginative lives of colonists. The British government did not neglect the colonies, nor could the colonies afford to ignore the imperial state.[53] The British government, as North Americans knew from reading their local newspapers and magazines, had the ability to pursue an aggressive foreign policy and at the same time energetically support colonial development. This ability to spend simultaneously on the military and civil society set it apart from its peers, which heavily prioritized the latter. George Grenville and his political allies who came to power after 1761 sought to bring British policy in line with those of France and Spain.

While in the French and Spanish Empires popular protests led to a relaxation of the policies of retrenchment, militarization, and increased colonial taxation—neatly characterized in the French case by the creation of the *Exclusif mitigé,* relaxed restrictions on colonial trade—the British Patriots succeeded in bringing down the Grenville government and restoring the energetic government of Patriot administrations.[54]

George Grenville's Patriotic opponents won in 1766. George III dismissed Grenville from office in July 1765. Within days Charles Wentworth-Watson, 2nd Marquess of Rockingham, had formed a new ministry filled with Patriots and Patriot sympathizers. Not only did the new government repeal the Stamp Act in March 1766, but it investigated a whole series of Patriot-inspired economic reform programs. The "intention," wrote the Bristol merchant Richard Champion, "is to remove the intolerable restrictions on the [American] trade, take off the burdensome part of the Admiralty Courts, and settle every other matter respecting America in a manner to give her entire relief." The London merchants Capel and Osgood Hanbury informed their American friends that they "were closely engaged in endeavoring to procure beneficial extensions and regulations of the American commerce." The Rockingham ministry demonstrated its commitment to opening trade with French and Spanish America by creating free ports in Jamaica and Dominica. These new, government-protected trading entrepôts were designed to entice French and Spanish merchants to purchase British manufactured goods and North American foodstuffs for hard currency, thereby putting an end to the shortage of specie in British America. The Patriot ministry and board of trade also solicited a wide variety of proposals for reforming the imperial constitution and offering more direct representation for British colonials. Presses on both sides of the Atlantic spewed out pamphlets offering reform proposals along Patriot lines. George Grenville was even convinced that Britain's relationship with Ireland would soon be renegotiated as well. Indeed, the Massachusetts Patriot James Otis Jr.'s call for radical parliamentary reform and the elimination of chattel slavery was but one particularly articulate voice among a growing chorus calling for a more diversified colonial economy. Both the Rockingham ministry and its successor were determined to modify or reverse the Grenville/Clive imperial program in India. They hoped to put an end to militarization and encourage a return to a policy of encouraging Bengali manufactures.[55]

The British Patriots who swept to power in the summer of 1765 sought to create a dynamic government that would reduce the nation's debt by stimulating economic growth rather than by cutting back on government spending. In 1766 Patriots like George Washington had reason to believe that the policies they had long advocated were being explored and implemented with renewed energy by the British imperial government.

III

Making a Patriot Government

The Patriot triumph was short-lived. While North Americans and Britons were celebrating the repeal of the Stamp Act and a return to Patriot imperial economic policies, George III dismissed the Rockingham ministry. Although the Patriot hero William Pitt, now earl of Chatham, became the new leading minister, he was compelled by the king to create a politically heterogeneous government. In imperial affairs, this meant that the new government reinstated George Grenville's policies. The new chancellor of the exchequer, Charles Townshend, immediately put in place new taxes on the American colonies with the intent of generating revenue to pay down the British national debt. These new duties, collectively known as the Townshend Acts, forced the Americans to pay duties on paper, paint, lead, glass, and tea. "The spirit of despotism and avarice, always blind and restless" had broken "forth again," commented the British Patriot Richard Price. British Americans responded to the new levies with a storm of protest, eventually adopting a coordinated set of nonimportation agreements. A new prime minister, Frederick North, 2nd earl of Guilford, took office in January 1770 and repealed most of Townshend's duties. But North, who hailed from an old Tory family, retained a lowered tea duty in order to bolster the financially failing East India Company. Colonial Americans were furious at the lowered tax on tea, reasoning that the repeal of the other duties was a temporary palliative. They were well aware that the East India Company's policies in Bengal were destroying the once booming economy in Britain's new colonies in South Asia. When news reached Britain that a band of Bostonians dressed as Indians had, in December 1773, tossed more than three hundred chests of tea into Boston Harbor, North and his government responded with vindictive fury. In March 1774 the ministry passed a series of measures known as the Coercive Acts. The acts shut Boston Harbor, transformed and limited the Massachusetts government, compelled Americans to house and quarter British troops, and offered colonial administrators immunity from prosecution in Massachusetts. North's government had demonstrated its deep commitment to defending British economic measures. And it was just as deeply committed to a political-economic model that prioritized colonial production over colonial consumption, much in the mold of George Grenville's policies.[1]

British Americans responded to the Coercive Acts with fury and disbelief. "The Ministry may rely on it," wrote George Washington, speaking for a growing segment of North American opinion in June 1774, "that Americans will never be taxed without their own consent, that the cause of Boston . . . now is and ever will be considered as the cause of America (not that we approve their conduct in destroying the tea) and that we shall not suffer ourselves to be sacrificed by piecemeal." Washington, like so many other Americans from Boston to Savannah, believed that the British "government is pursuing a regular plan" and that the principle of that plan was "that America must be taxed in aid of the British funds." To secure redress, and in order to procure imperial reform and the repeal of the Coercive Acts, a group of North Americans agreed to convene the first Continental Congress. That Congress, with representatives from twelve colonies, met in Carpenters' Hall in Philadelphia in September 1774. Because of "the present unhappy system of affairs" that was caused "by a ruinous system of colony administration adopted by the British ministry about the year 1763 evidently calculated for enslaving these colonies, and with them, the British Empire," the delegates adopted the Continental Association. George Washington, Thomas Jefferson, John Adams, Roger Sherman, and John Jay were among those who signed the 1774 Association, modeled no doubt on the association adopted by the English in 1696 designed to protect the principles of the Revolution of 1688–89. The delegates pledged nonimportation, nonconsumption, and nonexportation in order "to obtain redress of these grievances which threaten destruction to the lives, liberties and properties" of British North Americans. British North Americans were determined to put a temporary halt to the most important British export trade in order to force political change in Westminster.[2]

Once again Lord North and his ministers aggressively defended their economic system. Instead of repealing the offensive acts and returning to the Patriot imperial system, North chose to enforce the post-1763 plan. To enforce these measures more directly, in early 1774, North had employed General Thomas Gage as the new governor of Massachusetts Bay. Patriots in Massachusetts and other North American colonies meanwhile had called into being provincial congresses, shadow governments that existed outside British authority. This prompted both Houses of Parliament to declare, in February 1775, that the province of Massachusetts was in "rebellion" and was "countenanced and encouraged by unlawful combinations and engagements" in the other provinces.[3] In Massachusetts and elsewhere, ministerial forces and Patriots prepared for inevitable confrontation. Neither side would back down from its entrenched ideological commitments. On 19 April 1775 the first shots of an imperial civil war were fired at Lexington and Concord, just outside of Boston.

The contours of the deepening North American crisis are well known by students of the period. Scholars, authors of school textbooks, and politicians have told and retold the story of the actions of an increasingly oppressive British imperial state that prompted the reaction of Patriotic North Americans in defense of their liberty and against that government. American Patriots founded their new nation, we are told, in defense of small government and of local American culture against foreign imposition. By recovering the transatlantic and imperial contexts of Patriot political argument, it is possible to tell a radically different story. Instead of a local reaction against a distant oppressive regime, the Declaration of Independence needs to be understood as the ultimate statement of the eighteenth-century Patriot program in favor of a government that would aim to promote prosperity for the largest number of people.

In the 1770s the British ministry was faced with the quintessential problem of modern statecraft: how to address a large national debt while still steering the polity toward future prosperity. The crisis was an increasingly acute one. The expected massive injection of revenue from British India had failed to materialize. Many believed that the massive debt was doing significant damage to the British economy. Alexander Hamilton agreed with many British observers that "the continual emigrations from Great Britain to the continent are a glaring symptom that those islands are impoverished." North and his fellow ministers responded as have many governments in the twentieth and twenty-first centuries: they sought to curtail government spending, lower taxes on the wealthiest members of the electorate, and shift the burden offshore and onto the humbler and less electorally significant. "The money expended by this nation upon America," argued James Macpherson, the government apologist and notorious collator of the ancient Scottish poet Ossian, was an unnecessary and frivolous waste of resources.[4] The Patriots, by contrast, while acknowledging the extent and urgency of the problem, offered a very different solution. Instead of relieving the wealthy, they wanted the state to encourage the development and expansion of the consumer base, the buying power of the middle classes. These new and more prosperous consumers, Patriots thought, would purchase ever-larger amounts of British manufactured goods. They believed that by further stimulating growth in the colonies, the government would generate revenues indirectly, thereby trimming the debt. When it became clear that no amount of pressure would bring down the North government in Britain, American delegates to the First and Second Continental Congresses moved toward declaring independence in response to the austerity measures adopted by the British imperial government.

Both ministerial forces and Patriots agreed by April 1775 that the British Empire in America no longer existed. British North America was independent. The only question that remained was whether North America would be reconquered by British redcoats or would be able to maintain its independence by force of arms. In October, George III himself declared the colonies to be in "general revolt" with the "purpose of establishing an independent empire." The renowned Tory literary figure

Samuel Johnson agreed in 1775 that after the passage of the congressional Association, the Americans were "no longer subjects." British Americans, many of whom longed for imperial reform rather than imperial dissolution, reluctantly agreed. As early as September 1774, Patrick Henry claimed that "government is dissolved" by the military preparations of the North ministry. "The bands of civil society are broken," agreed the New York Episcopalian and future American bishop Samuel Seabury.[5]

Most, if not quite everyone, in the British Empire believed that a civil war had begun in North America. Patriots believed that British actions had made America independent and justified its citizens in taking up arms in their own defense. Defenders of the ministry, by contrast, believed that America was in rebellion and that only a reconquest would put an end to American independence. In Virginia, the Frederick County committee declared in no uncertain terms that enforcing the Coercive Acts "by a military power will have a necessary tendency to raise a civil war, thereby dissolving the union which has so happily subsisted between the Mother Country and her colonies." The nineteen British Lords who refused to support George III's October 1775 speech knew well that "a cruel civil war" was already taking place in America. The London Patriot leader John Wilkes feared the dreadful consequences of "a civil war of this magnitude and extent." "A Civil War is begun," bemoaned the Patriot Bishop of St. Asaph, Jonathan Shipley, in June 1775. From Newport, Ezra Stiles was deeply saddened by "the most unnatural civil war" that had already begun. The only options in play in 1775, Samuel Johnson averred uncontroversially, were "to allow their claim to independence, or to reduce them by force to submission and allegiance." The Battle of Lexington, Thomas Jefferson agreed, "has cut off our last hopes of reconciliation." America, George Washington wrote, explaining the significance of the April battle fought in Massachusetts, must "either be drenched with blood or inhabited by slaves. Sad alternative!"[6]

By the autumn of 1775, no one on either side of the Atlantic doubted that America was in practice independent. Royal governors had virtually no authority over their provinces. The colonies themselves had by then established shadow governments. Anarchy and civil war prevailed throughout North America. The British imperial state had ceased to function on the continent. Independence, many members of Congress claimed in June 1776, was "a fact which already exists." Why, then, did the Second Continental Congress feel compelled to issue a Declaration of Independence? Why did the influential Pennsylvanian John Dickinson think the debate over the Declaration "of such magnitude" that he claimed to "tremble" while "sharing in its determination"? Why did the Massachusetts lawyer John Adams, who often thought deeply indeed about history, deem the prospect of declaring independence "the greatest question" that "ever was debated in America, and a greater perhaps, never was or will be decided among men"? The answer, Adams himself made clear in his eloquent *Thoughts on Government,* published in the early spring, was precisely that the Americans had been "discharged" from their "allegiance," and it had become necessary "to assume government for our immediate security." The Declaration, the president of the Second Continental Congress, John Hancock, knew, was "the ground and foundation of a future government."[7] The Americans declared independence in July 1776 not because they loathed the oppression of British government but because they desperately needed a state. The Declaration of Independence was a call to state formation.

What kind of government did the American Founders want to create? America's Founders developed their answers to this question in the context of the century-long debate about the best form of imperial governance. British North Americans in the 1770s drew heavily on the Patriot tradition that had so influenced Lawrence Washington and the thousands who volunteered to serve with Edward Vernon in the 1730s. They rehearsed the arguments that Patriots on both sides of the Atlantic had honed in the bitter debates of the 1760s. The Framers of the Declaration of Independence advanced the arguments for an energetic and activist government in the Patriot tradition. Like previous generations of Patriots, they insisted that consumers provided the key to a growing economy, and that government activity was essential to create a dynamic consumer-driven economy. American Patriots announced their commitment to promote the very goals they had desperately wished the mother country had continued to embrace after the accession of George III.

Patriots and their antagonists framed their arguments in the 1770s, as they had throughout the eighteenth century, in the context of the burgeoning British national debt. Patriots, like their opponents, acknowledged the gravity of the imperial fiscal crisis. And they, like their opponents, knew that Britain's finances needed to improve if the empire was to survive. "It is notorious," stated the young Alexander Hamilton, that Britain "is oppressed with a heavy national debt." "There never was before in the world such a debt contracted or subsisting as the British," agreed the British Patriot MP Matthew Robinson-Morris. The influential Nonconformist preacher, actuarial expert, and leading public intellectual Richard Price carefully traced the growth of the debt "from 17 millions" in 1699 "to 140 millions" in 1774. On this point the supporters of the ministry agreed. William Knox, who shared none of Price's politics, arrived at a similar figure for the late 1760s. Britain, averred James Stewart, a Scottish defender of the North ministry, reeled under "an immense load of debt, hanging so heavy upon our shoulders."[8] The point of contention was what mode of imperial governance could best pay down the debt while at the same time promoting prosperity.

Supporters of the North ministry in the 1770s began their analysis, as had their predecessors, by claiming that the chief value of the colonies lay in the raw materials they produced. "It required no great sagacity to discover," observed William Knox, undersecretary of state for the American department and himself a former Georgia resident, that "there were many commodities which America could supply on better terms than they could be raised in England," including tobacco, timber, pitch, tar, rice, indigo, flax, and hemp.[9] It was these raw materials, many of them produced with significant support from British merchants, that made possible the prodigious prosperity of British America.

Ministerial supporters believed that the time had come to stop subsidizing American growth and instead to get the Americans to pay their fair share. They advocated austerity on the part of the imperial government and responsibility on the part of the North Americans. "It is now high time to adopt if we can, some useful scheme of frugality and economy in regard to America," argued the deeply influential dean of Gloucester Cathedral, Josiah Tucker. Not only should the government spend less on North America, ministry men were also convinced that Americans needed to do much more to pay down the debt. Knox, along with many other ministerial observers, pointed out that Britons were already suffering from high taxes. They could not be taxed any more. Inessential government spending had already been trimmed. "Financial regulations" and greater "diligence in collecting the taxes" in Britain could generate no great financial boon. In these circumstances, Knox and his fellow supporters of ministerial policies argued, the colonies should "contribute to the utmost of their ability to put Great Britain in a position, not only to maintain her public credit, by a regular payment of the interest of her debt, and a gradual reduction of the capital, but to have funds un-appropriated, and a revenue exceeding her expenses sufficient to mortgage for new loans." In short, the government needed to raise "a revenue" in America to help pay down the national debt.[10]

William Knox and Josiah Tucker established the framework. Other ministerial supporters echoed their sentiments. James Stewart argued for "taxing the Americans, and that lustily too," to pay down the debt that "had been incurred solely in defending and protecting these Americans." The Americans, agreed the Scottish philosopher Adam Ferguson, were now "able to support heavier burdens." The Americans must "contribute towards the expense of the state for the general protection," asserted James Macpherson.[11]

Ministerial supporters were at one in believing that the chief value of the colonies lay in their production, and that therefore taxing American consumers would have limited economic consequences. While admitting that American consumers purchased large quantities of British manufactured goods, ministerial supporters pointed out that British producers had other, equally profitable outlets. Tucker claimed that the records of the customs office demonstrated that "more English goods are sent up the two rivers of Germany, the Weser and the Elbe, than up any two rivers in North America." Sir James Steuart of Coltness, who was the most important Scottish political economist before Adam Smith, similarly argued that British manufacturers could just as easily vend their wares in Europe as in North America. Britain "would soon find a vent for all her manufactures in spite of all we could do," agreed Samuel Seabury in the guise of a Westchester farmer. Therefore the supporters of the North ministry believed the American non-importation and nonconsumption agreements would be of little economic consequence. "Notwithstanding their shutting their ports against our manufactures, permanent and profitable sources of commerce have been opened in other quarters," Macpherson chimed in; "our merchants find themselves capable of fulfilling their commissions from other states."[12]

Patriots on both sides of the Atlantic advanced a very different economic analysis. Patriots gave voice to and elaborated the same political economic arguments they had been advancing since the 1730s. Where the ministerialists insisted that the value of colonies lay in production, Patriots emphasized the centrality of colonial consumption. They readily accepted responsibility for paying down a share of the British debt. "The question is not whether the Americans shall contribute, but how they shall contribute," was how the Virginian Arthur Lee put it in 1776. The Patriots argued that Americans made significant and growing contributions to British state revenue, but that they did so indirectly. "The advantages derived from America in the circle of commerce are not so evident to a vulgar understanding, as so much palpable cash paid into the exchequer," the Patriot former governor of West Florida George Johnstone had condescended to explain to his fellows in the House of Commons in 1775.[13]

As late as the mid-1770s, the Patriots maintained that the massive and growing demand of colonial Americans for British manufactured goods contributed significantly to the British economy and to state revenue. It was American trade, they insisted, that kept the empire running. "With the population of the colonies has increased their trade; but much faster, on account of the gradual increase in luxury among them," argued Richard Price in a pamphlet that was mass marketed on both sides of the Atlantic in 1776. There was an "immense trade" between Britain and her colonies, agreed Alexander Hamilton. "It is a plain and incontestable fact," thundered the Patriot and future Prime Minister William Petty 2nd earl of Shelburne, in the House of Lords in October 1775, "that the commerce of America is the vital stream of this great empire." British American markets, Patriots maintained, were not ephemeral like European markets, in which British manufacturers faced continental competition and were at the mercy of the vagaries of continental politics. Whereas European markets were likely to be severed at any moment, British manufacturers could count on steady and increasing American demand. Trade with North America "was not only thus an increasing trade," explained Price, "but it was a trade in which we had no rivals; a trade certain, constant and uninterrupted." The colonial trade represented "a complete system in the exchange of all commodities" that "was established within your own dominion" and thus immune from "the fleeting principles" of international commerce," averred George Johnstone.[14]

In Britain and in North America, Patriots emphasized that the remarkable growth of North American consumption of British manufactures—growth that had resumed after the crisis of the 1760s—created thousands of new jobs and raised the value of British landed property. The "almost unlimited demand" of North Americans for British manufactures, reasoned the Virginian Richard Henry Lee in 1774, "produced employment for several hundred sail of ships and many thousand seamen," increased "the value of lands in Britain," and "entirely supported" the employment of "multitudes of people." "The consumption of [British] manufactures in these colonies supplies the means of subsistence to a vast number of her most useful inhabitants," agreed Alexander Hamilton.[15] This American view mirrored the sentiments of the lord mayor, aldermen, and commons of the City of London, who petitioned Parliament in October 1775 with the claim that the American trade was "the most valuable branch of our commerce, on which the existence of an infinite number of industrious manufacturers and mechanics entirely depends."[16]

Throughout the 1770s, Patriots continued to believe that their preferred imperial system would do far more to pay down the British debt than the extractive taxation demanded by the North ministry and its defenders. "Every man the least acquainted with the state and extent of our trade," Hamilton stated bluntly, "must be convinced, it is the source of immense revenues to the parent state." The Americans "spend the whole produce of all their land, and the profits of all their labor in a valuable commerce by which our manufactures are consumed, our laborers maintained, and our taxes are paid," argued Benjamin Franklin. Indeed, Franklin maintained, "but for the Grenvillian taxation scheme," the revenues generated by American consumption of British manufactures "would soon have come to be equal alone to the whole of our necessary annual expenses of government in time of peace." Had the Grenville ministry and its successors not abandoned Patriot attempts to stimulate colonial growth, Franklin and many other Patriots were sure, the British treasury would already have paid down the bulk of the enormous national debt. "By purchasing our goods," the British Patriot Richard Price noted, the Americans "paid our taxes" and thereby "helped us to bear our growing burdens." Had the Patriot imperial strategy continued after the

Seven Years' War, Price wrote, "a growing surplus in the revenue might have been gained, which invariably, applied to the gradual discharge of the national debt, would have delivered us from the ruin with which it threatens us."[17]

The Patriots insisted, correctly, that before the accession of George III the British imperial government had done a great deal to stimulate colonial economic development. Financial support and physical protection, not salutary neglect, characterized the British Empire before the fall of William Pitt's ministry in October 1761. This was "the beautiful system of empire our ancestors have been raising with so much pains and glory," as former colonial governor George Johnstone described it, that was being destroyed in "a mad career" by misguided statesmen. "The principle of commercial monopoly"—rather than seizing a "parliamentary revenue"—"runs through no less than twenty-nine acts of Parliament, from the year 1660 to the unfortunate period of 1764," averred Edmund Burke in his celebrated 1774 speech on American taxation. Colonists had accepted the trade restrictions, Burke explained, in part because they had received "pecuniary compensation" in the form of "immense capital" that enabled them "to proceed with their fisheries, their agriculture, their shipbuilding, and their trade." Thomas Jefferson, Benjamin Franklin, John Dickinson, and the members of the Second Continental Congress in July 1775 recalled wistfully "the mutual benefits" of the British imperial union. Jonathan Shipley, Bishop of St. Asaph— in an essay that the Delaware delegate to Congress Caesar Rodney deemed "one of the best pieces I ever read"—recalled that under the Patriot imperial system before the 1760s it was the policy to impart "liberality" to the British Americans, including "bounties to encourage their industry." It was this policy of state support for the Americans, rather than the new policy of extracting revenue, that the Patriots thought should be expanded.[18]

Patriots, always thinking on an imperial as well as on a local scale, believed that India provided a terrifying example of the consequences of the post-1760 imperial system. It was the specter of India that convinced North Americans that whatever the level of taxation that the North ministry currently demanded from them, their future aspirations for extraction were virtually limitless. In British India, seizing revenue rather than subsidizing commercial expansion had transformed the most prosperous provinces in Asia into an economic wasteland. By taxing arbitrarily the newly conquered provinces of Bengal, Behar, and Orissa, Britons had, Jonathan Shipley observed, "in the space of five or six years . . . destroyed and driven away, more inhabitants from Bengal, than are to be found at present in all our American colonies." It was, agreed Edmund Burke, "the same folly that has lost you at once the benefit of the West and the East." "Turn your eyes to India," Price advised, "there Englishmen actuated by a love of plunder and the spirit of conquest, have depopulated whole kingdoms, and ruined millions of innocent people by the most infamous oppression and rapacity." Colonial Patriots joined their British colleagues in perceiving an intimate connection between ministerial policy in India and North American. No wonder Americans, like the committee from Dunmore County, Virginia, thought the East India Company men to be "servile tools of arbitrary power." No wonder the American tobacco merchant John Norton remarked that Parliament had taken "such strides towards despotism for some time past with respect to the East India Company as well as America." "The measure of British crimes is running over," Richard Henry Lee warned; "the barbarous spoliation of the East is crying to heaven for vengeance against the destroyers of the human race."[19]

The obvious conclusion for Patriots was that the North ministry had pursued misguided economic policies. The best way to pay down the massive British debt was to stimulate increases in colonial consumption that would indirectly generate large sums for the British revenue. The taxation policies adopted by the Grenville and North ministries had the effect of suppressing American consumption. "If the minister seizes the money with which the American should pay his debts and come to market," the Virginian Arthur Lee explained, "the merchant and trader cannot expect him as a customer; nor can the debts already contracted be paid." The consequences were dire indeed. This was "cutting up commerce by the roots." "In order to gain a pepper-corn" through an "authoritative seizure," Richard Price lamented, the British administration "have chosen to hazard millions acquired by the peaceable intercourse of trade."[20]

For the Patriots, then, the emerging anarchy of the 1770s created a new problem. They were pleased to witness the diminishing power of the Grenville/North extractive and tyrannical state. But they knew all too well that the old British imperial state had done a great deal to support the infrastructure and provide the capital that made possible British America's remarkable and dynamic prosperity. North American Patriots, often comparing themselves with the successful Dutch independence struggle against the Spanish in the sixteenth century, understood they had to replace the British imperial state with a new state structure.

As British Americans discussed the adoption of resolutions endorsing nonimportation and nonconsumption of British manufactured goods in 1774, they began at the same time to discuss the necessity for state support for the North American economy. The Committee of Fairfax County, Virginia, chaired by George Washington, called for "subscriptions and premiums to the improvements of arts and manufactures in America." The Committee from Prince George County agreed "that manufactures ought to be encouraged." John Adams proposed a resolution to the First Continental Congress recommending that all colonies "encourage arts, manufactures, and agriculture by all means in their power." The Association ultimately adopted by Congress called on Americans to do all in their power to "promote agriculture, the arts, and the manufactures of this country, especially that of wool."[21] As early as 1774 American Patriots realized that economic reorientation required energetic government support.

By the time the Second Continental Congress convened in Philadelphia, in May 1775, state support of American economic development had gone from a desideratum to a necessity. The outbreak of the war meant both that British Americans needed to produce weapons and ammunition for fighting and that they could no longer rely on British exports to provide necessities for everyday life. The time had come for "an entirely new colony police," Ezra Stiles explained to Dr. Richard Price. British Americans needed state support for their survival. In February 1776 John Adams jotted down an urgent list of state building measures to be pursued by Congress, ranging from concluding foreign alliances and treaties of commerce, to regulating currency, to manufacturing cotton duck, gunpowder, and saltpeter. "America can never support her freedom till we have a sufficient source of arms and ammunition," explained Robert Treat Paine, so he eagerly acted on a congressional committee "who are laboring to push saltpeter and gunpowder making through all the colonies, and are also devising methods to establish a regular and extensive manufacture of muskets."[22]

But Congress wanted to do much more than create a warfighting machine. The provincial delegates were convinced they needed state support—at the congressional and at the provincial level—to jump-start the American economy. The delegates knew well that the British Empire had been prosperous and powerful before 1760 precisely because the British state had devoted substantial resources to economic development. The American delegates sought urgently to replace that state support. John Adams proposed that local governments be urged "to promote the culture of flax, hemp, and cotton and the growth of wool." These particular activities, he hoped, would be supplemented by state-supported societies "for the encouragement of agriculture, arts, manufactures and commerce." Congress needed to invest in the prosperity of future generations by providing them with the tools for development. "No expense" should be spared by the state in support of "the liberal education of youth, especially of the lower class of people," Adams advised in his *Thoughts on Government*. Others realized Congress needed to establish "different departments" of state, such as "a War Office, a Treasury Board," which would both satisfy immediate military needs and create the infrastructure for state borrowing for future developmental projects.[23]

American Patriots in the late 1770s continued the transatlantic Patriot tradition of insisting that states could play a constructive role in initiating development. But Patriots were relatively indifferent to where sovereignty lay within the state. They dismissed sixteenth- and seventeenth-century political theorists like Jean Bodin and Thomas Hobbes, who had insisted on unitary and clearly defined sovereign powers. Instead, Patriots, along with the former governor of West Florida, George Johnstone, believed that "a free government necessarily involves many clashing jurisdictions when pushed to the extreme." Johnstone, like so many Patriots, referred his British auditors to the examples of the overlapping sovereignties of Athenian committees and of the confused sovereignty in the Dutch confederation. Properly understood, "sovereignty," explained that most enthusiastic Patriot, Jonathan Shipley, bishop of St. Asaph, meant no more than "that just mixture of power and authority which is necessary to carry on the common interest, and on great occasions to exert the strength of the whole." Many North American Patriots similarly advocated notions of coordinated sovereignty. "We are dependent on each other—not totally independent states," Benjamin Rush insisted in debate. "Every man in America stands related to two legislative bodies," he elaborated; "he deposits his property, liberty, and life with his own state, but his trade and arms, the means of enriching and defending himself and his honor, he deposits with Congress."[24] Patriots were more concerned about constructing a state that could promote the common good than they were about delineating exact sovereign boundaries.

Why, then, did the members of the Second Continental Congress feel the necessity to declare independence in 1776? Until they formally declared independence, the delegates knew, they could not raise the money necessary to pursue their essential state building projects. The American army retreated ignominiously from Canada in the winter of 1775–76 in large part because Congress lacked the "hard money" necessary to support troops and to secure Canadian and Indian allies. "Can we hope to carry on a war without having trade or commerce somewhere? Can we ever pay any taxes without it?" asked the North Carolinian John Penn. "The consequence of making alliances is perhaps total separation with Britain," he explained, "and without something of that sort we may not be able to procure what is necessary for our defense." To secure trade with France, Benjamin Harrison concurred, "we must declare ourselves a free people." France would "lend her aid," Samuel Adams thought, only "if America would declare herself free and independent." No European power would be prepared to trade or treat with rebels, both because such actions might encourage uprisings within their own states and for fear that the rebels would negotiate a treaty with Britain to end the conflict. Without foreign alliances and treaties of commerce, the American war effort would collapse. "The war cannot long be prosecuted without trade, nor can taxes be paid until we are enabled to sell our produce," Richard Lee averred, "which cannot be the case without the help of foreign ships, whilst our enemy's navy is so superior to ours." The Americans needed much more than recognition—they needed commerce to support the war effort and to create a diversified American economy. It was precisely for this reason that immediately upon signing the Declaration, the Continental Congress ordered that copies be sent to the courts of Europe, translated into French, and "published" in European newspapers.[25]

American Patriots knew that like all modern statesmen and women, they could not hope to achieve all they aimed for with only the revenues immediately to hand. They knew they had to borrow money. The American state, they agreed, was never intended to be debt free. Even Thomas Paine, who was perhaps the century's fiercest critic of national debts, admitted that "no nation ought to be without debt" because "a national debt is a national bond." But without declaring independence it would be impossible for the North American Congress to borrow money to support its urgent state-building needs. Robert Morris floated the idea of borrowing money from European states, including the Dutch Republic, but with no possibility of offering "security" absent independence, he very much doubted that "any power in Europe will trust us." Others knew that a new American state needed to be created in order for Congress to issue stable paper currency secured against future revenues. This was why, when a declaration of independence appeared to be immediately forthcoming in mid-June 1776, the future vice president Elbridge Gerry expected that "loan offices will be established."[26] Independence, Gerry knew, would require the new republic to borrow money against the credit of the United States.

The Declaration of Independence was, then, less about unmaking the British Empire in North America than it was about announcing to the world the establishment of a new American government.[27] From the first, the Founders sought to create a government that would have all of the virtues but none of the vices of the British imperial state. In short, they wanted to fashion an American version of the Patriot state that had existed in Britain before the accession of George III.

Unmaking the empire and creating an American government were two very different enterprises. Perhaps no single piece of writing did more to articulate the importance of unmaking the British Empire than Thomas Paine's *Common Sense.* Paine's book, published in January 1776, was an immediate hit. In 1776 alone, Paine claimed, the book sold more than 100,000 copies. Many thought the book did "immense service" in the cause of independence, particularly persuading those in the middle and southern colonies that the time had come to sever ties with the British Empire. Paine, with the help of Dr. Benjamin Rush of Philadelphia, had deftly and powerfully summarized the arguments against reconciliation with Britain that had been voiced in the Second Continental Congress. He had done so with panache, in "a clear, simple, concise and nervous style."[28]

Paine's tract was popular because it used Patriot arguments to condemn George III and his ministry. The government Paine described in *Common Sense,* however, was a far cry from that envisioned by most Patriots. Whereas the Patriots had admiringly described the pre-1760 British imperial government as one that had positively promoted the development of the colonies, Paine denied that it could have had any such effect. Instead, he thought government could only act as a restraint on human vices. "Society is produced by our wants, government by our wickedness," he proclaimed. The whole purpose of government was merely to provide "security," he wrote; "even in its best state [it] is but a necessary evil." In his analysis of the state, Paine was far closer to the views of the ministerial writer and critic of the Declaration John Lind than he was to those of the Patriots. "His notions and plans of continental government" were perhaps unsurprisingly at the time "not much applauded."[29]

The more he mulled over Paine's principles, the more John Adams came to detest his views of government. In April 1776, Adams described Paine's notions as "poor and despicable"; by May they were "crude, ignorant." When he contemplated those notions later in life, he thought they "flowed from simple ignorance." While Adams pointedly took issue with Paine's institutional design, his defense of a single legislative house, his differences with Paine ran deeper. Whereas Paine understood government to be a necessary evil, and could imagine only a government that would prevent humans from harming one another, Adams believed government could and should play a more constructive role. Adams therefore wrote his own *Thoughts on Government,* published in April, in order "to counteract the effect" of *Common Sense.*[30]

It was Adams and not Paine who served on the Committee of Five appointed to draft the Declaration of Independence in June 1776. That committee also included Roger Sherman from New Haven, Robert R. Livingston of New York City, Dr. Benjamin Franklin, and Thomas Jefferson. Together they crafted a document that was "an expression of the American mind." They set forth no "new principles or new arguments, never before thought of," intending instead to express "the common sense of the subject." That sense derived from "the whole people," who had been "discussing it in newspapers and pamphlets, and debating it in Assemblies, Conventions, Committees of Safety and Inspection, in town and county meetings, as well as in private conversations." After the full committee "examined" the draft, it presented the document to Congress as a whole, where it was subjected to "severe criticism," leading to some final modifications. It was only then that the Declaration of Independence was "published to the world." It was precisely because it represented the "common sense" of the people, rather than the *Common Sense* of Thomas Paine, that the Americans "in every colony of the 13 have now adopted it as their own act."[31]

The Declaration was in many ways less the work of the Committee of Five than the collaborative effort of generations of Patriots in Britain and in North America. Since the English Revolution of 1688–89, Patriots had called for a strong state that would intervene to promote prosperity. They refined and honed their arguments in light of new developments. But throughout, they insisted that only a consumer-driven economy would generate lasting economic gains. Patriots believed the state needed to do all it could to augment the numbers and increase the economic wherewithal of these consumers. These were the principles that Lawrence Washington and thousands of American Patriots had imbibed from the Patriot Admiral Edward Vernon. These were the principles enunciated by the Patriot heroes of the midcentury: William Pitt, Isaac Barré, Henry Seymour Conway, John Wilkes, and the earl of Shelburne. These were the views still held by friends of the Americans in Britain, such as Richard Price, Edmund Burke, and Matthew Robinson.

These were also the views espoused, elaborated, and developed by North American Patriots Alexander Hamilton, James Otis Jr., Christopher Gadsden, and Benjamin Franklin. Only by reading the Declaration whole, and in the context of the Patriot tradition from which it emerged, is it possible to grasp its full meaning and its relevance today.

Contemporaries highlighted the importance of the Declaration as a state-forming document. When John Adams, one of the Committee of Five, wrote to his wife, triumphantly reporting on the adoption of the Declaration, he called attention not to the philosophical prologue but to the conclusion, which emphasized the document's state-making function. To Abigail he quoted the language "that these united colonies are, and of right ought to be free and independent states, and as such, they have, and of right ought to have full power to make war, conclude peace, establish commerce, and to do all the other acts and things, which other states may rightfully do." The ministerial enemies of the Patriots understood the Declaration as a state-making document as well. John Lind, for example, took "little or no notice" of the famous preamble to the Declaration, preferring instead to devote more than one hundred pages analyzing and rejecting the policy complaints of the American Patriots. The American loyalist Thomas Hutchinson likewise paid no attention to the philosophical preamble. He, similarly, trained his sights on the Continental Congress's grievances. For Hutchinson, as for many contemporary readers, the point of the Declaration was to create a new and energetic government. That is why Hutchinson pointed out that the Americans adopted the English state-builder Oliver Cromwell as "their favorite."[32]

The authors of the Declaration dated the origins of their misery to a very specific historical moment. Their difficulties had begun, they announced, with "the history of the present

King of Great Britain," the history of George III, who had come
to the throne only in October 1760, beginning "the history of
repeated injuries and usurpations" that now clearly constituted
"the establishment of an absolute tyranny over these states."
The congressional delegates framed their policy complaints in
terms not only of very recent events, but of "a long train of
usurpations and abuses, pursuing the same object." They complained, in other words, not only of individual misguided
policies but of a long series of actions that constituted a dangerous and pernicious ideology. The Founders dated the design
and implementation of this system not to the seventeenth
century, not to the beginning of the British Empire in America,
but to the period immediately following the Seven Years' War.

In claiming that British imperial "tyranny" commenced
only with the reversal of policies associated with the accession
of George III, the Founders were rehearsing a key Patriot argument. They insisted that the British imperial constitution had
worked well before 1760. The Virginian Arthur Lee referred
nostalgically to "the good days of George the Second."[33] Until
George III and his ministers began reversing three-quarters
of a century of imperial practices, British America had been
a flourishing place. Before Lord Bute, George Grenville, and
Lord North decided to replace state support for colonial development with illegitimate and unnecessary taxes, North Americans had lived happily under imperial rule. The problem was
not imperial sovereignty; the solution was not the end of empire.
The authors of the Declaration maintained that the problem
was recent imperial governance. When it became clear that
no action on the part of the American Patriots or their British
allies could bring down the North ministry and produce
imperial reform, the Patriots decided to initiate the policies
they desired themselves. Frustrated in their hopes for imperial

reform, the Patriots believed the solution was to create a new kind of state.

In advancing this specific historical claim, the authors of the Declaration were simply crystallizing deeply held Patriot beliefs. Patriots on both sides of the Atlantic dated the rise of discontent to the reversal of imperial economic policy in the 1760s. "No act avowedly for the purpose of a revenue" predated 1764, argued Edmund Burke; "the scheme of a colony revenue by British authority appeared therefore to the Americans in the light of a great innovation." The "rapid and bold succession of injuries" that began only with the accession of George III "is likely to distinguish the present from all other periods of American story," wrote Thomas Jefferson in 1774. It was only then that "a deliberate and systematical plan" was adopted for "reducing us to slavery." The earl of Shelburne "condemned in very severe terms the measures administration had pursued for ten years past." As late as July 1774 John Adams blamed "the political innovations of the last 10 years" for almost all the problems that Americans faced. "The present unhappy system of affairs," agreed the delegates to the First Continental Congress, "is occasioned by a ruinous system of colony administration adopted by the British ministry about the year 1763."[34] Patriots perceived the 1760s as a turning point not because it was their first contact with the British imperial state after two centuries of neglect. Rather, they perceived that before the accession of George III the imperial state had helped stimulate colonial development, whereas afterward it had sought merely to extract contributions to pay down the national debt.

The Committee of Five drew up a list of grievances against George III and Lord North's ministry that relied heavily on the economic principles Patriots had been defending at least since the 1730s. Having traced the emergence and development of those principles, it is now possible to unlock the ideological premises of the Declaration of Independence.

The Committee of Five made clear its belief that a broad-based consumer society was the key to future prosperity. The committee enunciated these views most clearly in its discussion of the older grievances. While the Committee of Five did cata-logue the crescendo of oppressive acts of the 1770s—the Quebec Act, the Boston Port Act, forced quartering troops with North Americans—the political economic thrust of the Declaration lies in the complaints dating from the reversal of ministerial policy in the 1760s.[35] The committee returned to three recurring Patriot concerns: (1) the British suppression of trade with Span-ish America, (2) the British refusal to support immigration to North America, and (3) British ministerial support for chattel slavery. All three of these grievances, the Patriots felt, had threatened American prosperity. By outlining these grievances the congressional delegates made clear that they expected a new American state would pursue entirely different policies. Finally, Congress felt compelled to explain why it was that their "British brethren," the inhabitants of the British Isles, were "deaf to the voice of justice and consanguinity." Unsurprisingly, the committee ascribed that failure to a political economic omission in the design of the imperial constitution that became increas-ingly manifest as North American populations grew in the late eighteenth century.

First, the Committee of Five, writing in the Patriot tradi-tion, accused George III and his Parliament of "cutting off our trade with all parts of the world." While Lord North, and more recent commentators, thought the colonists were com-plaining about Britain's Coercive Acts of 1774, this was a concern of far longer duration, becoming especially acute in the 1760s. This had been the Patriot complaint against the South Sea

Company in the 1730s. Patriots on both sides of the Atlantic had complained vociferously against George Grenville's executive orders that had shut down the vital illicit trade with Spanish America in the 1760s. By shutting down this trade, the British ministry had effectively deprived the colonies of their only source of hard currency. Spanish coin had long lubricated the wheels of American commerce. Benjamin Franklin was one of many Patriots who lamented the "bad results" of that policy. Patriots had enthusiastically embraced the Rockingham administration's plan to invigorate North American trade and inject "hard money" into the economy by establishing free ports in the mid-1760s.[36] Without trade with the Spanish territories, British Americans had little or no means of exchange.

Opening markets in Spanish America remained a central tenet of the Patriot economic model. Matthew Robinson proposed that the British ministry should "do almost directly the contrary of what we are about, that is to give a greater liberty and latitude of trade both to Ireland and to America including our West India islands." Benjamin Franklin, one of the Committee of Five, had called in 1775 for Britain to "give us the same privileges of trade as Scotland received at the union, and allow us a free commerce with all the rest of the world." Should the imperial government agree to that, Franklin averred as a member of Congress, "we shall willingly agree (and we doubt not it will be ratified by our constituents) to give and pay into the Sinking Fund £100,000 sterling per annum for the term of one hundred years," a sum "more than sufficient to extinguish all her present national debt." Jefferson, too, had called on the British imperial government not "to exclude us from going to other markets."[37] While neither Franklin nor Jefferson specified which foreign markets they meant, Patriots on both sides of the Atlantic knew full well about the immense riches that could be gained by supplying the fifteen million people of Spanish America with their consumer needs.

In many ways, of course, the authors of the Declaration's call for free trade was indeed a call for limits on government regulation. But it was at the same time a plea for *more* government involvement. A call for free trade in the eighteenth century had very different implications from a similar statement today. Benjamin Franklin, for one, argued as Adam Smith would the following year that "perhaps, in general, it would be better if government meddled no further with trade than to protect it, and let it take its course." But in the context of the 1770s to "protect" trade required significant state investment to allow commerce in the face of hostile governments. In other words, the Patriots very much wanted unfettered *access* to markets, but they had no interest in *unregulated* or *unprotected* markets. Trading with the Spanish and French American colonies, as Josiah Tucker was all too happy to point out, was "in disobedience to the injunctions of their Mother Countries."[38] The French and Spanish Empires forbade their subjects to trade directly with foreigners. British Americans knew well, after years of fighting off Spanish attempts to patrol the Caribbean, that they could trade "with all parts of the world" only with state gunboats protecting their commerce. At the very least they needed to create safe havens in North America where French and Spanish merchants could trade freely without fear of interference from either their home governments or the British navy. In foreign trade the post-1760 British imperial regime had both done too much to suppress American smuggling and too little to create the facilities and provide the protection necessary for a profitable commerce.

The American Founders' second complaint was about British immigration policy. Patriots believed that well-designed states should promote immigration. This was the reason the authors of the Declaration of Independence denounced George III for endeavoring "to prevent the population of these States." Since 1760 the British monarch had made emigration to America more difficult and less lucrative by "obstructing the Laws for Naturalization of Foreigners" and "raising the conditions of new Appropriations of Lands." And George III had reversed generations of imperial policy by "refusing to pass" laws "to encourage . . . migrations hither."[39]

Immigration had become a contentious issue again in the 1760s and 1770s. It had become "of late years a common idea that the population of England is declining very fast," noted the famous British agricultural writer Arthur Young. Those holding this widespread view, a view "not only found in political pamphlets, but which often occurs in Parliament," blamed Britain's plight in large part "on emigrations to the colonies." Richard Price, for example, spoke of "depopulation so great as to have reduced the inhabitants in England and Wales near a quarter in eighty years." On this, if little else, Josiah Tucker agreed, lamenting "the late prodigious swarms of emigrants" to America. Britons were right to sense a tremendous surge of emigration: more than 125,000 people left the British Isles for North America between 1760 and 1775. From the 1760s, Grenvillians and their supporters had fretted about the economic consequences of this outmigration. Because they were obsessed with the size of the national debt and the role economic production would play in paying down that debt, Grenville and his supporters were desperate to keep workers within the British Isles. In this they were reviving concerns about migration and British population from the seventeenth century. As early as February 1763 a government memorandum advised that "an immediate and effective check" be placed "on the migration of our common people by confining our settlements in America within common limits."⁴⁰ No doubt sentiments such as these were, in part, responsible for the Proclamation of 1763, which placed strict limits on the western extension of British American settlements.

As concerns of British emigration escalated, along with the development of various North American plans for expanding into and settling in western lands, the British ministry reversed decades of immigration policy. Not only had the imperial state ceased to subsidize immigration, as it had done in the 1730s for Georgia, but it increasingly vetoed colonial legislation that offered assistance to new immigrants. The press overflowed with comments on the local and national consequences of migration to America. "What South America has been to Spain, North America has been to us," proclaimed one ministerial spokesman: "a downright depopulation of our country." In 1773 the government leaked a proposed bill to the press that would have severely restricted British emigration.⁴¹

The British ministry's recent efforts to limit migration to the colonies, reversing decades of state support for immigration, infuriated the members of the Second Continental Congress. From their perspective, efforts to limit migration to North America not only were unjust, they also made little economic sense. Migrants left Britain in search of greater prosperity. With their new wealth they would become more prolific consumers, purchasing more British manufactured goods, and would thereby strengthen the empire. High wages, the very reason migrants came to the new world, proved that North America still desperately needed labor to continue to develop. It was "madness in the extreme" to attempt to "diminish" the population of North America, argued Arthur Lee; "were these men, these plantations, these cities trebled, the profits would center in Great Britain, and add so much more to her strength and opulence." The ministry, complained Thomas Jefferson, referring no doubt to Hillsborough's long and successful opposition to colonial westward expansion, had adopted new land policies by which "the population of our country is likely to be checked." The local Committee of Darien, Georgia, made a similar point. Restrictive land policies formed "a principal part of the unjust system of politics adopted by the present Ministry," they said, with the aim "to prevent as much as possible the population of America and the relief of the poor and distressed of Britain and elsewhere."[42]

Immigration, Patriots were convinced, should receive government support, not restrictions or prohibitions. New immigrants provided necessary labor and skills. Opening up new lands "on easy terms" would "invite emigrants to settle," argued the members of the Mississippi Land Company, including George Washington, "and the inhabitants of the infant settlement, finding their labor most profitably bestowed on agriculture," would inevitably generate "a large and never falling demand" for British manufactured goods, thereby enlarging the British "revenue." Benjamin Franklin, the self-proclaimed "friend of the poor," made clear his commitment to the same Patriot political economic principles in his more pointed attack on the proposed legislation to limit emigration from Britain. "New settlers to America," he argued, reproduce far more quickly than they would had they remained in Britain because land was cheaper and prosperity more easily attained. As a result "new farms are daily everywhere forming in those immense forests, new towns and villages rising; hence a growing demand for our merchandise to the greater employment of our manufacturers and the enriching of our merchants." Far from weakening Britain, immigration was a positive boon: "by this natural increase of people, the strength of the Empire is increased." Increasing the population of the colonies necessarily augmented Britain's trade, agreed the authors of *The Crisis,* so it was in Britain's "interest to encourage their increase."[43] America's founders made clear that they expected the new republic to pursue its interest and support new immigrants who would soon become consumers in a vibrant economy.

Third, America's founders signaled their commitment to a political economy of consumption in their treatment of chattel slavery. In the draft of the Declaration initially presented to Congress the Committee of Five accused George III of having "waged war against human nature itself, violating its most sacred rights of life and liberty in the persons of a distant people who never offended him, captivating and carrying them into slavery in a another hemisphere or to incur miserable death in their transportation thither." To keep the slave trade open, the committee insisted, George III "prostituted his negative for suppressing every legislative attempt to prohibit or restrain this execrable commerce."[44] This intended clause of the Declaration of Independence, with its powerful language, neatly captured the spirit of the Patriot antislavery movement.

Loyalists and Tories at the time berated the Patriots for their hypocritical acceptance of chattel slavery. "I would wish to ask the delegates of Maryland, Virginia and the Carolinas, how their constituents justify their depriving more than an hundred thousand Africans of their right to liberty and the pursuit of happiness, and in some degree to their lives, if these rights are so absolutely inalienable," sneered Thomas Hutchinson. "Slaves there are in America, and where there are slaves, there liberty is alienated," pointed out another commentator on the Declaration. "How is it that we hear the loudest yelps for liberty among the drivers of negroes?" asked the great Tory literary figure Samuel Johnson.[45] In fact, far from being insensitive to the miserable plight of hundreds of thousands of slaves in North America, the Patriots took a strong stance against the cruel and inhumane institution.

Patriots had long opposed the institution of slavery as being inconsistent with the aims and values of a modern commercial society. In the 1730s, many Patriots on both sides of the Atlantic had denounced the pernicious economic and moral consequences of slavery. Some, like William Byrd of Virginia, himself a slaveholder, had called for a parliamentary statute banning slavery. The Patriot trustees of Georgia had outlawed slavery in their new province. While many continued to voice concerns about chattel slavery in British America, and others objected to the inhumanity of the slave trade, it was in the 1760s and 1770s that a broad and powerful antislavery movement reemerged.

A variety of interventions on both sides of the Atlantic framed a lively public debate on the merits and demerits of chattel slavery. The Massachusetts Patriot James Otis Jr., perhaps drawing on the marquis de Mirabeau's denunciation of slavery, declared the slave trade to be "the most shocking violation of the law of nature, [which] has a direct tendency to diminish the idea of the inestimable value of liberty and makes every dealer in it a tyrant." In 1769 the prolific Granville Sharp launched his career as an abolitionist. Sharp, whose work was quickly circulated in abridged form in America, soon befriended the Americans Benjamin Rush and Benjamin Franklin, and was throughout the crisis of the 1770s a firm ally of the American cause. Rush himself penned two widely circulated pamphlets condemning slavery, inspired by the writings of the Quaker abolitionist Anthony Benezet. These were followed in quick succession with a slew of other tracts and sermons on the subject.[46] Discussions were further animated by William Murray 1st earl of Mansfield's celebrated, though narrow, June 1772 judgment in the case of *Somerset v. Stewart* that slavery was illegal in England.

Pro-slavery advocates, though less prolific, were not silent in defense of the institution. Most in the "Southern provinces" and the West Indies, John Laurens told his father, did "obstinately recur to the most absurd arguments in support of slavery" but ultimately fell back on economic claims: "Without slaves how is it possible for us to be rich?" Only African slaves were capable of the hard labor in difficult climates required "in the southern continental province[s], and in the sugar islands," maintained the West Indian Edward Long. In this context Harvard College staged a public dispute on the legality of chattel slavery in July 1773.[47]

The widespread Patriot belief that British America was in the process of an epochal transition gave urgency to the anti-slavery movement as it gathered steam. Patriots, like most in the eighteenth century, divided human history in stages of sociocultural development. British America, Patriots believed, was poised on the transition from a primitive agrarian stage to a modern civilized society. Patriots argued that further commercial development required the elimination of slavery. Patriots thought that slave societies tended to be ones in which wealth was concentrated in the hands of a few rich oligarchs who squeezed all the wealth they could through the exploitive harvesting of single crops like tobacco, rice, or sugar. Because of this extreme concentration of wealth, slave societies could never develop into broad-based consumer societies. Such societies were less likely to develop quickly, were more likely to remain at primitive stages of development, and were also far more dependent on an increasingly intransigent mother country. Many in North America agreed with the influential Scottish Enlightenment writer John Millar that when "a people became civilized" they came to appreciate the economic inefficiencies of slavery. They learned that a slave had no incentive either to consume or "to exert much vigor or activity in the exercise of any employment," that "the work of a slave who receives nothing but a bare subsistence, is really dearer than that of a freeman to whom constant wages are given in a proportion to his industry." Millar determined that "it is a matter of regret that any species of slavery should still remain in the dominions of Great Britain." Edward Wigglesworth, holder of the prestigious Hollis Chair of Divinity at Harvard College, was one among many American readers of Millar who concluded that it was "to the disgrace of America [that] slavery still prevails here." In this Wigglesworth was echoing the views of the prominent British legal thinker Francis Hargrave, who had been retained as James Somerset's lawyer by Granville Sharp. Hargrave, whose brief in the Somerset case was reprinted in North America, denounced slavery as a "pernicious institution" typical of the "early and barbarous state of society."[48]

Beginning in the late 1760s an increasing number of Patriots, not a few of them slaveholders, began to voice their belief that the abolition of the slave trade, at a minimum, and possibly the abolition of slavery itself was necessary for British America to become fully civilized. Slaveholders reasoned that only government legislation prohibiting the slave trade, or outlawing slavery, would allow them to do what they believed was right without simultaneously destroying their economic livelihoods. The wealthy South Carolina merchant Christopher Gadsden, soon to be owner of the largest wharf in America, thought slavery a "crime" that weakened his home province. It was under Gadsden's leadership that the South Carolina Sons of Liberty—radicals to be sure but radicals in a rice-producing province—proposed to outlaw the slave trade. Gadsden's fellow South Carolinian and future president of the Second Continental Congress Henry Laurens had come to "abhor slavery," declaring that "the day I hope is approaching when from principles of gratitude as well as justice every man will strive to be foremost in showing his readiness to comply with the Golden Rule" and abolish slavery. Laurens's son John, who would later propose to create a black regiment in the Continental Army, argued in March 1776 that "the Southern colonies cannot contend with a good grace for liberty until we shall have enfranchised our slaves." William Whipple of New Hampshire, a signer of the Declaration, enthusiastically endorsed John Laurens's plans for a black regiment, hoping it would lead to "emancipation" and "the means of dispensing the blessings of freedom to all the human race in America." Benjamin Franklin, though a slave owner, had long been skeptical about slavery. After the *Somerset* case he publicly declared his wish that the freedom accorded James Somerset be made general. In the short term he pleaded for "a law for abolishing the African commerce in slaves and declaring the children of present slaves free after they become of age." The celebrated president of the College of New Jersey, and a signer of the Declaration, John Witherspoon, also warned that slaves had been historically "grievously oppressed" in free states, urging that measures be taken to prevent this in the future. Rush was one among many who perceived a tidal wave of sentiment "in favor of the poor negroes" in North America. The editors of the *New York Journal* opined in December 1774 "that a spirit of opposition to the enslaving of others prevails among the British colonists."[49]

North American Patriots did not merely speak out against slavery and the slave trade. They took decisive action. The

Pennsylvania Assembly in 1773 passed such a stiff duty on imported slaves that its effect amounted "to an almost total prohibition." The Rhode Island Assembly in 1774, despite the huge profits reaped by many Rhode Island slave traders, "prohibited the importation of negro slaves under a large penalty, and have enacted that such slaves shall be free as soon as they set foot on the shore within the colony." Connecticut soon followed suit, leading one American journalist to claim that this action entirely refuted "the argument of those who say, that while they are struggling, and willing to brave every difficulty and hardship for their own freedom, they encourage the violation of other men's liberty." In 1772 the Virginia House of Burgesses, with many slaveholders among them, had addressed George III, arguing against the "great inhumanity" of the slave trade and insisting that the institution of slavery "greatly retards the settlement of the colonies." Two years later county after county in Virginia—eight in all—passed resolutions against the slave trade. Most, like George Washington's home county of Fairfax, linked their pleas for a permanent end to this "wicked, cruel and unnatural trade" to their desire to diversify and modernize the Virginia economy. For Virginians the end of slavery would necessarily create a broader and more equal consumer base and play a large role in promoting the province's transition from a more primitive to a more advanced stage of development. The Committee of Darien, Georgia, drawing on its region's long tradition of opposition to slavery, indicated its "disapprobation and abhorrence of the unnatural practice of slavery in America" and pledged to work for "the manumission of our slaves in this colony." The Provincial Congress of Georgia pledged in January 1775 to end the importation of slaves.[50]

There could be no doubting the broad-based antislavery movement in North America in the 1770s. Many in North

Carolina were lobbying the Assembly there to address the king against the slave trade, reported one essayist in 1774. "The chief justices of both North and South Carolina are interesting themselves against the traffic," this essayist continued; "the people of Maryland also are roused on this matter; the Assemblies of Pennsylvania and New Jersey are applied to by petition from a great number of the inhabitants of those provinces; the Assembly of New York passed an act laying a duty on any further importation, but it was refused by the Governor; Connecticut hath prohibited any further importation, and ordered all that may be born in the colony to be free; and the Massachusetts Assembly passed an act at their last session, prohibiting any further importation and ordered that none should be bought or sold in the colony and all born after to be free, but it was negatived by the Governor." In April 1776, the Continental Congress itself—in a step that has received scant notice from most historians—no doubt responding to this wave of sentiment from New Hampshire to Georgia, resolved to ban the slave trade.[51]

Despite this widespread desire to put an end to the slave trade and in some instances to abolish slavery itself, the Committee of Five's antislavery clause was omitted in the final draft of the Declaration. Seeking to maintain "unanimity" in the Congress, Jefferson recalled, the committee "struck out" the clause "reprobating the enslaving the inhabitants of Africa." This was done, he said, "in complaisance to South Carolina and Georgia, who had never attempted to restrain the importation of slaves, and who on the contrary still wished to continue it." In fact, Georgia had sought to limit the slave trade and was anyway too small to represent a threat. Wealthy and powerful South Carolina was another matter. With the fiery critic of slavery Christopher Gadsden back in Charleston, Edward Rutledge attempted to organize opposition to the Declaration and the proposed Articles of Confederation on the grounds that they advanced "leveling principles." Rutledge and his supporters, in essence, believed that British America had not yet reached the level of refinement achieved in Europe. In its current state, American commerce required hierarchy and slavery. Rutledge understood well that his political opponents intended to create a strong state that would be inimical to oligarchical slave societies. His fellow delegate from South Carolina Thomas Lynch warned in late July that any attempt to threaten slavery would constitute "an end of the confederation." South Carolina successfully postponed the vote on the Declaration to secure amendments that Josiah Bartlett worried might spoil an already "pretty good" document.[52] The Declaration that the Carolinians finally agreed to no longer included the explicit condemnation of slavery and the slave trade.

The Committee of Five and the majority in the Continental Congress did not, however, fully concede the point. The first complaint against George III in the restructured Declaration was that he had "refused to assent to laws, the most wholesome and necessary for the public good." Taken out of historical context, this phrase is vague and enigmatic. But it was language frequently deployed by Patriot critics of slavery and the slave trade. In his widely circulated and oft-reprinted *Observations,* Richard Price had pointed out that "it is not the fault of the colonies that they have among them so many of these unhappy people." The colonists had "made laws to prohibit the importation of them," he insisted, "but these laws have always had a negative put upon them here, because of their tendency to hurt our negro trade." Benjamin Franklin, a member of the drafting committee, had previously called attention to the "several laws heretofore made in our colonies to discourage the importation of slaves" that were "disapproved and repealed by your government here as being prejudicial forsooth to the interest of the African Company." This was Thomas Jefferson's view as well. In 1774 he had blamed George III for rejecting colonial anti-slavery laws "of the most salutary tendency." "The abolition of domestic slavery is the great object of desire in those colonies," Jefferson insisted. They had made "repeated attempts" to put an end to the slave trade. All of these were "defeated by his Majesty's negative." George III had, Jefferson fumed, preferred "the immediate advantage of a few African corsairs to the lasting interests of the American states, and to the rights of human nature deeply wounded by this infamous practice."[53] Patriots had long believed that George III had put a stop to colonial efforts to end the slave trade even though those efforts manifestly aimed to promote "the public good."

So deeply did American Patriots believe that they could now be counted among the most civilized societies that they denounced George III and his minions for conducting war in an uncivilized manner. The Founders blamed George III and his ministers for "transporting large armies of foreign mercenaries to complete the works of death, desolation and tyranny, already begun with circumstances of cruelty and perfidy scarcely paralleled in the most barbarous ages and totally unworthy of the head of a civilized nation." As part of this barbarous strategy of warfare, a strategy that violated the accepted laws of war, George III was also exciting "domestic insurrections amongst us" and endeavoring "to bring on the inhabitant of our frontiers, the merciless Indian savages, whose known rule of warfare, is an undistinguished destruction of all ages, sexes and conditions." In these powerful clauses the Founders were not, at base, commenting on the Indians. Rather they were denouncing George III for having eschewed the rules of civilization in favor of a return to a more primitive means of conducting foreign affairs. Indeed, members of Congress held a bewildering array of sentiments toward the Indians. Some hoped for Indian neutrality in the conflict with George III. They treated the Indians as civilized noncombatants. Others wanted to employ Indians among the regular troops of the army. Still others sought to strengthen and expand Indian alliances. All, however, condemned the barbarous ways in which they perceived the British to be deploying Indians. Most members of Congress knew from their reading the great theorist of international conflict Emmerich de Vattel that "the common laws of war, those maxims of humanity, moderation and probity, which we have before enumerated and recommended, are in civil wars to be observed by both sides." In particular, Vattel insisted, and the Founders agreed, that women, children, the sick, and the aged "are enemies who make no resistance, and consequently give us no right to treat their persons ill, or use any violence against them, much less to take away their lives."[54] In the view of the Founders, the British were encouraging the Indians to employ just these barbarous military tactics. Just as the Founders insisted that their own transition into a higher state of civilization made the use of chattel slaves inappropriate, so they denounced George III for dragging Britain into a state of barbarism through his military tactics.

In the Declaration of Independence, Patriots made clear their intentions to create a government that would promote a dynamic consumer economy in their treatment of the hot button issues of foreign trade, immigration, and slavery. They believed that in preventing the colonies from gaining hard currency and new and skilled workers, and in preventing them from diversifying their economies by eliminating slave societies devoted to the production of a single crop, such as rice, George III and his ministerial allies had done all they could to prevent colonial prosperity. American Patriots intended the Declaration to lay the foundation for a new state that would remedy these deficiencies. They wanted to create a state that would guarantee the rights and provide the support that the Patriot imperial state had delivered before the accession of George III.

The authors of the Declaration did, of course, denounce George III for "imposing taxes on us without our consent." Patriots were not averse to paying taxes. They were already willingly paying large sums to support the war effort. Why, then, did they find taxation without representation to be such a heinous breach of their privileges? Over and over again, we are often reminded, the American Patriots had pointed out that the right to tax themselves was a right long guaranteed by the British constitution.[55] But Patriots on both sides of the Atlantic had also emphasized that taxation *without representation*—not taxation in general—generated bad economic policies. It was the lack of representation, rather than their antipathy to taxation, that propelled the Patriots to action.

An unrepresented population was, Patriots argued, a population that could not provide needed economic information nor press the government to remove grievous exactions. Lord John Cavendish was typical of many Patriots in believing that the origins of the "injurious and inefficacious" ministerial policies lay in the "want of full and proper information being laid before Parliament." As long as Americans were not represented in an imperial Parliament, the English and Scots would have every incentive to remove the tax burden from themselves and their electors and extract revenue from those who could not vote them out of office. The "British Parliament with a view to the ease and advantage of itself and its constituents," thought Alexander Hamilton, "would oppress and grind the Americans as much as possible." "The people of England would pull down the Parliament house if their present heavy burdens were not transferred from them to you," he explained. This was also the conclusion of the County Committee for Fairfax Virginia, chaired by George Washington. It concluded that Britain was adopting a "species of tyranny and oppression" precisely because with no American representation Parliament was acting on "information" that "must be always defective, and often false." With no American representation, the imperial Parliament "may have a separate, and in some [instances] an opposite interest to ours." At the heart of the famous call for no taxation without representation was an analysis of what went so terribly wrong in the British Empire after 1760. A sovereign imperial legislature with imperfect information and accountable only to English and a few Scottish voters was badly designed to promote the prosperity of the whole. "Equal interests among the people, should have equal interests in the representative people," according to the principle pithily expressed by John Adams.[56] A future American state, they implied, needed to represent all Americans; informed by, and accountable to, the broadest swath of the population.

Knowing that the Declaration of Independence was a call to state formation in the Patriot mode, it becomes possible to reexamine the most cited and best-known lines of the document: "We hold these truths to be self-evident, that all men are created equal, that they are endowed by their Creator with certain unalienable Rights, that among these are Life, Liberty and the pursuit of Happiness.—That to secure these rights, Governments are instituted among Men." That governments were "instituted among men" to protect not only life and liberty, but "the pursuit of happiness" as well, had become a commonplace in eighteenth-century political argument. For precisely this reason "the pursuit of happiness" had many potential meanings. Patriots, by and large, however, had a more specific meaning in mind. They interpreted the phrase to mean the promotion of the public good or welfare. States, they believed, were instituted to do much more than merely provide security: they were much more than a necessary evil.

Patriots believed passionately that states had a responsibility positively to promote the happiness of their populations. This had long been the view of those revered by the American Patriots. Statesmen, argued John Trenchard and Thomas Gordon in *Cato's Letters*, were responsible for the "wealth, security and happiness of kingdoms." Joseph Priestley was certain "that the happiness of the whole community is the ultimate end of government can never be doubted." "All civil government, as far as it can be denominated free, is the creature of the people," agreed Priestley's great friend Richard Price; it therefore "has in view nothing but their happiness." "The true end of civil regimen is the happiness and prosperity of the governed," asserted the Patriot Charles Lennox, 3rd duke of Richmond, in the House of Lords. "A state ought to have but one object in view," insisted the great French philosophe the Abbé Raynal in 1776, "and that is, public felicity." The rulers of a state should do "everything necessary" to promote "the felicity" of the people, agreed the Swiss theorist Vattel, by which he meant providing "the necessities, conveniencies, and even accommodations of life."[57]

American Patriots shared this conviction. Because "every individual is to seek and find his happiness in the welfare of the whole," preached the Connecticut Patriot Levi Watson, and because all governments "must tend to promote the general welfare, this is the test by which they must be tried." The most powerful evidence that the framers of the Declaration understood "the pursuit of happiness" in this way comes from the members of the Continental Congress themselves. They had a very broad view of the positive obligations of government. "All speculative politicians will agree that the happiness of society is the end of government," posited John Adams. "The form of government which communicates ease, comfort, security, or in one word happiness to the greatest number of persons and in the greatest degree," Adams concluded simply, "is the best." Almost a year before they promulgated the Declaration of Independence, the Second Continental Congress issued a much less famous declaration, "The Declaration of the Causes and Necessity for Taking up Arms." The committee that wrote this earlier declaration included Thomas Jefferson and Benjamin Franklin. "Government," they said baldly, "was instituted to promote the welfare of mankind and ought to be administered for the attainment of that end."[58] Read this way, back to front, there can be no doubt that the Declaration of Independence was a call for the creation of a powerful state that would actively promote the welfare of the people.

The Declaration, John Adams proudly proclaimed, "completes a Revolution which will make as good a figure in the history of mankind as any that has preceded it." Benjamin Rush thought it inaugurated "a new era."[59] Both men understood that because no means had been found to resurrect the British Patriot state, it was time to create a Patriot state in the Western Hemisphere. Both men knew that the Declaration had inaugurated a new era of state making in North America. Independence from Britain had existed for more than a year in July 1776. America's founders issued their Declaration to kick-start the creation of a Patriot state. They made their intentions clear by drawing on almost a century of Patriot economic thinking. Like the British Patriots who had governed the empire before 1760, America's Patriots believed in government-supported trade with Spanish America, they believed in state-supported immigration, and they believed in state-supported efforts to diversify the economy. This last position would almost certainly begin with an assault on the slave trade. The American Patriots began and ended their manifesto with paeans to the state.

Perhaps no one understood the implications of the Declaration better than John Adams. "The advantages" that the Declaration will bring are "very numerous and very great," he told John Winthrop. The various colonies would hasten to complete their own governments, and the newly created states would "exert themselves to manufacture saltpeter, sulfur, powder, arms, cannon, mortars, clothing and everything necessary for the support of life." A state with such a broad remit would not be cheap. Adams knew that a government that sought to promote the greatest happiness for the greatest number would require substantial contributions from the people. This is why he admitted to William Gordon that postindependence Americans could look forward to "taxes, heavy taxes for many years."[60]

Epilogue

I n his undelivered first inaugural address, George Washington outlined a remarkable vision for an energetic American government. It was a Patriot blueprint for governance. At the beginning of the conflict with Britain, Washington recalled, "money, the nerve of war, was wanting." The "sword was to be forged on the anvil of necessity" by the fledgling American republic: "the treasury to be created from nothing." And against all odds, from out of nothing, the Americans created a treasury and prevailed in the bloody conflict. Along with peace came the realization that the war had left the new American state with "a load of debt" that needed to be repaid. It was Congress's inability to find means to repay this debt that led America's first president to lament "the impotence of Congress under the former confederation." He therefore called on the new Congress "to raise the supplies for discharging the interest on the national debt." Washington knew that to build a flourishing new polity required Congress to levy new taxes. Washington was not, however, interested in balancing the books. He did not aim only to eliminate the wartime debt. Instead, he proposed a tremendously ambitious program for state-supported economic development. He called for the creation of "a grand provision of warlike stores, arsenals, and dockyards." But Washington did not merely want to prepare the American republic for future wars. He wanted the government to create an economic infrastructure to promote long-term prosperity. "While the individual states shall be occupied in facilitating the means of transportation by opening canals and improving roads," Washington continued, "you will not forget that the purposes of business and society may be vastly promoted by giving cheapness, dispatch and security to communications through the regular posts." Washington knew that the United States was not yet prepared to become a manufacturing nation on the scale of Britain. Nevertheless he thought that "many articles" made of "wool, flax, cotton and hemp; and all in leather, iron, fur and wood may be fabricated at home with great advantage." To that end, he hoped Congress would offer "encouragement"—presumably financial and legislative—to their manufacture. Above all, Washington concluded, Congress should "take measures for promoting the general welfare."[1]

President Washington's commitment to promoting the general welfare was not a postrevolutionary discovery. At an early age Washington, along with many North Americans, had imbibed Patriot views on the importance of state-supported development. Constantly reminded of his own Patriot commitments every time he signed his letters from his ancestral home of Mount Vernon, Washington made clear his support of a Patriot vision for a British imperial government that would financially support colonial development in the midst of the crisis of the 1760s. When he read the Declaration of Independence to his troops in New York in July 1776, he believed that that document embodied long-held Patriot support for the British constitution. That constitution, Washington knew, not only protected the rights of its subjects but also guaranteed their happiness through government support, through the privileges it granted its subjects. When he became the first president of the United States, then, George Washington reiterated arguments for state-supported development he and tens of thousands of Patriots had long held on both sides of the Atlantic. Washington reaffirmed the Patriot commitment to an energetic government that would simultaneously protect its citizens and actively promote their welfare.

In the 1780s, however, many believed that the American government created by the Declaration of Independence and then codified by a separate but simultaneously functioning committee in the Articles of Confederation was not strong enough. Eighteenth-century commentators and modern scholars alike have emphasized the fragility of the polity created by the Articles of Confederation. A series of crises after the Articles of Confederation were finally ratified by all thirteen states in 1781 convinced many that the confederation constitution had created a central government that was far too impotent. Alexander Hamilton maintained that "the confederation of the United States is defective" as a result of "confining the power of the federal government within too narrow limits, withholding from it that efficacious authority and influence in all matters of general concern which are indispensable to the harmony and welfare of the whole." The following year Thomas Jefferson observed that the "conviction was growing strongly that nothing can preserve our confederacy unless the Band of Union, their common council be strengthened." James Madison spoke of "dangerous defects in the Confederation."[2] If the Articles created such an ineffectual state, one might reasonably ask, does that not imply that the Patriots were narrowly committed to winning the war? Does this not suggest that creating an energetic government was at best an afterthought? Doesn't the weakness of America's first constitution imply that the Patriots were in fact merely fighting to rid themselves of the coercive British imperial state?

In fact, the members of the Second Continental Congress were determined to create a confederation that was stronger than any the world had ever seen. Hamilton, Jefferson, and Madison were expressing the same concerns that they and other Patriots had expressed in the 1770s. They were merely pointing out that their first experiment in creating an American constitution had failed to achieve all of their aims. The intentions of the framers of the Articles of Confederation, like those of all historical actors, need to be understood not from the perspective of the unintended consequences of their actions but rather from their aims.

The Articles were from the first conceived as part of a "revolutionary portfolio" of state formation—along with the Declaration, the state constitutions, and the Model Commercial Treaty of July 1776—with the intention of demonstrating to foreign imperial governments other than Britain that the new American republic had the strength not only to conduct a war against the world's strongest imperial power but also to raise money to pay back loans. The Model Commercial Treaty established the new republic's commitment to free trade and a willingness to defend those choosing to trade with the United States, along Patriot lines. The newly independent American states needed the Articles to make clear that theirs was not merely a defensive alliance but a confederated polity that would outlive the war against Britain. That is why all versions of the Articles discussed between 1776 and the passage by Congress of the final Articles in November of 1777 emphasized that the states entered into "a firm league of friendship with each other" not only "for their common defense" but also for the "security of their liberties" and the promotion of "their mutual and general welfare." The Articles were intended, the Second Continental Congress claimed in urging their ratification, to create states "forever bound and connected together by ties the most intimate and indissoluble." Such a confederation, the members of the Second Continental Congress hoped, would "support our public credit, restore the value of our money, enable us to maintain our fleets and armies and add weight and respect to our councils at home and to our treaties abroad."[3] Energetic government, not the location of sovereignty, was the central concern.

British Americans were by no means the first people to have serious discussions of confederation. Members of the Continental Congress drew on a robust discussion of the virtues of confederation that had been conducted since at least the middle of the seventeenth century. These discussions of confederation mushroomed in the wake of the war of Spanish Succession (1701–13) as Europeans sought desperately to avoid the bloodshed that had resulted from this first pan-European struggle over empire. Patriots, in particular, embraced the proposals for perpetual peace advanced by Charles-Irénée Castel, abbé de Saint-Pierre. Saint-Pierre, whose later works the Patriots would embrace in their attacks on Sir Robert Walpole, called for a European "union and perpetual Congress" modeled on the Dutch Republic, the Swiss confederation, or the sovereignties of Germany. Saint-Pierre's ideas resurfaced in the wake of the even bloodier Seven Years' War. They were popularized and widely disseminated by no less a figure than Jean-Jacques Rousseau. In 1776, in the midst of the revolutionary crisis, Richard Price and Adam Smith, both of whom embraced the Patriot political economy of consumption, proposed confederations as the last best hope to avoid imperial civil war and promote peace. It was upon this tradition, central to Patriot thinking on both sides of the Atlantic, that the New Jersey delegate and president of the College of New Jersey John Witherspoon drew when he predicted to the Second Continental Congress in July 1776 "that in future times all the states in one quarter of the globe may see it proper by some plan of union, to perpetuate security and peace." He was certain that "a well planned confederacy among the states of America may hand down the blessings of peace and public order to many generations."[4]

America's Founders were drawing upon a well-established Patriot discussion of confederation—of notions of coordinated sovereignty—when they began to debate their own Articles of Confederation in 1776. Over and over again North American Patriots focused their discussions on ancient and modern confederations, ranging from the Greek Achaean League to the Swiss Confederation. In particular, they discussed the Dutch Republic.[5] The confederation of the seven United Provinces of the Netherlands seemed both a model and a warning. The Dutch Republic, they knew, had been formed in 1579 as a defensive alliance of seven provinces to fight against the greatest power of the day, the Spanish Empire. Together the provinces successfully prosecuted a brutal eighty-year war against Spain that ended ultimately with Dutch independence in 1648. In the process the Dutch emerged as a major power on the European scene, fueled by Europe's most dynamic economy. Patriots marveled at the political, military, and economic success of the Dutch confederation.[6]

Most Patriots, however, were also familiar with the less glorious eighteenth-century history of the Dutch Confederation. In a period in which most European states built military leviathans, the Dutch remained committed to the notion that sovereignty lay exclusively at the local level. They required unanimity among the provinces to go to war. Each maritime province had its own admiralty. Taxation was levied at the provincial and city level. When the provinces were convened at the States General in The Hague, voting took place province by province. Wealthy and populous Holland had as many votes as Friesland. The cumbersome Dutch confederation increasingly made the republic irrelevant in European power politics. The Dutch, while still prosperous, suffered relative economic decline. American Patriots like Benjamin Rush and James Wilson followed the widely read and admired French *philosophe* the Abbé Raynal in blaming Dutch political impotence and economic regression on a confederation in which "each province is supreme."[7]

It was with this history of European confederationalism very much in mind that American Patriots approached the problem of creating their own confederation in 1776 and 1777. Members of the Continental Congress wanted to create a confederation that would both protect liberty and create a powerful government that would not soon relegate the new republic to a tertiary role on the global stage.

Crafting the Articles of Confederation proved to be a difficult task. "Every speck of ground is disputed and very jarring claims and interests are to be adjusted among us," noted William Williams of Connecticut. In a particularly dark moment Joseph Hewes of North Carolina was "inclined to think we shall never model it so as to be agreed by all the colonies." While few were as pessimistic as Hewes, there could be no doubting the enormity of the task. State delegations differed over how to regulate relations with Indians, the geographical limits of the various states, the mode of voting and representation in Congress, and the means of assessing taxation.[8] These issues and the pressing demands of administering the war effort delayed consideration and ultimately finalization of the Articles of Confederation for more than a year.

While the final document was not to prove lasting, the members of the Continental Congress did succeed in creating a confederation that was stronger than any heretofore created. Despite the best efforts of some, like the Irish immigrant and North Carolina delegate Thomas Burke, to maintain the sovereignty of the states along Dutch lines, in November 1777 the members of Congress signed off on a document that granted new and significant powers to the central government.[9]

After months of delay, the members of the Continental Congress did in the end rush to complete their confederation. Forced to flee the American capital of Philadelphia by General Howe's advancing forces, having to deal with the reality of a collapsing currency and dwindling credit, members of Congress agreed to minimize controversy and move forward with confederation. Once again, political economic consideration moved forward the process of American state formation. Edward Rutledge of South Carolina, whose doubts about central power were not so different from those of Thomas Burke, saw as early as October 1776 that "necessity requires" confederation. Agreeing to the Articles is "necessary to our salvation," agreed Daniel Roberdeau of Pennsylvania a year later. In the view of William Williams and many others, only agreeing to "a firm union" could put an end to runaway inflation and the "depreciation of the currency." "There is nothing in my opinion so threatening to us as our depreciating currency," agreed Samuel Adams in the midst of the debates on the Articles. The military and above all the economic situation had worsened sufficiently that by the middle of 1777 "a very great majority of Congress" had become "anxious for a confederacy." The obvious "necessity of the measure" meant, in the view of Charles Carroll of Carrollton, that the confederacy would "not be formed on principles so mutually advantageous as it ought and might be." But the Marylander Carroll concluded that "an imperfect and somewhat unequal confederacy is better than none."[10]

Because of their differences, the members of the Continental Congress were forced into accepting compromises in order to pass the Articles. "Partial interests" had to be "laid aside." "In this great business," Richard Henry Lee of Virginia explained to the New Haven radical Roger Sherman, "we must yield a little to each other, and not rigidly insist on having everything correspondent to the partial views of every state." Yield the states did on a number of issues. Perhaps one of the most important compromises was on the matter of taxation. By October 1777 taxation remained the single most outstanding issue. The New England states wanted taxes to be levied on the basis of population. Southerners demurred, however, realizing that such a principle would punish them heavily for their large numbers of slaves. The issue of slavery, it had been clear since the July 1776 debate over the Committee of Five's proposed antislavery clause in the Declaration of Independence, was one of the most divisive in North America. While a great wave of antislavery sentiment accompanied the Patriot program, it was also true that many wealthy and powerful slaveholders, particularly in South Carolina, would resist any attack on the basis of their wealth. Already in July 1777 John Adams recommended delaying a Massachusetts bill for "freeing negroes" on the grounds that the American states already had "causes enough for jealousy, discord and division." It was this principle of compromise that shaped the eighth article of the confederation, dealing with taxation. Despite the opposition of all of the New England states, Congress decided to tax on the basis of land rather than population. This meant, in the view of the irate New Hampshire man Nathaniel Folsom, that "one third part of the wealth of the southern states which consists in negroes, is entirely left out and no notice taken of them in determining their ability to pay taxes." Had the taxation quota been set "by the number of inhabitants including slaves," Cornelius Harnett of North Carolina pointed out, "this would have ruined poor North Carolina." In South Carolina, which had a much larger slave population, the effects would have been at least as significant. Pressed by the urgency of the situation, members of the Continental Congress made a vital concession on taxation in the Articles of Confederation. Slavery had gained a reprieve.[11]

Nevertheless, the Articles of Confederation that were adopted in November 1777 and finally ratified after years of debate in 1781 created a much stronger confederal government than any that had gone before. Thomas Burke complained perceptively that the Articles adopted by Congress gave the central government "many powers" beyond questions of foreign affairs, including the "regulating of alloy of coin struck by authority of any of the states, fixing the standards of weights and measures, regulating the trade and affairs with Indians, and all that appertains to the naval force." Burke was more alive than later commentators have been to the immense power granted to Congress in the clause in Article 9, which granted Congress the "power to borrow money and emit bills." While Burke was no doubt exaggerating the power of the confederacy when he claimed that central authority had been awarded "an unlimited power over the property of individuals," he was right that Congress had been given much more power over political economy than the Dutch States General had ever received or assumed. The chief justice of South Carolina, William Henry Drayton, after studying the Articles of Confederation closely, concluded that even though Thomas Burke's second article "speaks of the sovereignty of the respective states," the totality of the document had given to Congress "almost all the important powers of government."[12]

While members of Congress had disagreed about the contours of confederal coordination, the vast majority of them agreed that union was essential to resolving the critical political economic crises facing the infant republic. Without confederation, they feared with good cause, inflation would run rampant, trade would stagnate, and the war effort would suffer. Life for humble folks throughout North America would become intolerably hard. Confederation was necessary to increase the coordinated power of the American government to alleviate these problems. Charles Carroll of Maryland was sure that "a good confederation" would give the American republic "great strength and new vigor." Whereas many scholars and politicians imagine that the Patriots had gone to war to avoid the financial rigors of a powerful state, in fact the Founders welcomed confederation precisely because union made possible taxation to promote the common good. Congressional passage of the Articles would address the currency crisis, argued James Lovell of Massachusetts, and that meant "taxation, high and payable at short periods." John Adams agreed that in order to address the "real danger" that America faced, "large taxation" was now urgently necessary. Now that Congress "have at length finished the Confederation," Richard Henry Lee of Virginia reported, it was now possible to turn to "taxation, finance, and recruiting the army." Confederation achieved, Cornelius Harnett of North Carolina agreed, the states could now "agree immediately to tax as high as the people can possibly bear."[13]

Those who drafted the Articles of Confederation thought they were creating the blueprint for a strong union with

coordinated powers. They expected that Congress would iden-
tify the needs and aims of the union, while the states would
pass the necessary laws and resolutions to implement that
agenda. That the Articles of Confederation were ultimately to
prove too weak to coordinate the union was an unintended
consequence of the compromises the delegates were forced to
make in the face of crisis. It was not the delegates' desired out-
come. The weakness may have come about, as many Federalists
would later claim, because of a fundamental flaw in institutional design. Above all, optimistic that the states would recog-
nize the urgency of their situation, Congress had not given the
central government the right to tax. Nevertheless, at the time
and later, delegates were unanimous in asserting that they had
created "the best confederacy that could be formed, especially
when we consider the number of states, their different interests"
and "customs." No less an authority than Thomas Jefferson
looked back on the Articles as "a wonderfully perfect instru-
ment, considering the circumstances in which it was formed."
He agreed with John Adams that the American confederation
approved in November 1777 and ratified in 1781, whatever its
defects, was an improvement over "the confederations which
have existed hitherto."[14] While the Articles ultimately proved to
be a failed constitutional experiment, the delegates of the Second Continental Congress had designed the first constitution
of the United States to create a more powerful confederation
than had hitherto existed. They had attempted—and failed—to
create a Patriot government.

It was because the Articles had not created the energetic
government that the Patriot framers of the Declaration had
foreseen that George Washington warned his fellow citizens
when he lay down his arms in June 1783 that even in victory his
country was in "crisis." This was the moment, Washington

declared in his "Circular to the States," "to give such a tone to our Federal Government, as will enable it to answer the ends of its institution, or this may be the ill-fated moment for relaxing the powers of the union, annihilating the cement of the Confederation, and exposing us to become the sport of European politics." This was a crisis not of sovereignty but of the "system of policy." Washington insisted that it was his "duty and that of every true Patriot" to allow Congress "to exercise those prerogatives they are undoubtedly invested with" by the Articles of Confederation. He demanded "a faithful and pointed compliance on the part of every state, with the late proposals and demands of Congress, or the most fatal consequences will ensue." He called on his fellow citizens to "strengthen the hands of government, and be happy under its protection." "Who will grudge to yield a very little of his property to support the common interest of Society, and insure the protection of government?" asked the triumphant general.[15] The federal government, Washington believed, could do a great deal to promote the happiness of its citizens in peace and war. But it needed the power to do so.

American Patriots framed the Declaration of Independence, the founding document of the new American republic, to proclaim their preference for an energetic imperial government. Until well into the 1770s Patriots on both sides of the Atlantic had hoped for a political reversal in Britain. They hoped that a new British ministry would return to the pre-1760 policies of state-supported imperial development. When they lost all hope for British political transformation, American Patriots took it upon themselves to create a powerful Patriot government in North America. Patriots called for a strong government, with coordinated sovereignty, which would support the growth of a dynamic consumer economy. They imagined that the

Continental Congress would set the agenda, and that the newly founded states would implement that agenda.[16] They drew up a Declaration affirming their determination to promote the happiness, the general welfare, of all North Americans. They believed, as had British Patriots for several generations, that the government should promote economic development by opening up markets for American products, thereby gaining currency to lubricate the economy, subsidize and support immigration to foster a stronger consumer base, and put an end to slavery in order to accelerate North America's transformation from a primitive to a civilized society.

American Patriots did not declare independence to put an end to empire. The British Empire under Patriot leadership, they knew well, had done a great deal to promote the well-being of its colonies by spending heavily on development. That is why Washington praised "the foundation of our Empire" in 1783. In this Washington was echoing a common, almost ubiquitous theme. The New England Patriot and abolitionist Ezra Stiles said in April 1775 that Americans were "laying the foundations of a glorious future empire." William Hooper of North Carolina proclaimed the following year that "America must become the seat of Empire."[17] Patriots on both sides of the Atlantic opposed the extractive policies and austerity measures of the British ministers after 1760 because they wanted a return to a policy of state-supported growth, not because they wanted to call to a close the age of empires. Empires, like other polities, the Patriots believed, gained their character not by the forms they took but from the policies they pursued.

George Washington framed his first inaugural address in the spirit of the Declaration of Independence. In 1789, just as in 1776, Washington gave voice to Patriot arguments that he had embraced as a young man. Like the British Patriot Admiral

Edward Vernon, whom Lawrence Washington had so admired, George Washington believed that governments could and should play a significant role in promoting a happier, a more equal, and a more prosperous society. He believed that states were created to promote the common good. Governments were much more than a necessary evil that existed merely to provide security for property. Washington and his fellow Patriots on both sides of the Atlantic wanted an energetic government. They wanted a government that could quickly and efficiently gather the resources necessary to fight foreign wars. They also wanted to create a government that could promote economic prosperity in peacetime. They believed that the state needed to provide subsidies to develop key industries and products. They wanted the state to provide the infrastructure to make communications easier and commerce more profitable. Patriots, because they believed it was necessary to empower a broad consumer base to promote economic growth, wanted the government to subsidize immigration and eventually eliminate chattel slavery. Slave societies, most Patriots believed, were necessarily primitive rather than modern commercial societies. Energetic and popular governments, in the view of Washington and Patriots on both sides of the Atlantic, could simultaneously provide security and promote social and economic transformation. These were the views that Washington endorsed when writing his farewell circular in 1783 and his inaugural address in 1789. These were the views that Washington knew he was defending when he read America's founding document to his troops in July 1776. Like Emmerich de Vattel, of whose writings Washington was so fond, he believed that the pre-1760 British constitution was "happy" and "admirable" because it was designed to promote "the public welfare." It did so, according to Vattel, in the text so beloved by the members of the Continental Congress, because it was a state happy to devote resources "to encourage labor, to animate industry, and to excite abilities; to propose honors, rewards, privileges."[18] American Patriots declared independence and defended the virtues of the British constitution in the same breath because they believed deeply that a well-designed government, responsive to the people, was essential to promoting the greatest prosperity for the greatest number. In July 1776 American Patriots issued a clarion call for an energetic government.

Notes

Abbreviations

Add	Additional manuscripts
Beinecke	Beinecke Rare Book and Manuscript Library, Yale University
BL	British Library
BRO	Bristol Record Office
CUL	Cambridge University Library
HBS	Harvard Business School, Baker Library
HEH	Henry E Huntington Library, San Marino, CA
IOR	India Office Records, British Library
LOC	Library of Congress
MHS	Massachusetts Historical Society
NYHS	New-York Historical Society
NYPL	New York Public Library
SCHS	South Carolina Historical Society (now housed at the College of Charleston)
TNA	National Archives, United Kingdom
WCL	William Clements Library, University of Michigan

Introduction

1. I owe the phrase to Pauline Maier, *American Scripture: Making the Declaration of Independence* (New York: Knopf, 1997); see similarly Robert Bellah, "Civil Religion in America," *Daedalus* 34, no. 4 (2005), 47.

2. George Washington (New York) to John Hancock, 10 July 1776, in *The Papers of George Washington, Digital Edition,* ed. Theodore J. Crackel (Charlottesville: University of Virginia Press, 2008), Revolutionary War

Series, 5: 258 (hereafter *Digital Washington Papers*); *Gentleman's Magazine* 46 (September 1776), 434.

3. Charles-Guillaume-Frédéric Dumas (The Hague) to Benjamin Franklin, 30 June 1775, *Benjamin Franklin Papers Online*, vol. 22; Benjamin Franklin (Philadelphia) to Charles-Guillaume-Frédéric Dumas, 9 December 1775, ibid.; James Bowdoin (Boston) to Benjamin Franklin, 19 August 1776, ibid.; Emmerich de Vattel, *The Law of Nations* (London: J. Coote, 1759), 1: 14; Edmund Burke, *The Speech of E. Burke, Esq. on American Taxation*, 19 April 1774, 3rd ed. (Philadelphia: Benjamin Towne, 1775), 29–30; Resolves of Fairfax County, 18 July 1774, in *Revolutionary Virginia: The Road to Independence*, ed. Robert L. Scribner (Charlottesville: University of Virginia Press, 1973), 1: 128. The radical Thomas Paine reprinted a petition expressing similar sentiments in February 1775: Petition and Memorial of the Assembly of Jamaica, 28 December 1774, *Pennsylvania Magazine*, February 1775, p. 98.

4. Merrill Jensen, *The Articles of Confederation* (Madison: University of Wisconsin Press, 1940), 163; Hannah Arendt, *On Revolution* (London: Penguin, 1963), 149; John Philip Reid, *The Concept of Liberty in the Age of the American Revolution* (Chicago: University of Chicago Press, 1988), 56; Gordon S. Wood, *Empire of Liberty* (Oxford: Oxford University Press, 2009), 10; Jack P. Greene, *The Constitutional Origins of the American Revolution* (Cambridge: Cambridge University Press, 2010), xiii; Ronald Hamowy, "The Declaration of Independence," in *A Companion to the American Revolution*, ed. Jack P. Greene and J. R. Pole (Oxford: Basil Blackwell, 2003), 260; Thomas P. Slaughter, *Independence* (New York: Hill and Wang, 2014), xvi, 436.

5. Earlier generations of American historians relied on the then cutting edge scholarship of Lewis Namier and J. H. Plumb: Bernard Bailyn, *The Origins of American Politics* (New York: Knopf, 1968), 15–16, 32–33, 35–36; Edmund S. Morgan, "The American Revolution: Revisions in Need of Revising," *William and Mary Quarterly* 14, no. 1(1957), 4. More recent historians have insisted that we integrate the newest findings from British historiography: Pauline Maier, *From Resistance to Revolution* (New York: Knopf, 1972); T. H. Breen, "Ideology and Nationalism on the Eve of the American Revolution: Revisions Once More in Need of Revising," *Journal of American History* 84, no. 1 (1997), 14–16. This book is an attempt to bring to bear the latest findings in British historiography on interpreting America's founding document.

6. John Brewer, *Sinews of Power* (New York: Knopf, 1989). Max Edling has also highlighted the development of the British state, but is wrong to see it as narrowly "made for war." Max Edling, *A Revolution in Favor of Government* (Oxford: Oxford University Press, 2003), 51.

7. This paragraph relies heavily on chapter 3 of my *1688: The First Modern Revolution* (New Haven: Yale University Press, 2009).

8. Jon Butler, *Becoming America* (Cambridge: Harvard University Press, 2000), 2; John J. McCusker, "Measuring Colonial Gross Domestic Product," *William and Mary Quarterly* 56, no. 1 (1999), 5; George Washington (Williamsburg) to Robert Cary and Company, 1 June 1774, in Crackel, *Digital Washington Papers,* Colonial Series, 10: 83.

9. Benjamin Franklin, *The Interest of Great Britain Considered with Regard to Her Colonies,* 2nd Boston ed. (1760), 54.

10. Ibid., 57; *The Crisis,* no. 80, 27 July 1776, p. 505; Ezra Stiles (Newport) to William Leechman (Glasgow), 2 December 1760, Correspondence Box 3, 1760–63, Beinecke, MS Vault Stiles/Folder 323; Samuel Langdon (Portsmouth, New Hampshire) to Ezra Stiles, 5 October 1761, ibid., Folder 347; "The Number of People in the Colony of Rhode Island taken by the King's Order in the Year 1730," Beinecke, MS Vault Stiles, Misc. papers, 25; Ezra Stiles (Newport) to Dr. James Fordyce (London), 22 November 1763, Correspondence Box 5, 1763–65, Beinecke, MS Vault Stiles/Folder 406; Ezra Stiles (Newport) to Nathaniel Lardner, 20 June 1764, ibid., Folder 435; Edward Wigglesworth, *Calculations on American Population* (Boston: John Boyle, 1775), 5. Spanish America was about five times the size of British America in the 1770s: James Belich, *Replenishing the Earth* (Oxford: Oxford University Press, 2009), 30–36; Stanley Engermann, Kenneth Sokoloff, Miguel Urquiola, and Daron Acemoglu, "Factor Endowments, Inequality, and Paths of Development among New World Economies," *Economia* 3, no. 1 (2002), 50. In addition to the works cited above, this paragraph and the prior one draw on Butler, *Becoming America;* John J. McCusker and Russell R. Menard, *The Economy of British America, 1607–1789* (Chapel Hill: University of North Carolina Press, 1991); Marc Egnal, *New World Economies* (New York: Oxford University Press, 1998); Emma Hart, *Building Charleston: Town and Society in the Eighteenth-Century British Atlantic-World* (Charlottesville: University of Virginia Press, 2010); Jessica Roney, *Governed by a Spirit of Opposition: The Origins of American Political Practice in Colonial Philadelphia* (Baltimore: Johns Hopkins University Press, 2014).

11. When Bernard Bailyn referred to the "weak" "overall structure of the English government," he was relying on a British historiography that has since been superseded: Bailyn, *Faces of Revolution* (New York: Vintage, 1990), 64. See Lawrence Stone, ed., *An Imperial State at War: Britain from 1689 to 1815* (New York: Routledge, 1994).

12. Sir John Sinclair, *The History of the Public Revenue of the British Empire* (London: W. and A. Strahan, 1785–90), 1: 4–5; Brewer, *Sinews of Power,* 40.

13. Daniel Defoe, *An Essay upon Projects* (London: R.R., 1697), 1, 10–11, 25; John Houghton, *A Collection of Letters for the Improvement of Husbandry and Trade,* 8 September 1681, p. 21; "Essay on the Interest of the Crown in American Plantations and Trade," 1685, BL, Add 47131, ff. 24–25.

14. Perry Gauci, *The Politics of Trade: The Overseas Merchant in State and Society, 1660–1720* (Oxford: Oxford University Press, 2001), 165; *Spectator,* 1, no. 10 (12 March 1711), 55; Charles Davenant, *Discourses on the Public Revenues and Trade of England* (London: James Knapton, 1698), 2: 320; James Brydges, Journal, 4, 6 February 1697, HEH, ST 26, Vol. 1.

15. *An Essay upon the Government of the English Plantations on the Continent* (London: Richard Parker, 1701), 1–2; Henry Martin, *Considerations upon the East-India Trade* (London: A. and J. Churchill, 1701), sig. A2v; Joseph Addison (Cock-Pit) to Manchester, 27 February 1708, Beinecke, Osborn fc 37/13/33; Steve Pincus, "Rethinking Mercantilism: Political Economy, the British Empire, and the Atlantic World in the Seventeenth and Eighteenth Centuries," *William and Mary Quarterly* 69, no. 1 (2012), 3–34. I disagree with Jack Rakove's recent assertion that the British government's "mercantilist conviction" drove British policymaking after 1760 in ways that were "wholly unsurprising." Political economy was highly contested in eighteenth-century Britain. The novel policies pursued after 1760 were completely surprising to many: Jack Rakove, "Got Nexus?" *William and Mary Quarterly* 68, no. 4 (2011), 637.

16. Julian Hoppit and Joanna Innes, "Introduction," *Failed Legislation, 1660–1800* (London: Hambledon, 1997); William Blathwayt (Breda) to George Stepney, 21 July 1701, Beinecke OSB MSS 2/Box 2/Folder 32; William Blathwayt (Darien) to George Stepney, 26 August 1701, Beinecke, OSB MSS 2/ Box 2/ Folder 33; James Brydges to Nicholas Philpott, 29 September 1714, HEH, ST 57/11, p. 10; *Spectator* 2, no. 101 (26 June 1711), 11; *Spectator* 2, no. 112 (9 July 1711), 167; *Spectator* 2, no. 126 (25 July 1711), 250. All quotations from the 1758 Tonson edition. Lawrence Klein, "Joseph Addison's Whiggism," in *Cultures of Whiggism,* ed. David Womersley, Paddy Bullard, and Abigail Williams (Newark: University of Delaware Press, 2005), 108–26.

17. Daniel Finch 8th earl of Winchilsea, 15 November 1739, *Cobbett's Parliamentary History of England,* vol. 11, p. 64; John Wilkes, 26 October 1775, in *Proceedings and Debates of the British Parliaments Respecting North America, 1754–1783,* ed. R. C. Simmons and P. D. G. Thomas, vol. 6, *April 1775–May 1776,* (White Plains, NY: Kraus International, 1982–87), 98; John Brewer, *Party Ideology and Popular Politics at the Accession of George III* (Cambridge: Cambridge University Press, 1976).

18. Amy Watson's Yale doctoral dissertation is tracing these dense social networks of belief in Scotland, New York, and Georgia.

19. Michael Eamon, *Imprinting Britain: Newspapers, Sociability, and the Shaping of British North America* (Montreal: McGill-Queen's University Press, 2015); Geoffrey Alan Cranfield, *The Development of the Provincial Newspaper, 1700–1760* (Oxford: Clarendon, 1962); David A. Copeland, *Colonial American Newspapers: Character and Content* (Newark: University of Delaware Press, 1997); William Byrd II (Virginia) to Mr. Smyth, 6 September 1740, in *The Correspondence of the Three William Byrds of Westover, Virginia, 1684–1776*, ed. Marion Tinling (Charlottesville: University of Virginia Press, 1977), 2: 557; Abigail Franks to Naphtali Franks, 12 December 1735, in *Letters of the Franks Family, 1733–1748*, ed. Leo Hershkowitz and Isidore S. Meyer (Waltham, MA: American Jewish Historical Society, 1968), 50; Abigail Franks to Naphtali Franks, 3 December 1736, ibid., 55.

20. Bernard Bailyn, *Ideological Origins of the American Revolution* (Cambridge: Harvard University Press, 1967), 43 (first quotation); Jack N. Rakove, " 'How Else Could It End?' Bernard Bailyn and the Problem of Authority in Early America," in *The Transformation of Early American History*, ed. James A. Henretta, Michael Kammen, and Stanley N. Katz (New York: Knopf, 1991), 52 (second quotation); Gordon S. Wood, *The Creation of the American Republic, 1776–1787* (1969; Chapel Hill: University of North Carolina Press, 1998), 14–15 (third quotation); Steve Pincus, "Neither Machiavellian Moment nor Possessive Individualism: Commercial Society and the Defenders of the English Commonwealth," *American Historical Review* 103, no. 3 (1998), 705–36; Robert Brenner, *Merchants and Revolution* (Princeton: Princeton University Press, 1993); Gabriel Glickman, "Empire, 'Popery,' and the Fall of English Tangier," *Journal of Modern History* 87, no. 2 (2015), 247–80; Abigail Swingen, *Competing Visions of Empire: Labor, Slavery, and the Origins of the British Atlantic Empire* (New Haven: Yale University Press, 2015); Carl Wennerlind, *Casualties of Credit: The English Financial Revolution, 1620–1720* (Cambridge: Harvard University Press, 2011); Carl Wennerlind and Philip Stern, eds., *Mercantilism Reimagined: Political Economy in Early Modern Britain and Its Empire* (Oxford: Oxford University Press, 2014); Steve Pincus, *1688: The First Modern Revolution* (New Haven: Yale University Press, 2009); Alan C. Houston, *Benjamin Franklin and the Politics of Improvement* (New Haven: Yale University Press, 2008); Pincus, "Rethinking Mercantilism"; Steve Pincus, "Addison's Empire: Whig Conceptions of Empire in the Early 18th Century," *Parliamentary History* 31, no. 1 (2012), 99–117; James Vaughn, "The Politics of Empire," Ph.D. diss., University of Chicago, 2008. Bailyn himself has recovered the important imperial debate over immigration in the 1770s: Bernard Bailyn, *Voyagers to the West* (New York: Knopf, 1986), 29–66; Gordon Wood, *The Radicalism of the American Revolution* (New York: Knopf, 1992), 101.

21. Charles A. Beard, *An Economic Interpretation of the Constitution of the United States* (New York: Macmillan, 1913). It is a profound irony that many of those most critical of Beardian interpretations of American history happily adopt interpretations of eighteenth-century Britain inspired by Lewis Namier, whose historical method was inspired by Beard. I am grateful for this point to Namier's biographer David Hayton. The loyalist Joseph Galloway came the closest to offering a Beardian interpretation of the Declaration when he suggested that the independence party included "men of bankrupt fortunes, overwhelmed in debt to the British merchants": Joseph Galloway's Statement on His Plan of Union, 28 September 1774, in *Letters of Delegates to Congress,* ed. Paul H. Smith (Washington, DC: Library of Congress, 1976), 1: 120. In fact, at the moment of the Association, most refused to repudiate their debts.

22. Here I follow Andrew Gelman, Boris Shor, Joseph Bafumi, and David Park, "Rich State, Poor State, Red State, Blue State: What's the Matter with Connecticut?" *Quarterly Journal of Political Science* 2 (2007), 345–67. They modify the findings of Thomas Frank, *What's the Matter with Kansas? How Conservatives Won the Heart of America* (New York: Metropolitan, 2004).

23. Arthur Lee, *An Appeal to the Justice and Interests of the People of Great Britain,* 4th ed. (London: J. Almon, 1776), 3; James Duane's Speech to the Committee on Rights, 8 September 1774, Smith, *Letters of Delegates to Congress,* 1: 53; Ezra Stiles (Newport) to Catherine Macaulay, 15 April 1775, Beinecke, MS Vault Stiles, Correspondence Box 12; Mercy Otis Warren (Plimouth) to Abigail Adams, 19 January 1774, in *Adams Family Correspondence,* ed. L. H. Butterfield (Cambridge: Belknap Press of Harvard University Press, 1963), 1: 91; George Washington (Philadelphia) to Captain Robert Mackenzie, 9 October 1774, in Smith, *Letters of Delegates to Congress,* 1: 167; Robert Morris (Philadelphia) to Silas Deane, 5 June 1776, ibid., 4 (1979): 147; Benjamin Rush, *Autobiography,* ed. George W. Corner (Princeton: Princeton University Press, 1948), 119. I agree with Bailyn that "it is not much of an exaggeration to say that one had to be a fool or a fanatic in early January 1776 to advocate American independence"; *Faces of Revolution,* 69.

24. Maier, *American Scripture,* xvi–xxi; Garry Wills, *Inventing America: Jefferson's Declaration of Independence* (New York: Doubleday, 1978); Carl Lotus Becker, *The Declaration of Independence: A Study in the History of Ideas* (New York: Vintage, 1970); Morton White, *The Philosophy of the American Revolution* (New York: Oxford University Press, 1978); Jay Fliegelman, *Declaring Independence: Jefferson, Natural Language, and the Culture of Performance* (Stanford: Stanford University Press, 1993).

1
Mount Vernon

1. Remarks, 1787–88, in *The Papers of George Washington, Digital Edition,* ed. Theodore J. Crackel (Charlottesville: University of Virginia Press, 2008), Confederation Series, 5: 515; Richard Harding, *Amphibious Warfare in the Eighteenth Century: The British Expedition to the West Indies, 1740–1742* (Woodbridge, UK: Boydell, 1991), 205; Stephen Saunders Webb, *Marlborough's America* (New Haven: Yale University Press, 2013), 392–98; J. R. McNeil, *Mosquito Empires: Ecology and War in the Greater Caribbean, 1620–1914* (Cambridge: Cambridge University Press, 2010), 153–64.

2. *London Evening Post,* 5 November 1757; Memoirs of James Vernon Junior, 13 March 1740, 23 March 1740, 22 April 1740, 12 November 1740, 23 November 1740, 1 December 1740, British Library, Additional MSS 40794, ff. 18–19; *Vernon's Glory* (London: W. Webb, 1740); *Vernon's Glory Part II* (London: W. Webb, 1740); Henry Fielding, *The Vernon-iad* (London: Charles Corbett, 1741); Elizabeth Robinson (Bulstrode) to Sarah Robinson Scott, 12 September 1740, Henry E. Huntington Library, Montague Papers, Box 3, MO 5552; Kathleen Wilson, *The Sense of the People* (Cambridge: Cambridge University Press, 1995), 140–65; "Empire, Trade, and Popular Politics in Mid-Hanoverian Britain: The Case of Admiral Vernon," *Past and Present,* no. 121 (1988), 74–109; Gerald Jordan and Nicholas Rogers, "Admirals as Heroes: Patriotism and Liberty in Hanoverian England," *Journal of British Studies* 28, no. 3 (1989), 201–24.

3. *London Evening* Post, 5 November 1757; *A New Song to the Tune of You Fair Ladies Now at Land* [1740]; *The Good Patriot's Security* (London: T.R., 1740), 8–9; "On Admiral Vernon's Taking His Seat in the House of Commons," in *The Foundling Hospital for Wit* (London: G. Lion, 1743), 53; *Boston Evening-Post,* 24 March 1740; James Thomson and David Mallet, *Alfred: A Masque,* Presented at Cliveden 1 August 1740 (London: A. Millar, 1740), 43–44.

4. William Wood (Paris) to Horace Walpole, 23 January 1726, CUL, Ch(H) Corresp/1276.

5. John Lord Carteret, 1 February 1739, *Cobbett's Parliamentary History of England,* 10: 926; John Lord Carteret, 1 March 1739, ibid., 10: 1187; George Lyttelton, *Considerations upon the Present State of our Affairs* (1739), 13; *Gentleman's Magazine* 9 (December 1739), 643 (reprinting an essay from *The Craftsman,* 15 December 1739); *Common Sense,* 19 August 1738; *Common Sense,* 12 April 1740; *New York Weekly Journal,* 24 July 1738. Zenger returned to this theme: *New York Weekly Journal,* 25 September 1738.

6. *The Importance of the Sugar Colonies to Great-Britain Stated* (London: J. Roberts, 1731), 4, 7, 35–36; *Observations on the Case of the Northern*

Colonies (London: J. Roberts, 1731), 4–5; [Arthur Zouch,] *Considerations on the Dispute Now Depending before the Honourable House of Commons between the British Southern and Northern Plantations in America* (London: J. Roberts, 1731), 23–24; William Wood, *Survey of Trade,* Part III (1719), 179; Joshua Gee, *Trade and Navigation* (1729), 25–26.

7. Philip Yorke 1st earl of Hardwicke, 1 March 1739, *Cobbett's Parliamentary History of England,* 10: 1155–56; Horace Walpole, 3 March 1739, ibid., 10: 1255; Horace Walpole, *The Grand Question, Whether War or No War with Spain* (London: J. Roberts, 1739), 8.

8. Memoirs of James Vernon Junior, 1722–23, BL, Add 40794, f. 6r; *The Good Patriot's Security* (1740), 33.

9. Hugh Jones, *The Present State of Virginia* (1724), 112–13; Sir John Barnard, 30 March 1737, *Cobbett's Parliamentary History of England,* 10: 156–57. See similar arguments in *Gentleman's Magazine* 8 (June 1738), 286; and reprinted from *The Craftsman* in *Gentleman's Magazine* 8 (December 1738), 642.

10. *Common Sense,* 18 March 1738, No. 59. Both George Lyttelton and the earl of Chesterfield were among the brain trust behind *Common Sense.* Cadwallader Colden, *The Interest of the Country in Laying Duties* (New York: J. Peter Zenger, [1726]), 6–7; *Gentleman's Magazine* 9 (October 1739), 536, reprinting an essay from *The Craftsman,* 13 October 1739; Diary of John Perceval, 10 February 1732, Historical Manuscripts Commission, *Manuscripts of the Earl of Egmont* (London: His Majesty's Stationery Office, 1920), 1: 220; Jordan and Rogers, "Admirals as Heroes," 207; John Viscount Perceval (London) to John Perceval, 16 March 1732, BL, Add 47013A, f. 1v; Sir Edward Knatchbull, 24 February 1729, in *The Parliamentary Diary of Sir Edward Knatchbull, 1722–1730,* ed. A. N. Newman, Camden Society, Third Series, vol. 94 (1963), 87; Diary of John Perceval, 4 April 1733, HMC, *Egmont,* vol. 1, p. 349. For discussion of the opposition to the excise scheme, see Paul Langford, *The Excise Crisis: Society and Politics in the Age of Walpole* (Oxford: Oxford University Press, 1975); Clyve Jones, "The House of Lords and the Excise Crisis: The Storm and the Aftermath," *Parliamentary History* 33, no. 1 (2014), 160–200.

11. Sir John Barnard, 30 March 1737, *Cobbett's Parliamentary History of England* 10: 160; Sir William Keith, "A Short Discourse on the Present State of the Colonies in America," November 1728, in *A Collection of Papers and Other Tracts* (London: J. Mechell, 1740), 171–72.

12. *The Craftsman,* 4 November 1738, no. 643; George Lyttelton, *Considerations upon the Present State of our Affairs* (London: T. Cooper, 1739), 4; *Gentleman's Magazine* 9 (January 1739), 32; John Campbell 2nd duke of Argyll, 1 March 1739, *Cobbett's Parliamentary History of England* 10: 1136; Samuel Sandys, 16 November 1739, ibid., 11: 102.

13. John Perceval 1st earl of Egmont's Journal, 4 February 1740, BL, Add 47070, f. 19v; William Byrd II (Virginia) to Egmont, 12 July 1736, in *The Correspondence of the Three William Byrds of Westover, Virginia, 1684–1776,* ed. Marion Tinling (Charlottesville: University of Virginia Press, 1977), 2: 487–88; *Gentleman's Magazine* 10 (July 1740), 341. By this point the magazine had wholeheartedly plumped for the Patriots; Harman Verelst (Georgia Office, Westminster) to William Stephens, 29 March 1740, TNA, CO 5/667, f. 160v; *An Account Shewing the Progress of the Colony of Georgia in America* (1741), 10. This argument had previously been made with respect to the West Indies: Diary of John Perceval, 16 May 1733, HMC, *Egmont,* vol. 1, p. 376; Benjamin Martyn, *An Impartial Enquiry into the State and Utility of the Province of Georgia* (London: W. Meadows, 1741), 35.

14. James Knight, *Some Observations on the Assiento Trade* (London: H. Whitridge, 1728), 2; John Leveson-Gower 1st earl Gower, Memorandum, June 1738, TNA, PRO 30/29/1/12/4, f. 352v; William Pulteney, 30 March 1738, *Cobbett's Parliamentary History of England* 10: 649; John Lord Carteret, 2 May 1738, ibid., 10: 751.

15. Sir William Keith, *Some Useful Observations on the Consequences of the Present War with Spain* (London: J. Mechell, [1740]), 7–8; Hugh Hume Campbell, Lord Polwarth, *State of the Rise and Progress of our Disputes with Spain* (London: T. Cooper, 1739), 4–5, 30.

16. Sir Edward Knatchbull, 21 January 1729, *Parliamentary Diary,* Newman, 80; *The Good Patriot's Security* (1740), 11; Diary of John Perceval, 23 February 1731, HMC, *Egmont,* vol. 2, p. 143; Petition of the Merchants in Glasgow trading to the British Plantations in America, 16 March 1738, *Cobbett's Parliamentary History of England* 10: 641–42; Micaiah Perry, 2 March 1738, in *A Collection of the Parliamentary Debates in England* (London, 1741), 16: 3–4; *Gentleman's Magazine* 8 (August 1738), 393; William Pitt, 3 March 1739, *Cobbett's Parliamentary History of England* 10: 1280; Alderman Robert Willimot, 9 March 1739, ibid., 10: 1320; William Pulteney, 9 March 1739, ibid., 10: 1297–98.

17. Memoirs of James Vernon junior, BL, Add 40794, ff. 1–3; Egmont, An Account of Georgia, March 1731, BL, Add 47000, ff. 53–54; Memoirs of James Vernon Junior, 29 March 1732, BL, Add 40794, ff. 9–10; Verner W. Crane, *The Southern Frontier 1670–1732* (New York: Norton, 1981 [originally 1928]), 303; Verner W. Crane, "The Origins of Georgia," *Georgia Historical Quarterly* 14, no. 2 (1930), 94–107; Geraldine Meroney, "The London Entrepôt Merchants and the Georgia Colony," *William and Mary Quarterly* 25, no. 2 (1968), 230–44.

18. Diary of John Perceval, 25 April 1733, 30 April 1733, HMC, *Egmont,* vol. 1, pp. 367, 370; *Daily Courant,* 2 September 1732; *Daily Journal,* 2 September 1732; *Fog's Weekly Journal,* 9 September 1732; *Daily Journal,* 4 December 1732;

St. James Evening Post, 3 March 1733; *Daily Courant,* 1 May 1733; *Daily Journal,* 8 August 1733; *Grub Street Journal,* 6 September 1733. The private donations toward the colony never rose higher than £4,000 in a single year. The yearly parliamentary grants averaged more than £10,000. Diary of John Perceval, 10 May 1733, HMC, *Egmont,* vol. 1, p. 373; *Daily Journal,* 14 June 1733; "Accounts of Net Public Income and Expenditure of Great Britain and Ireland," 1868–69, House of Commons Parliamentary Papers Online (2005), 89–103.

19. Diary of John Perceval, 10 May 1733, HMC, *Egmont,* vol. 1, pp. 372–73; Egmont, An Account of Georgia, 1731, BL, Add 47000, f. 54r.

20. Egmont, An Account of Georgia, 1731, BL, Add 47000, f. 54r; *Daily Journal,* 4 July 1732; *Grub Street Journal,* 6 July 1732; *Fog's Weekly Journal,* 5 August 1732.

21. *Some Account of the Trustees for Establishing the Colony of Georgia in America* [London, 1732]; *London Journal,* 5 August 1732; *The Craftsman,* 12 August 1732; James Oglethorpe, *A New and Accurate Account* (1732), 34; James Oglethorpe (Frederica, Georgia) to Georgia Trustees, 4 July 1739, TNA, CO 5/640/2, f. 340r.

22. *Grub Street Journal,* 20 July 1732; London *Journal,* 29 July 1732; *Some Account of the Trustees for Establishing the Colony of Georgia in America* [London, 1732]; *London Journal,* 5 August 1732; *The Craftsman,* 12 August 1732.

23. Memoirs of James Vernon Junior, 29 June 1732, BL, Add 40794, f. 10r; Benjamin Martyn, *Some Account of the Designs of the Trustees* (1732); *London Journal,* 5 August 1732; *The Craftsman,* 12 August 1732; James Oglethorpe, *A New and Accurate Account of the Provinces of South-Carolina and Georgia* (London: J. Worrall, 1732), ii–iii, 44–45; Harrington (Whitehall) to Georgia Trustees, 26 November 1734, TNA, CO 5/636/1, f. 8r; Samuel Eveleigh (Charles Town) to James Oglethorpe, 19 October 1734, TNA, CO 5/636/3, ff. 253–54; Daniel MacLachlan (London) to James Oglethorpe, 9 May 1735, TNA, CO 5/636/3, f. 327; William Stephens (Savannah) to Georgia Trustees, 27 May 1738, TNA, CO 5/640/1, f. 112r; Egmont's Journal, 13 December 1738, BL, Add 47069, f. 9r; Petition of the Georgia Trustees, 26 February 1739, *Cobbett's Parliamentary History of England* 10: 1057; Martyn, *An Impartial Enquiry,* 38–39; *An Account Shewing the Progress of the Colony of Georgia* (1741), 5, 13, 15, 18, 20, 23–24, 28, 32.

24. *London Journal,* 29 July 1732; James Oglethorpe to Granville Sharp, 3 October 1776, *Memoirs of Granville Sharp, esq.* (London, 1820), 157; Harman Verelst (Georgia Office, Westminster) to Thomas Causton, 14 December 1737, TNA, CO 5/667, f. 48r; Harman Verelst (Georgia Office, Westminster) to William Stephens, 25 February 1740, TNA, CO 5/667, f. 153r; Egmont's Journal, 4 February 1740, BL, Add 47070, f. 20; Benjamin Martyn (Georgia Office, Westminster) to Messrs. Andrew Grant, Thomas Baillie, and David Douglas,

25 March 1740, TNA, CO 5/667, f. 155r; Harman Verelst (Georgia Office, Westminster) to James Oglethorpe, 29 March 1740, TNA, CO 5/667, f. 160r (discusses antislavery sermon delivered to the trustees by William Crowe); Betty Wood, *Slavery in Colonial Georgia* (Athens: University of Georgia Press, 1984), 1–3; *An Account Shewing the Progress of the Colony of Georgia in America* (London, 1741), 8–10; Harman Verelst (Georgia Office, Westminster) to William Stephens, 29 March 1740, TNA, CO 5/667, f. 160v; Egmont's Journal, 29 April 1739, BL, Add 47069, f. 54v; Petition of the Inhabitants of New Inverness, 3 January 1739, in Martyn, *An Impartial Enquiry,* 81–84. The inhabitants of Ebenezer, Georgia, also wrote to Oglethorpe against slavery: Inhabitants of Ebenezer to Oglethorpe, 13 March 1739, in Martyn, *An Impartial Enquiry,* 71–72; William Byrd II (Virginia) to Egmont, 12 July 1736, in *The Correspondence of the Three William Byrds of Westover, Virginia, 1684–1776,* ed. Marion Tinling (Charlottesville: University of Virginia Press, 1977), 2: 487–88; Jonathan Belcher (Boston) to John Perceval earl of Egmont, 13 November 1739, MHS, Jonathan Belcher Letterbooks, 6: 135. For the mutual antipathy between Bladen and Belcher, see Belcher (Boston) to Colonel Martin Bladen, 3 December 1739, ibid., 6: 173. Their hatred almost certainly arose from Belcher's support of some kinds of low-end manufactures in Massachusetts against Bladen's objections: see the thinly veiled criticism of Belcher in Martin Bladen, "Reasons for Appointing a Captain General for the Continent of North America," 27 December 1739, CUL, Ch (H) Papers 84/38.

25. James Oglethorpe (Frederica, Georgia) to Georgia Trustees, 16 November 1739, TNA, CO 5/640/3, f. 415v; Egmont's Journal, 27 January 1739, BL, Add 47069, f. 20r.

26. Memoirs of James Vernon Junior, June–July 1739, BL, Add 40794, ff. 15–16.

27. John Brooke has called attention to ideological divisions in the colonies not dissimilar to the ones I am describing: John L. Brooke, *The Heart of the Commonwealth* (Cambridge: Cambridge University Press, 1992), 53–65; William Pulteney, 15 November 1739, *Cobbett's Parliamentary History of England* 11: 87; Hugh Hume Campbell, Lord Polwarth, *State of the Rise and Progress of Our Disputes with Spain* (1739), 75.

28. Alexander Spotswood to Charles 2nd Viscount Townshend, 1727, BL, Add 32694, ff. 3–4. This dispatch was included among Lord Cathcart's papers. Townshend, despite his political alliance with Walpole in the 1720s, was the author of the radical 1709 proposed treaty that would have pried open Spanish American markets for British trade. His fall from power in May 1730 ultimately led to the alienation of other radicals from the Walpolian regime. Jonathan Belcher was one prominent example: Jonathan Belcher (Boston) to Captain

John Dean, 20 October 1739, MHS, Jonathan Belcher Letterbooks, 6: 71–72; William Dummer, A Short Sketch for Attempting the Havana, 6 November 1730, LOC, Vernon-Wager MSS, Peter Force Papers 8D/4. For Jeremiah Dummer's radical political economy, see Dummer, *A Defence of the New England Charters* (London: W. Wilkins, 1721), 64, 68, 78; John Dalrymple 2nd earl of Stair, Memorial, 9 December 1739, in *A Selection from the Papers of the earls of Marchmont,* ed. George Henry Rose (London: John Murray, 1831), 2: 170–71; "A Plan for Attacking the Spanish Settlements in the West Indies," ca. 1738, CUL, Ch(H) Papers 51/78/1.

29. *Boston Weekly Post-Boy,* 28 April 1740; *Boston Weekly Post-Boy,* 5 May 1740; *Boston Weekly Post-Boy,* 14 July 1740. See also the identical essay to the one quoted in *Boston Evening-Post,* 28 April 1740; *Pennsylvania Gazette,* 12 March 1740; *Pennsylvania Gazette,* 13 December 1739; *New York Weekly Journal,* 2 October 1738; *New York Weekly Journal,* 21 April 1740; *New York Weekly Journal,* 28 April 1740; *New York Weekly Journal,* 19 May 1740. Zenger added a description of Havana harbor in June: *New York Weekly Journal,* 9 June 1740.

30. Sir William Gooch (Virginia) to Board of Trade, 26 May 1740, TNA, CO 5/1325, f. 2r; *Boston Weekly Post-Boy,* 26 May 1740; William Byrd II (Virginia) to Sir Charles Wager, 26 May 1740, Tinling, *Correspondence of the Three William Byrds,* 2: 547; William Byrd II (Virginia) to Sir Charles Wager, 6 September 1740, ibid. 2: 558–59; William Shirley (Boston) to Newcastle, 12 May 1740, BL, Add 32693, f. 279; Jonathan Belcher (Boston) to Richard Partridge, 20 May 1740, MHS, Jonathan Belcher Letterbooks, 6: 351; Jonathan Belcher (Boston) to Newcastle, 4 June 1740, ibid. 6: 372; Letter from Boston, 1 August 1740, CUL, Ch (H) Corresp/2958; "A Scheme for Attacking some part of the Spanish West Indies," ca. 1739, CUL, Ch(H) Papers 51/78/2; Abigail Franks (New York) to Naphtali Franks, 6 July 1740, in *Letters of the Franks Family, 1733–1748,* ed. Leo Hershkowitz and Isidore S. Meyer (Waltham, MA: American Jewish Historical Society, 1968), 72; *New York Weekly Journal,* 15 September 1740; *Boston Weekly Post-Boy,* 28 April 1740; James Logan (Philadelphia) to Thomas Story, 8 November 1740, in *The Correspondence of James Logan and Thomas Story, 1724–1741,* ed. Norman Penney (Philadelphia: Friends Historical Association, 1927), 81; *Boston Weekly Post-Boy,* 19 May 1740; *Boston Weekly Post-Boy,* 26 May 1740.

31. Colonel William Blakeney (Hampton, Virginia) to Newcastle, 23 October 1740, TNA, CO 5/41, f. 250v; Egmont (Charlton) to William Taylor, 24 July 1740, BL, Add 46991, f. 35r; Charles Lord Cathcart (The Buckingham, St. Hellens) to Newcastle, 16 August 1740, TNA, CO 5/41, f. 104r; Cathcart (Spithead) to Newcastle, 30 September 1740, TNA, CO 5/41, f. 172r; Sir Chaloner

Ogle (Dominica) to Newcastle, 23 December 1740, TNA, CO 5/41, f. 208v. Only 3,119 troops arrived in the Caribbean: Harding, *Amphibious Warfare*, 205; William Blakeney (New York) to Newcastle, 25 June 1740, TNBA, CO 5/41, f. 215r; William Blakeney (New York) to Newcastle, 11 September 1740, TNA, CO 5/41, f. 231r.

32. Douglas Southall Freeman, *George Washington: A Biography* (New York: Scribner, 1948), 1: 65–71; Ron Chernow, *Washington* (New York: Penguin, 2010), 9.

2
Patriots and the Imperial Crisis of the 1760s

1. The two pamphlets in question were *A Specimen of Naked Truth from a British Sailor* (London: W. Webb, 1746) and *Some Seasonable Advice from an Honest Sailor* (London, 1746); Edward Vernon, Memorandum to self, April 1746, National Maritime Museum, VER/1/4/A; *Old England*, 11 March 1749. I owe these references to the kindness of Dr. Sarah Kinkel.

2. The arguments in the preceding paragraphs are based on the work of Sarah Kinkel: "Disorder, Discipline, and Naval Reform in Mid-Eighteenth Century Britain," *English Historical Review* 128, no. 535 (2013), 1451–82; "The King's Pirates? Naval Enforcement of Imperial Authority, 1740–1776," *William and Mary Quarterly* 71, no. 1 (2014), 3–34.

3. *London Evening Post*, 1 November 1757; *Lloyd's Evening Post and British Chronicle*, 2 November 1757; *London Evening Post*, 5 November 1757; *Leeds Intelligencer*, 8 November 1757; *Pennsylvania Gazette*, 2 February 1758; *New York Gazette or Weekly Post-Boy*, 6 February 1758; *Boston Gazette and Country Journal*, 20 February 1758; *New Hampshire Gazette*, 3 March 1758.

4. Figures come from ukpublicspending.co.uk. By comparison US federal debt as a percentage of GDP in 2015 was just over 100 percent.

5. Steve Pincus and James Robinson, "Wars and State-Making Reconsidered: The Rise of the Developmental State," *Annales* (forthcoming, 2016). The British state at midcentury did not conform to Max Edling's assertion that the eighteenth century was "an age when the central government gave little in return for the subjects' tax money." Edling, *A Revolution in Favor of Government* (Oxford: Oxford University Press, 2003), 55; Ezra Stiles, Memoirs and Extracts, 1766–1767, Beinecke, MS Vault Stiles, MP/Folder 402, pp. 43–47.

6. For the standard accounts: Edmund S. Morgan and Helen M. Morgan, *The Stamp Act Crisis: Prologue to Revolution* (Chapel Hill: University of North Carolina Press, 1962); Jack P. Greene, *The Constitutional Origins of*

the American Revolution (Cambridge: Cambridge University Press, 2011), 68; Eliga H. Gould, *The Persistence of Empire* (Chapel Hill: University of North Carolina Press, 2000); P. D. G. Thomas, *British Politics and the Stamp Act Crisis* (Oxford: Clarendon, 1975); Philip Lawson, *George Grenville: A Political Life* (Oxford: Clarendon, 1984); John L. Bullion, *A Great and Necessary Measure* (Columbia: University of Missouri Press, 1982); Fred Anderson, *Crucible of War* (New York: Vintage, 2002), 562.

7. Paul W. Mapp has also noted Britain's "imperial change of direction" in ideological terms in 1762–63: *The Elusive West and the Contest for Empire* (Chapel Hill: University of North Carolina Press, 2011), 416.

8. George Grenville (Wotton) to duke of Bedford, 6 November 1767, Henry E Huntington Library, ST 7/II; George Grenville (London) to duke of Bedford, 5 September 1763, in *The Grenville Papers,* ed. William James Smith (New York: AMS, 1970), 2: 108–9; George Grenville (London) to Edward Harley 4th earl of Oxford, 1 September 1763, HEH, ST 7/I; George Grenville (Downing Street) to earl of Northumberland, 28 October 1763, HEH, ST 7/I.

9. Charles Garth (London) to South Carolina Committee of Correspondence, 21 January 1764, WCL, Charles Garth Letterbook, f. 92r.

10. George Grenville (Bath) to Thomas Whately, 13 October 1765, HEH, ST 7/II.

11. R. Wolters (Rotterdam) to Charles Jenkinson, 25 September 1763, BL, Add 38201, f. 126r; Charles Jenkinson to R. Wolters, 7 August 1764, BL, Add 38304, f. 41r; R. Wolters (Rotterdam) to Charles Jenkinson, 12 October 1764, BL, Add 38203, f. 186; Charles Jenkinson to R. Wolters, 19 October 1764, BL, Add 38304, f. 78r; Charles Jenkinson to John Larpent Jr., 7 December 1764, BL, Add 38304, f. 97r; John Larpent Jr. (Paris) to Charles Jenkinson, 13 January 1765, BL, Add 38204, f. 27v; John Campbell (Ormond Street, London) to Charles Jenkinson, 15 November 1764, BL, Add 38203, f. 261; Charles Jenkinson (London) to Sir Robert Jenkinson, 25 May 1766, BL, Add 38305, f. 21v; Marquis de Montcalm (Governor of Quebec) to Monsieur Berryer Ministre de la Marine, 1 October 1758, BL, Add 38335 (Charles Jenkinson's papers), f. 35r; Earl of Sandwich, Debates in House of Lords, 1766, BL, Add 35912, f. 84r.

12. For some examples, see *Gentleman's Magazine* 9 (January 1739), 34; preface to Nicolas Dutot, *Political Reflections upon the Finances and Commerce of France* (London: A. Millar, 1739), iii–iv; John Lord Carteret, 1 March 1739, *Cobbett's Parliamentary History of England* 10: 1187; John Lord Hervey, 1 March 1739, ibid., 10: 1206; *Considerations on the American Stamp Act and on the Conduct of the Minister who Planned it* (London: W. Nicoll, 1766), 26.

13. *Gentleman's Magazine* 34 (July 1764), 325; Thomas Whately, *Considerations on the Trade and Finances of this Kingdom,* 2nd ed. (London:

J. Wilkie, 1766), 3–4; George Grenville (London) to earl of Northumberland, 28 October 1763, HEH, ST 7/I; George Grenville (London) to earl of Northumberland, 26 November 1763, HEH, ST 7/I; George Grenville (Wotton) to George Chalmers, 5 October 1766, HEH, ST 7/II; Thomas Whately to George Grenville, 20 October 1766, BL, Add 42084, ff. 198–99; *London Evening Post,* 29 June 1765; Hugh Bailley (London) to Robert Clive, 4 January 1765, IOR, MSS Eur G37/33/1, f. 9r; Thomas Ramsden (Pontefract) to Charles Jenkinson, 11 December 1763, BL, Add 38201, f. 312r; Thomas Whately, *Regulations Lately Made Concerning the Colonies* (1765), 3; George Grenville, 6 February 1765, in *Proceedings and Debates of the British Parliaments Respecting North America, 1754–1783,* ed. R. C. Simmons and P. D. G. Thomas, vol. 2, *1765–1768* (White Plains, NY: Kraus International, 1982–87), 10; George Grenville, 14 January 1766, ibid., 2: 87; Charles Garth (London) to South Carolina Committee of Correspondence, 17 April 1764, WCL, Charles Garth Letterbook, f. 98r; Charles Jenkinson, "My Account of the Optional Offers about the Stamp Duty," ca. 1768, BL, Add 38337, f. 259r.

14. Whately, *Considerations on the Trade and Finances,* 8; Robert Melvill (Grenada) to Dunk Halifax, 26 August 1765, TNA, CO 101/10, f. 342r; Charles Jenkinson to James Stuart-Mackenzie, 11 September 1764, BL, Add 38304, f. 59v; John Watts (New York) to Gedney Clarke, 9 August 1763, NYHS, John Watts's Copybook of Letters, 1762–1765, p. 103.

15. Whately, *Regulations Lately Made Concerning the Colonies,* 88–89, 91, 94; Henry McCulloh, *Miscellaneous Essay* (1755), 101–2; George Grenville (London) to earl of Bath, 30 April 1763, HEH, ST 7/I; George Grenville (London) to Horatio Walpole, 8 September 1763, HEH, ST 7/I; Dunk Halifax (Great George Street, London) to George Grenville, 5 December 1763, BL, Add 57808, f. 129r; Oliver M. Dickerson, *The Navigation Acts and the American Revolution* (Philadelphia: University of Pennsylvania Press, 1951), 161–89; Thomas C. Barrow, *Trade and Empire: The British Customs Service in Colonial America* (Cambridge: Harvard University Press, 1967), 173–212.

16. Charles Garth (London) to South Carolina Committee of Correspondence, 21 January 1764, WCL, Charles Garth Letterbook, f. 92r.

17. Steve Pincus and Alice Wolfram, "A Proactive State? The Land Bank, Investment, and Party Politics in the 1690s," in *Regulating the British Economy 1650–1850,* rd. Perry Gauci (Burlington, VT: Ashgate, 2011), 41–62; Henry McCulloh, *Wisdom and Policy of the French* (1755), 129; McCulloh, *Miscellaneous Essay,* 63; Whately, *Regulations Lately Made Concerning the Colonies,* 41; Charles Garth (London) to South Carolina Committee of Correspondence, 21 January 1764, WCL, Charles Garth Letterbook, f. 92r; Joseph Albert Ernst, *Money and Politics in America, 1755–1775* (Chapel Hill: University

of North Carolina Press, 1973), 70–88; Jack P. Greene and Richard M. Jellison, "The Currency Act of 1764 in Imperial-Colonial Relations, 1764–1776," *William and Mary Quarterly* 18, no. 4 (1961), 485–518.

18. See the failed "Plan of 1764" carefully described by Daniel K. Richter, "The Plan of 1764: Native Americans and a British Empire that Never Was," in Richter *Trade, Land, and Power* (Philadelphia: University of Pennsylvania Press, 2014), 177–201; Richard Grosvenor, "Hints Respecting the Military Establishments in the American Colonies," 25 February 1763, BL, Add 38335, ff. 27–28; Francis Bernard (Castle William, Massachusetts) to John Pownall, 18 August 1765, in *The Papers of Francis Bernard*, ed. Colin Nicolson (Boston: Colonial Society of Massachusetts, 2012), 2: 308; Francis Bernard (Castle William) to Richard Jackson, 24 August 1765, ibid., 2: 321–22; Eliphalet Dyer (London) to Jared Ingersoll, 14 April 1764, New Haven Museum, MSS 68, Box I/Folder O.

19. Richard Grosvenor, Lord Grosvenor, "Hints Respecting the Settlement of our American Provinces," 25 February 1763, BL, Add 38335, ff. 14–18. Jonathan Mayhew thought the entire Grenvillian strategy sought to "retard the population of the colonies." Jonathan Mayhew (Boston) to Thomas Hollis, 8 August 1765, in "Thomas Hollis and Jonathan Mayhew: Their Correspondence, 1759–1766," ed. Bernhard Knollenberg, *Proceedings of the Massachusetts Historical Society*, Third Series, 69: 173.

20. Jared Ingersoll, Notes on Thomas Whately, New Haven Museum, MSS 68, Box III/Folder W; Jared Ingersoll to Thomas Fitch, 11 February 1765, New Haven Museum, MSS 68, Box III/Folder W; John Bretell (Stamp Office) to Charles Jenkinson, 26 March 1765, BL, Add 38204, f. 166r; McCulloh, *Miscellaneous Essay*, 94; Whately, *Regulations Lately Made Concerning the Colonies*, 101; Justin du Rivage and Claire Priest, "The Stamp Act and Political Origins of American Legal and Economic Institutions," *Southern California Law Review* 88, no. 4 (2015), 875–912.

21. Whately, *Regulations Lately Made Concerning the Colonies*, 44–45.

22. My thinking on the East India Company has been decisively shaped by James Vaughn, "The Politics of Empire: Metropolitan Socio-Political Development and the Imperial Transformation of the British East India Company, 1675–1775," Ph.D. diss., University of Chicago, 2008. A blow-by-blow account of the struggle is provided by Robert McGilvary, *Guardian of the East India Company: The Life of Laurence Sulivan* (London: Tauris, 2006), 130–46.

23. Charles Jenkinson to R. Wolters, 4 May 1764, BL, Add 38304, f. 20r; John Walsh (London) to Robert Clive, 14 February 1765, IOR, MSS Eur G37/33/2, f. 65v; John Walsh (Chesterfield Street, London) to Robert Clive, 5 April 1765, IOR, MSS Eur G37/34/1, ff. 7–8. Unsurprisingly, Grenville detested Sulivan: John

Stewart (London) to Robert Clive, 8 February 1765, IOR, MSS Eur G37/33/2, f. 28r; George Grenville (Downing Street) to Humphry Morice, 10 March 1764, HEH, ST 7/I; Charles Jenkinson to Solomon Salvador, 12 April 1764, BL, Add 38304, f. 14r; George Grenville (Stoke) to duke of Bedford, 24 April 1764, HEH, ST 7/I; Joseph Salvador (White Hart Court, London) to Charles Jenkinson, 6 March 1764, BL, Add 38202, f. 147r; Joseph Salvador (White Hart Court, London) to Charles Jenkinson, 7 March 1764, BL, Add 38202, f. 148r; Joseph Salvador (Bath) to Charles Jenkinson, 22 April 1764, BL, Add 38202, f. 248r; George Grenville (Bath) to Charles Jenkinson, 29 April 1764, HEH, ST 7/I; Charles Jenkinson (London) to George Grenville, 1 May 1764, BL, Add 57809, f. 105r.

24. Robert Clive (London) to Robert Palk, 15 December 1762, IOR, MSS Eur G37/3/1, f. 42; Robert Clive, *Letter to the Proprietors of the East India Stock* (London: J. Nourse, 1764), 4. This analysis circulated widely in government circles: Paper, ca. 1762, TNA, PRO 30/47/20/2, ff. 12–13 (papers of the earl of Egremont); "A Brief Statement of the English and French Territories," WCL, Shelburne Papers, vol. 98, pp. 1–2; Robert Clive (Calcutta) to John Andrews, 26 January 1759, IOR, MSS Eur G37/3/1, f. 20. For Sulivan's critique: see Laurence Sulivan (East India House) to William Pitt, 26 July 1761, WCL, Shelburne Papers, vol. 99, no. 1; Earl of Sandwich (Whitehall) to Robert Clive, 8 January 1765, IOR, MSS Eur G37/33/1, f. 15r.

25. Robert Clive (Calcutta) to William Pitt, 1 January 1759, HEH, STG Box 18 (12); Robert Clive (Berkeley Square, London) to Court of Directors, 27 April 1764, IOR, Mss Eur G37/3/1, f. 132r; Robert Clive (Calcutta) to Court of Directors, 30 September 1765, HEH, STG Box 20 (17).

26. Robert Clive (Calcutta) to William Pitt, 1 January 1759, HEH STG Box 18 (12); Robert Clive to Directors of the East India Company, 30 September 1765, WCL, Shelburne Papers, vol. 99, nos. 45–47; Robert Clive to the Select Committee of Bengal, 30 September 1765, ibid., 99, nos. 62–63.

27. Ezra Stiles, Memoirs and Extracts, 1766–67, 25 July 1766, Beinecke, MS Vault Stiles, MP/Folder 402, pp. 18–21. Like Sulivan, Stiles predicted that "grasping at power and internal dominion in India will prove the ruin of the [East India] Company and the commerce."

28. James C. Riley, *The Seven Years War and the Old Regime in France* (Princeton: Princeton University Press, 1986), 193–207.

29. Stanley J. Stein and Barbara H. Stein, *Apogee of Empire: Spain and New Spain in the Age of Charles III* (Baltimore: Johns Hopkins University Press, 2003), 37–41, 58–80; Allan J. Kuethe and Kenneth J. Andrien, *The Spanish Atlantic World in the Eighteenth Century* (Cambridge: Cambridge University Press, 2014), 231–47; Allan J. Kuethe, *Cuba, 1753–1815: Crown, Military, and Society* (Knoxville: University of Tennessee Press, 1986), 25–28; Frances Ramos,

Identity, Ritual, and Power in Colonial Puebla (Tucson: University of Arizona Press, 2012), 154; Manuel Lucena-Giraldo, "The Limits of Reform in Spanish America," in *Enlightened Reform in Southern Europe and Its Atlantic Colonies,* ed. Gabriel Paquette (Farnham, UK: Ashgate, 2009), 312–18; John Huxtable Elliott, *Empires of the Atlantic World: Britain and Spain in America, 1492–1830* (New Haven: Yale University Press, 2006), 306–8; Jeremy Adelman, *Sovereignty and Revolution in the Iberian Atlantic* (Princeton: Princeton University Press, 2006), 22–31; R. Wolters (Rotterdam) to Charles Jenkinson, 11 October 1765, BL, Add 38201, f. 179v; William Henry van Nassau van Zuylestein 4th earl of Rochford (Madrid) to Dunk Halifax, 8 July 1765, TNA, SP 94/171, f. 18v; William Henry van Nassau van Zuylestein 4th earl of Rochford (San Ildefonso) to Henry Seymour Conway, 17 September 1765, TNA, SP 94/171, f. 210v; Henry Seymour Conway (London) to earl of Rochford, 19 September 1765, TNA, SP 94/171, f. 143; William Henry van Nassau van Zuylestein 4th earl of Rochford (Madrid) to Henry Seymour Conway, 24 March 1766, TNA, SP 94/173, f. 193v; William Henry van Nassau van Zuylestein 4th earl of Rochford (Aranjuez) to Henry Seymour Conway, 5 May 1766, TNA, SP 94/174, f. 21v. Throughout I cite British perceptions of French and Spanish imperial developments to demonstrate that this was part of the British imperial imagination.

30. All of the major uprisings compared by Anthony McFarlane "took place at moments of abrupt changes of policy in the Spanish state." "Rebellions in Late Colonial Spanish America: A Comparative Perspective," *Bulletin of Latin American Research* 14, no. 3 (1995), 317; Carlos Marichal, *Bankruptcy of Empire: Mexican Silver and the Wars between Spain, Britain, and France, 1760–1810* (Cambridge: Cambridge University Press, 2007), 49; Kuethe, *Cuba,* 67–71; José Andres-Gallego, *El Motín de Esquilache* (Madrid: Fundación Mapfre Tavera, 2003), 194; William Henry van Nassau van Zuylestein 4th earl of Rochford (Madrid) to Henry Seymour Conway, 12 March 1766, TNA, SP 94/173, ff. 184–85; George Henry Lennox (Aubigny) to Henry Seymour Conway, 9 April 1766, TNA, SP 78/269, f. 306r; *New York Mercury,* 15 July 1765; *Gentleman's Magazine* 35 (August 1765), 389; Josiah Hardy (Cadiz) to Dunk Halifax, 23 July 1765, TNA, SP 94/171, f. 58; Henry Seymour Conway (St. James's London) to William Henry Lyttelton, 23 September 1765, TNA, CO 137/62, f. 51v; Aaron Lousada (Kingston, Jamaica) to William Henry Lyttelton, 11 December 1765, TNA, CO 137/62, f. 158r; Ezra Stiles, Incidents at Newport, 20 March 1766, Stamp Act Notebook, Beinecke, MS Vault Stiles, MP/Folder 372, p. 22; Kenneth Andrien, "Economic Crisis, Taxes, and the Quito Insurrection of 1765," *Past and Present,* no. 129 (November 1990), 104–31; Anthony McFarlane, "The Rebellion of the Barrios: Urban Insurrection in Bourbon Quito," *Hispanic American Historical Review* 69, no. 2 (1989), 285–87. Andrien

differs from McFarlane's account by pointing to the long-term structural cause of unrest in Quito—the decline of local textile manufacturing—and highlighting the radical nature of plebeian demands. They agree, however, that fiscal reforms sparked the uprising. William Henry van Nassau van Zuylestein 4th earl of Rochford (Escorial) to Henry Seymour Conway, 4 November 1765, TNA, SP 94/172, ff. 106–7; William Henry van Nassau van Zuylestein 4th earl of Rochford (Madrid) to Henry Seymour Conway, 12 March 1766, TNA, SP 94/173, ff. 185–86. Sir William Burnaby (Leguanea, Jamaica) to William Henry Lyttelton, 14 December 1765, TNA, CO 137/62, f. 163r; "Account of the New Disturbances at Quito," 11 April 1766, TNA, SP 94/173, ff. 224–25; Lewis de Visme (Aranjuez) to Duke of Richmond, 30 June 1766, TNA, SP 94/174, f. 124r; Elliott, *Empires of the Atlantic World*, 311–12; Kuethe and Andrien, *Hispanic Atlantic World*, 255–56. The numbers were clearly greatly exaggerated: McFarlane, "Rebellion of the Barrios," 305.

31. Kuethe, *Cuba*, 68–70; Andrien, "Economic Crisis," 122–23; McFarlane, "Rebellion of the Barrios," 293, 297–301.

32. William Henry van Nassau van Zuylestein 4th earl of Rochford (Madrid) to Henry Seymour Conway, 24 March 1766, TNA, SP 94/173, ff. 191–92; Rochford (Madrid) to Henry Seymour Conway, 31 March 1766, TNA, SP 94/173, ff. 207–15; George Henry Lennox (Paris) to Henry Seymour Conway, 4 May 1766, TNA, SP 78/270, f. 6v; Lewis de Visme (Aranjuez) to Duke of Richmond, 18 June 1766, TNA, SP 94/174, f. 68; Stein and Stein, *Apogee of Empire*, 83–88; Kuethe and Andrien, *Hispanic Atlantic World*, 256–60; Laura Rodriguez, "The Spanish Riots of 1766," *Past and Present*, no. 53 (1973), 117–46; George Henry Lennox (Aubigny) to Henry Seymour Conway, 9 April 1766, TNA, SP 78/269, f. 306r. Stein and Stein maintain that the "immediate objective" of the riots "was the ouster of Esquilache, spearhead of the reforms that followed the arrival of Charles III in 1759"; *Apogee of Empire*, 83; Earl of Rochford (Madrid) to Henry Seymour Conway, 24 March 1766, TNA, SP 94/173, f. 191v.

33. Edmond Dziembowski, *Un Nouveau Patriotisme Français, 1750–1770* (Oxford: Voltaire Foundation, 1998), 263–76; Pernille Roge, "A Natural Order of Empire: The Physiocratic Vision of Colonial France after the Seven Years' War," in *The Political Economy of Empire in the Early Modern World*, ed. Sophus A. Reinert and Pernille Roge (Basingstoke: Palgrave Macmillan, 2013), 34–40; Loïc Charles and Paul Cheney, "The Colonial Machine Dismantled: Knowledge and Empire in the French Atlantic," *Past and Present*, no. 219 (2013), 142–46; François-Joseph Ruggiu, "India and the Reshaping of the French Colonial Policy, 1759–1789," *Itinerario* 35, no. 2 (2011), 27–28; John Shovlin, "Rethinking Enlightenment Reform in a French Context," in Paquette, *Enlightened Reform in Southern Europe*, 47–61; Jean Tarrade, *Le Commerce Colonial*

de la France à la fin de l'Ancien Regime (Paris: Presse Universitaire de France, 1972), 1: 73–81; John D. Garrigus, *Before Haiti* (New York: Palgrave Macmillan, 2006), 117; Jean-Pierre Guicciardini, ed., *Mémoires du Duc de Choiseul* (Paris: Mercure de France, 1982), 213–30; H. M. Scott, "The Importance of Bourbon Naval Reconstruction to the Strategy of Choiseul after the Seven Years War," *International History Review* 1, no. 1 (1979), 17–35.

34. John Larpent Jr. (Paris) to Charles Jenkinson, 27 January 1765, BL, Add 38204, f. 53v; Charles Jenkinson to George Grenville, 6 December 1765, BL, Add 57809, f. 204v; *London Evening Post,* 13 June 1765; Garrigus, *Before Haiti,* 119–24; Jean Tarrade, "L'Administration Coloniale en France à la Fin de l'Ancien Regime," *Revue Historique* 229 (1963), 108; Charles and Cheney, "The Colonial Machine Dismantled," 152–53; Roge, "Natural Order of Empire," 40–43.

35. Henry Seymour Conway (London) to Francis Seymour Conway, 29 November 1764, Lewis Walpole Library, vol. 84/31; Francis Seymour Conway earl of Hertford (Paris) to Dunk Halifax, 1 July 1765, TNA, SP 78/267, ff. 13–14; David Hume (Compiègne) to Henry Seymour Conway, 12 August 1765, TNA, SP 78/267, f. 121v; *Annual Register, or a View of the History, Politics and Literature for the year 1764* (London: J. Dodsley, 1765), 6–10; *Gentleman's Magazine* 34 (January 1764), 41; R. R. Palmer, *The Age of Democratic Revolutions* (Princeton: Princeton University Press, 2014), 67–75; Riley, *Seven Years War,* 207–17. According to Michael Kwass, "the scale, language and publicity of fiscal dispute reached heights unprecedented since the Fronde of the mid-seventeenth century"; Michael Kwass, *Privilege and the Politics of Taxation in Eighteenth-Century France* (Cambridge: Cambridge University Press, 2000), 161; Julian Swann, *Politics and the Parlement of Paris under Louis XV, 1754–1774* (Cambridge: Cambridge University Press, 1995), 218–19.

36. John Brewer long ago pointed out that political argument traveled easily back and forth across the Atlantic in this period: John Brewer, *Party Ideology and Popular Politics at the Accession of George III* (Cambridge: Cambridge University Press, 1976), 202–5; Richard Champion (Bristol) to Caleb Lloyd, 15 February 1766, BRO, MSS 38083/1, p. 148.

37. Francis Fauquier (Williamsburg) to Henry Seymour Conway, 5 November 1765, TNA, CO 5/1345, f. 97r; John Penn (Philadelphia) to Henry Seymour Conway, 19 February 1766, TNA, CO 5/1280, f. 176r; Jonathan Mayhew (Boston) to Thomas Hollis, 8 August 1765, Knollenberg, 173; William H. Smith Jr. (New York) to Robert Monckton, 8 November 1765, in *Historical Memoirs from 16 March 1763 to 9 July 1776 of William Smith,* ed. William Sabine (New York, 1956), 31.

38. Morgan and Morgan, *Stamp Act Crisis,* 125–86; Ezra Stiles, ca. 1769, Stamp Act Notebook, Beinecke, MS Vault Stiles, MP/Folder 372, pp. 65, 68;

James Wright (Savannah) to Board of Trade, 9 November 1765, TNA, CO 5/649, ff. 48–49; James Wright (Savannah) to Board of Trade, 15 January 1766, TNA, CO 5/649, ff. 142–43; James Wright (Savannah) to Board of Trade, 1 February 1766, TNA, CO 5/649, f. 152; James Wright (Savannah) to Board of Trade, 7 February 1766, TNA, CO 5/649, f. 154r; James Wright (Savannah) to Henry Seymour Conway, 24 June 1766, TNA, CO 5/658, f. 104v; James Habersham (Savannah) to William Knox, 30 October 1765, in *The Letters of Hon. James Habersham 1756–1775, Collections of the Georgia Historical Society* (Savannah: Georgia Historical Society, 1904), 6: 47–48; Habersham (Savannah) to Knox, 4 December 1765, ibid., 6: 50; Habersham (Savannah) to George Whitefield, 27 January 1766, ibid., 54–55. The South Carolina Assembly coordinated efforts with the Assembly in Georgia: Peter Manigault (Charlestown, SC) to Alex Wylly (Speaker of the House of Assembly of Georgia), Autumn 1765, SCHS, 1068/11/278/2, pp. 33–34; General Thomas Gage to Board of Trade, 4 November 1765, BL, Add 33030, f. 62r; Montagu Wilmot (Halifax, Nova Scotia) to Board of Trade, 19 November 1765, TNA, CO 217/21, f. 140; *Connecticut Gazette,* 22 November 1765; John Bartlet Brebner, *The Neutral Yankees of Nova Scotia* (New York: Columbia University Press, 1937), 157–62; Elizabeth Mancke, *The Fault Lines of Empire* (New York: Routledge, 2005), 72, 84; James Carr, Merchant, Committee on the American Papers, 17 February 1766, BL, Add 33030, ff. 185–86; Petition of Stephen Fuller, Agent of Jamaica, 11 February 1766, Simmons and Thomas, *Proceedings and Debates*, 2: 184; James Irwin, Planter, Committee on the American Papers, 17 February 1766, BL, Add 33030, f. 187r; William Henry Lyttelton (Jamaica) to Board of Trade, 2 April 1764, TNA, CO 137/33, ff. 131–32; Samuel Martin Sr. (Antigua) to Samuel Martin Jr., 5 August 1765, BL, Add 41347, f. 205r; John Howell (Spanish Town, Jamaica) to Henry Seymour Conway, 31 May 1766, TNA, CO 137/62, f. 208r; Samuel Adams (Boston) to John Smith, 20 December 1765, in *The Writings of Samuel Adams,* ed. Henry Alonzo Cushing (New York: Octagon, 1968), 1: 59; Stephen Fuller (London) to William Henry Lyttelton, 24 December 1765, WCL, William Henry Lyttelton Papers, Box 17; Stephen Fuller (London) to Jamaica Committee of Correspondence, 22 February 1766, WCL, William Henry Lyttelton Papers, Box 17; James Harris Diary, 15 February 1765, Simmons and Thomas, *Proceedings and Debates,* 2: 13; Jared Ingersoll (London) to Thomas Fitch, 6 March 1765, New Haven Museum, MSS 68, Box III/Folder W; compare Donna J. Spindel, "The Stamp Act Crisis in the British West Indies," *Journal of American Studies* 11 (1977), 203–22; John Adams, Diary, 2 January 1766, in *Diary and Autobiography of John Adams,* ed. L. H. Butterfield (Cambridge: Belknap Press of Harvard University Press, 1961), 1: 285; Lovell Stanhope, Reasons in Support of the Bill to Restrain Exorbitant Grants to Negroes,

13 June 1763, TNA, CO 137/33, f. 34r (on the two regiments in Jamaica); Ezra Stiles, History of Jamaica, 22 March 1763, Beinecke, Vault Stiles, M&P/Folder 315/5; Extract of a Letter from a Gentleman in Charles Town to William Tryon, 13 December, 1765, in *The Correspondence of William Tryon*, ed. William S. Powell (Raleigh: Division of Archives and History, 1980), 1: 168; Capel Hanbury, Committee on the American Papers, 11 February 1766, BL, Add 33030, f. 106v; Jonathan Mayhew (Boston) to Thomas Hollis, 19 August 1765, Knollenberg, 175; Thomas Gage (New York) to Henry Seymour Conway, 4 November 1765, in *The Correspondence of General Thomas Gage*, ed. Clarence Edwin Carter (New Haven: Yale University Press, 1931), 1: 71.

39. Samuel Adams (Boston) to John Smith, 20 December 1765, Cushing, *Writings of Samuel Adams*, 1: 58; *Connecticut Gazette*, 30 August 1765.

40. George Rude, *Wilkes and Liberty* (Oxford: Clarendon Press, 1962), 17–36; Charles Jenkinson, Diary, 14 May 1763, BL, Add 38335, f. 120r; Charles Jenkinson, Diary, 15 May 1763, BL, Add 38335, f. 121r; *Gentleman's Magazine* 35 (May 1765), 244; *Providence Gazette Extraordinary*, 24 August 1765; *New York Mercury*, 5 August 1765; Duke of Bedford (Bedford House) to Duke of Marlborough, 19 May 1765, in *Correspondence of John Fourth Duke of Bedford*, ed. Lord John Russell (London: Longman, Brown, Greene and Longmans, 1846), 3: 279; Richard Rigby to Duke of Bedford, 20 May 1765, ibid., 3: 282; Hew Dalrymple (London) to Duke of Bedford, 22 May 1765, ibid., 3: 283; Edmund Burke to Henry Flood, 18 May 1765, in *The Correspondence of Edmund Burke*, ed. Thomas W. Copeland (Chicago: University of Chicago Press, 1958), 1: 194; George Cooke, 17 December 1765, Simmons and Thomas, *Proceedings and Debates*, vol. 1, *1754–1764*, 59.

41. *The Examination of Benjamin Franklin* ([London]: J. Almon, 1767), 11; Henry Seymour Conway, 3 February 1766, Simmons and Thomas, *Proceedings and Debates*, 2: 135; William Smith Jr. (New York) to Robert Monckton, 8 November 1765, Sabine, *Historical Memoirs*, 30. Compare this broader context from Smith with the quotation presented by the Morgans: *Stamp Act Crisis*, 93; Gordon S. Wood, *The American Revolution: A History* (New York: Modern Library, 2002), 24; T. H. Breen, *The Marketplace of Revolution* (Oxford: Oxford University Press, 2004), 218.

42. Daniel Mildred, Committee on the American Papers, 11 February 1766, BL, Add 33030, f. 113r; Emmanuel Elam, Committee on the American Papers, 12 February 1766, BL, Add 33030, ff. 143–44; Josiah Bunry, Committee on the American Papers, 12 February 1766, BL, Add 33030, f. 140v; Capel Hanbury, Committee on the American Papers, 11 February 1766, BL, Add 33030, f. 106r; Barlow Trecothick, Committee on the American Papers, 11 February 1766, BL, Add 33030, ff. 88–89.

43. Jared Ingersoll (London) to Thomas Fitch, 11 February 1765, New Haven Museum, MSS 68, Box III/Folder W; Charles Garth (London) to South Carolina Committee of Correspondence, 23 December 1766, WCL, Charles Garth Letterbook, f. 162v; Petitions Received by the House of Commons, 17 January 1766, Simmons and Thomas, *Proceedings and Debates*, 2: 96–97; Petitions Received by the House of Commons, 20 January 1766, ibid., 2: 100–101; Petition Received by the House of Commons, 21 January 1766, ibid., 2: 103–4; Petitions Received, 27 January 1766, ibid., 2: 108; Petition Received by the House of Commons, 29 January 1766, ibid., 2: 115; James E. Bradley, *Popular Politics and the American Revolution in England* (Macon, GA: Mercer University Press, 1986), 127, 133; Richard Champion (Bristol) to Caleb Lloyd, 23 February 1766, BRO, MSS 38083/1, p. 149; George Thomas Keppel 6th earl of Albemarle, ed., *Memoirs of the Marquis of Rockingham and his Contemporaries* (London: Bentley, 1852), 1: 284–85.

44. John Watts (New York) to Sir William Baker, 30 March 1765, NYHS, John Watts's Copybook of Letters, 1762–65, p. 227; John Hancock (Boston) to Barnards and Harrison, 25 February 1766, HBS, Hancock Family Papers, Vol. JH-6, p. 173; John Hancock (Boston) to Harrison and Barnard, 30 June 1766, HBS, Hancock Family Papers, Vol. JH-6, p. 186; Richard Champion (Bristol) to Caleb Lloyd, 15 February 1766, BRO, MSS 38083/1, p. 149; Capel and Osgood Hanbury (London) to George Washington, 27 March 1766, in *The Papers of George Washington, Digital Edition,* ed. Theodore J. Crackel (Charlottesville: University of Virginia Press, 2008), Colonial Series, 7: 431; Breen, *Marketplace of Revolution,* 226.

45. John Huske, "Observations on the Trade of Great Britain to her American Colonies," ca. 1765–66, BL, Add 33030, f. 318. Tim Breen has recovered much of this ideology but presents it as if this were a uniquely "American perspective": Breen, *Marketplace of Revolution,* 205–6.

46. Samuel Garbett, "Thoughts on the Colonies," 1766, WCL, Shelburne, 49: 4.

47. William Bollan, *A Succinct View of the Origin of Our Colonies* (London, 1766), 7, 32–37.

48. John Dickinson, *The Late Regulations Respecting the British Colonies* (Philadelphia: William Bradford, 1765), 4–5, 8, 30, 32. Dickinson also condemned Grenville's restrictions on trade with Spanish America, especially in the case of West Florida: ibid., 37. Dickinson is usually described in a constitutionalist context, not a political economic one: Greene, *Constitutional Origins,* 114–16, 133–34; Bernard Bailyn, *Ideological Origins of the American Revolution* (Cambridge: Harvard University Press, 1967), 215–16. But see Jane Calvert, *Quaker Constitutionalism and the Political Thought of John Dickinson*

(Cambridge: Cambridge University Press, 2009), 210; Breen, *Marketplace of Revolution*, 92–93.

49. Daniel Dulany, *Considerations on the Propriety of Imposing Taxes in the British Colonies*, 2nd ed. (London: J. Almon, 1765), 35. The Morgans' elegant treatment of Dulany's constitutional position misses this Patriot political economic argument: Morgan and Morgan, *Stamp Act Crisis*, 75–91. But see Breen, *Marketplace of Revolution*, 211. James Otis Jr., *Considerations on Behalf of the Colonists*, 2nd ed. (London: J. Almon, 1765), 17, 29–30; Thomas Cushing and Samuel Adams (Boston) to Reverend George Whitfield, 11 November 1765; Cushing, *Writings of Samuel Adams*, 1: 32.

50. Sir William Meredith, 5 February 1766, Simmons and Thomas, *Proceedings and Debates*, 2: 158. Meredith presented the Virginia petition against the Stamp Bill: Jared Ingersoll (London) to Thomas Fitch, 6 March 1765, New Haven Museum, MSS 68, Box III/Folder W; Henry Seymour Conway, 3 February 1766, Simmons and Thomas, *Proceedings and Debates*, 2: 135; D. H. Watson, "William Baker's Account of the Debate on the Repeal of the Stamp Act," *William and Mary Quarterly* 26, no. 2 (1969), 261. The Duke of Grafton expressed similar views in the Lords: Augustus Fitzroy 3rd Duke of Grafton, Debates in the House of Lords, 1766, BL, Add 35912, f. 85r; *South Carolina Gazette*, 9 June 1766; Dennys de Berdt (London) to Colonel White, 16 January 1766, LOC, MSS 18036; Charles Garth (London) to South Carolina Committee of Correspondence, 19 January 1766, WCL, Charles Garth Letterbook, f. 163v; William Pitt, 14 January 1766, Simmons and Thomas, *Proceedings and Debates*, 2: 81, 88.

51. *New York Mercury*, 30 January 1764; Memorial of the Merchants of the City of New York, 1764, NYPL, William Smith Papers, Box 1/Lot 180 (1); Petition of the Merchants of the City of New York, 28 November 1766, WCL, Shelburne, 49: 33; Petition of the General Assembly of New York, 11 December 1766, TNA, CO 5/378, f. 226; *Resolutions of the South Carolina Assembly, 29 November 1765* (Charles Town: Peter Timothy, 1765); South Carolina Committee of Correspondence (Charles Town) to Charles Garth, 16 December 1765, WCL, Charles Garth Letterbook, f. 159r; Samuel Ward (Newport, Rhode Island) to Henry Seymour Conway, 25 June 1766, TNA, CO5/1280, f. 39; Petition of Edward Montagu, Agent for the Colony of Virginia, 21 January 1766, Simmons and Thomas, *Proceedings and Debates*, 2: 104; William Pitkin (Hartford) to Henry Seymour Conway, 4 August 166, TNA, CO 5/1280, f. 73; Resolves of the Lower House of the Connecticut Assembly, 24 October 1765, Beinecke, MS Vault Stiles, MP/Folder 379, p. 3; Representation of the House of Burgesses to Governor Francis Fauquier, May 1763, WCL, Shelburne, 49: 28; Thomas Cushing and Samuel Adams (Boston) to Reverend G[eorge]

W[hitefield], 11 November 1765, Cushing, *Writings of Samuel Adams,* 1: 31; James Otis, Thomas Cushing, Samuel Adams, and Thomas Gray (Boston) to Dennys de Berdt, 20 December 1765, ibid., 1: 62; Samuel Adams (Boston) to John Smith, 19 December 1765, ibid., 1: 43.

52. George Washington (Mt. Vernon, Virginia) to Francis Dandridge, 20 September 1765, Crackel, *Digital Washington Papers,* Colonial Series, 7: 395; Washington (Mt. Vernon) to Robert Cary and Company, 20 September 1765, ibid., 7: 395–96; Washington (Mt. Vernon) to Capel and Osgood Hanbury, 25 July 1767, ibid., 8: 15.

53. Joshua Piker, *Okfuskee: A Creek Indian Town in Colonial America* (Cambridge: Harvard University Press, 2004), 40–41; John J. McCusker and Russell R. Menard, *The Economy of British America* (Chapel Hill: University of North Carolina Press, 1985), 355; Gould, *Persistence of Empire,* 16.

54. McFarlane, "Rebellion in the Barrios," 321; Tarrade, *Le Commerce Colonial,* 1: 166, 296–302; Roge, "A Natural Order of Empire," 47; Swann, *Politics and the Parlement of Paris,* 193.

55. Richard Champion (Bristol) to Caleb Lloyd, 23 February 1766, BRO, MSS 38083/1, pp. 154–55; Capel and Osgood Hanbury (London) to George Washington, 27 March 1766, Crackel, *Digital George Washington Papers,* Colonial Series, 7: 431; Dennys de Berdt (London) to William Smith, March 1766, LOC, MSS 18036; Frances Armytage, *The Free Port System in the British West Indies* (London: Longmans, Green, 1953); Memo on Free Port in Dominica, 1766, BL, Add 33030, f. 251r; "Thoughts on the expediency of opening the ports of Dominica," ca. 1766, BL, Add 33030, ff. 253–56; John Huske, "Observations on the Trade of Great Britain to her American Colonies," ca. 1765–66, BL, Add 33030, ff. 318–22; William Smith (New York) to George Whitfield, 6 December 1765, Historical Manuscripts Commission, *The Manuscripts of the earl of Dartmouth* (London: HMSO, 1887), 1: 331–32; Richard Stockton to Samuel Smith, 21 March 1767, HMC, *Dartmouth,* vol. 1, p. 332; Propositions Regarding American Colonies, 1768, BL, Add 35912, ff. 49–50; Charles Yorke, Observations on Propositions Regarding American Colonies, 1768, BL, Add 35912, ff. 49–50. These memoranda represent but the tip of a very large iceberg. George Grenville (Wotton) to Robert Nugent, 21 May 1766, HEH, ST 7/II; George Grenville (Wotton) to Thomas Whately, 25 May 1766, HEH, ST 7/II; James Otis Jr., *The Rights of the Colonies Asserted and Proved,* 3rd ed. (London: J. Williams, 1766), 43–44, 53–54; *East India Examiner,* 6, 10, 13, 17, 20, 23 September 1766. The pro-Clive *East India Observer* accused those calling for an inquiry of pursuing "Patriot" policies: no. 1 (1766), 2. On the Grafton/Pitt parliamentary enquiries: H. V. Bowen, *Revenue and Reform: The Indian Problem in British Politics, 1757–1773* (Cambridge:

Cambridge University Press, 1991), 48–66; Lucy S. Sutherland, *The East India Company in Eighteenth-Century Politics* (Oxford: Clarendon, 1952), 138–76. Contemporaries understood full well that the Declaratory Act was toothless, comparing it to the Irish Declaratory Act of 1720: Duke of Newcastle, Debates in House of Lords, 1766, BL, Add 35912, f. 79v; Paul Langford, *The First Rockingham Administration, 1765–1766* (Oxford: Oxford University Press, 1973), 197. Parliament did not use the constitutional power asserted in the 1720 act to tax Ireland directly.

3

Making a Patriot Government

1. Richard Price, *Observations on the Nature of Civil Liberty, the Principles of Government, and the Justice and Policy of the War with America,* 9th ed. (London: Edward and Charles Dilly and Thomas Cadell, 1776), 25; Edmund Burke, *The Speech of E. Burke Esq. on American Taxation, 19 April 1774,* 3rd ed. (Philadelphia: Benjamin Towne, 1775), 5. North had a more conciliatory style than some of his predecessors, but he shared their economic principles; see Andrew O'Shaughnessy, *The Men Who Lost America* (New Haven: Yale University Press, 2013), 50–51.

2. George Washington (Williamsburg) to George William Fairfax, 10–15 June 1774, in *Papers of George Washington Digital Edition,* ed. Theodore J. Crackel (Charlottesville: University of Virginia Press, 2008), 10: 96–97; George Washington (Mount Vernon) to Bryan Fairfax, 4 July 1774, ibid., 10: 109–10; George Washington (Mount Vernon) to Bryan Fairfax, 20 July 1774, ibid., 10: 129–30; The Association, 20 October 1774, in *The Papers of Thomas Jefferson Digital Edition,* ed. Barbara Oberg and J. Jefferson Looney (Charlottesville: University of Virginia Press, 2008–15), Main Series, 1: 149–50 (hereafter *Digital Jefferson Papers*); Richard Henry Lee's Draft Address to the People of Great Britain and Ireland, 11–18 October 1774, in *Letters of Delegates to Congress,* ed. Paul H. Smith (Washington, DC: Library of Congress, 1976), 1: 178. Numerous local calls for association before and after that of the First Continental Congress made the same point: Delaware Committee (George Read, Thomas McKean, John McKinley) to Virginia Committee, 26 May 1774, in *Revolutionary Virginia: The Road to Independence,* ed. Robert L. Scribner (Charlottesville: University of Virginia Press, 1973), 2: 83; New York Committee of Correspondence to Committee for Correspondence for Connecticut, 24 June 1774, in *American Archives,* Fourth Series, ed. Peter Force and M. St. Clair Clarke (Washington, 1837), 1: 306; North Carolina Committee to Committee of Correspondence for Virginia, 21 June 1774, Scribner,

Revolutionary Virginia, 2: 125; Address of Fincastle County Committee, 20 January 1775, ibid., 2: 255.

3. *Humble Address of the Right Honourable the Lords Spiritual and Temporal, and Commons in Parliament Assembled* (Philadelphia: John Dunlap, 1775).

4. Alexander Hamilton, *A Full Vindication of the Measures of Congress* (New York: James Rivington, 1774), 15; Richard Price, *An Appeal to the Public,* New Edition (London: T. Cadell, 1774), 45; Burke, *Speech of E. Burke,* 12; James Macpherson, *The Rights of Great Britain Asserted* (London: T. Cadell, 1776), 74–75.

5. *His Majesty's Most Gracious Speech,* 26 October 1775 [London, 1775]; Samuel Johnson, *Taxation no Tyranny,* 3rd ed. (London: T. Cadell, 1775), 56–57; John Dyke Acland, 26 October 1775, in *Proceedings and Debates of the British Parliaments Respecting North America, 1754–1783,* ed. R. C. Simmons and P. D. G. Thomas, vol. 6, *April 1775–May 1776* (White Plains, NY: Kraus International, 1982–87), 94; John Adams, Notes of Debates, 6 September 1774, Smith, *Letters of Delegates to Congress,* 1: 27–28; Samuel Seabury, *Free Thoughts on the Proceedings of the Continental Congress* ([New York], 1774), [3], 16 November 1774.

6. Resolves of Frederick County, 8 June 1774, Scribner, *Revolutionary Virginia,* 1: 136; Daniel Hulsebosch, *Constituting Empire* (Chapel Hill: University of North Carolina Press, 200), 145; Lords Dissenting to Address on the King's Speech, 26 October 1776, Simmons and Thomas, *Proceedings and Debates,* 6: 73; John Wilkes, 26 October 1775, ibid., 6: 97; James Duane (Philadelphia) to Peter Van Schaak, 2 October 1774, Smith, *Letters of Delegates to Congress,* 1: 136. The radical Whig historian Catherine Macaulay shared this fear: Catherine Macaulay, *An Address to the People of England, Scotland, and Ireland,* 3rd ed. (New York: John Holt, 1775), 14; Jonathan Shipley to Benjamin Franklin, June 1775, *Benjamin Franklin Papers Online,* vol. 22; Ezra Stiles (Newport) to Isaac Karigal, 7 July 1775, Beinecke, MS Vault Stiles, Correspondence Box 12; *The Crisis,* 6 January 1776; Temple Luttrell, 26 October 1775, Simmons and Thomas, *Proceedings and Debates,* 6: 112; Johnson, *Taxation no Tyranny,* 68–69; Richard Rigby, 27 October 1775, Simmons and Thomas, *Proceedings and Debates,* 6: 139; Thomas Jefferson (Virginia) to William Small, 7 May 1775, in Oberg and Looney, *Digital Jefferson Papers,* Main Series, 1: 165; Thomas Paine, *Common Sense,* 3rd ed. (London: J. Almon, 1776), 15–16, 23; George Washington (Philadelphia) to George William Fairfax, 31 May 1775, *The Papers of George Washington, Digital Edition,* ed. Theodore J. Crackel (Charlottesville: University of Virginia Press, 2008), Colonial Series, vol. 10, p. 368; Samuel Adams (Philadelphia) to James Warren, 16 April 1776, Smith,

Letters of Delegates to Congress, 3: 530; Richard Henry Lee (Philadelphia) to Landon Carter, 2 June 1776, ibid., 4 (1979): 117; Abraham Clark (Philadelphia) to Elias Dayton, 4 July 1776, ibid., 4, p. 376.

7. Thomas Jefferson's Notes of Proceedings in Congress, 8 June 1776, Smith, *Letters of Delegates to Congress*, 4: 161; Francis Lightfoot Lee (Philadelphia) to Landon Carter, 19 March 1776, ibid., 3: 407; Richard Henry Lee (Philadelphia) to Landon Carter, 1 April 1776, ibid., 3: 470; Jonathan Dickinson Sergeant (Princeton) to John Adams, 11 April 1776, ibid., 3: 508; John Dickinson's Notes for a Speech in Congress, 1 July 1776, ibid., 4: 351; John Adams (Philadelphia) to Abigail Adams, 3 July 1776, ibid., 4: 374; John Adams, *Thoughts on Government* (Philadelphia: John Dunlap, 1776), 16–17; John Hancock (Philadelphia) to New Jersey Convention, 5 July 1776, Smith, *Letters of Delegates to Congress*, 4: 392. The centrality of state-making at this moment was precociously emphasized by Bradburn: Douglas Bradburn, *The Citizenship Revolution: Politics and the Creation of the American Union 1774-1804*. (Charlottesville: University of Virginia Press, 2009), pp. 46–47.

8. Hamilton, *Full Vindication*, 15; Matthew Robinson-Morris, *Considerations on the Measures Carrying on with Respect to the British Colonies* (London: R. Baldwin, 1774), 80; Price, *Appeal to the Public,* iv; William Knox, *Present State of the Nation* (London: J. Almon, 1768), 53; James Stewart, *A Letter to the Rev. Dr. Price* (London: J. Bew, 1776), 45–46.

9. William Knox, *The Interest of the Merchants and Manufacturers of Great Britain* (London: T. Cadell, 1774), 10–15.

10. Josiah Tucker, *An Humble Address and Earnest Appeal,* 2nd ed. (Gloucester: R. Raikes, 1775), 26. Tucker was unusual among the ministry's supporters in calling for the abandonment of America. But internal evidence makes it clear that he was receiving valuable statistical information from inside the ministry; Knox, *Present State of the Nation*, 35, 40, 55.

11. Stewart, *A Letter to the Rev. Dr. Price,* 45–46; Adam Ferguson, *Remarks on Dr. Price's Observations* (London: G. Kearsley, 1776), 46; James Macpherson, *The Rights of Great Britain Asserted* (London: T. Cadell, 1776), 79.

12. Josiah Tucker, *Four Tracts on Political and Commercial Subjects,* 2nd ed. (Gloucester: R. Raikes, 1774), 207; James Steuart (Coltness) to Archibald Hamilton, 25 January 1775, in "Sir James Steuart: Nine Letters on the American Conflict, 1775–1778," ed. David Raynor and Andrew Skinner, *William and Mary Quarterly* 51, no. 4 (1994), 762. Steuart's *An Inquiry into the Principles of Political Oeconomy* (London: A. Millar and T. Cadell, 1767) led the North government to consult him on political economic issues. Adam Smith aimed to confute his principles. Samuel Seabury, *Free Thoughts on the Proceedings*

of the Continental Congress ([New York], 1774), 10; Tucker, *Humble Address and Earnest Appeal*, 71–72; Macpherson, *The Rights of Great Britain Asserted*, p. 11.

13. Arthur Lee, *An Appeal to the Justice and Interests of the People of Great Britain* 4th ed. (London: J. Almon, 1776), 33; George Johnstone, 26 October 1775, Simmons and Thomas, *Proceedings and Debates*, 6: 106. On Johnstone and his remarkable family, see Emma Rothschild, *The Inner Life of Empires* (Princeton: Princeton University Press, 2011).

14. Price, *Observations on the Nature of Civil Liberty*, 28. On the pamphlet's popularity, see John Lind, *Three Letters to Dr. Price* (London: T. Payne, J. Sewell and T. Emsly, 1776), ii–iv. Many newspapers on both sides of the Atlantic summarized Price's arguments: *New England Chronicle*, 4 July 1776; *New-York Gazette and Weekly Mercury*, 22 July 1776; *Connecticut Courant*, 29 July 1776; *Dunlap's Maryland Gazette*, 13 August 1776; Caesar Rodney (Philadelphia) to Thomas Rodney, 10 July 1776, Smith, *Letters of Delegates to Congress*, 4: 433; Hamilton, *Full Vindication*, 12; John Adams, Notes of Debates, 26–27 September 1774, Smith, *Letters of Delegates to Congress*, 1: 103; William Petty 2nd earl of Shelburne, 26 October 1775, Simmons and Thomas, *Proceedings and Debates*, 6: 85; *America Vindicated* (Devizes: T. Burrough, 1774), 9; Jonathan Shipley (Bishop of St. Asaph), *The Whole of the Celebrated Speech* (Newport: R. Southwick, Sept. 1774), 5; George Johnstone, 26 October 1775, Simmons and Thomas, *Proceedings and Debates*, 6: 108–9; Lords Dissenting to Address on the King's Speech, 26 October 1775, ibid., 6: 73.

15. Hamilton, *Full Vindication*, 12.

16. Richard Henry Lee, Draft Address to the People of Great Britain and Ireland, 11–18 October 1774, Smith, *Letters of Delegates to Congress*, 1: 175; Hamilton, *Full Vindication*, 12; Lee, *Appeal to the Justice and Interests*, 30; Petition of the Lord Mayor, Aldermen and Commons of the City of London, 27 October 1775, Simmons and Thomas, *Proceedings and Debates*, 6: 124.

17. Hamilton, *Full Vindication*, 14; Richard Henry Lee, Draft Address to the People of Great Britain and Ireland, 11–18 October 1774, Smith, *Letters of Delegates to Congress*, 1: 177; Lee, *Appeal to the Justice and Interests*, 39; Benjamin Franklin, in *The Public Advertiser*, 9 March 1774; Benjamin Franklin, in *The Public Advertiser*, 29 January 1770. "Our" in this sentence refers to the British. Price, *Observations on the Nature of Civil Liberty*, 17, 27–29; Robinson-Morris, *Considerations on the Measures*, 79.

18. George Johnstone, 26 October 1775, Simmons and Thomas, *Proceedings and Debates*, 6: 106; Emma Rothschild, *The Inner Life of Empires* (Princeton: Princeton University Press, 2011), 72; Mercy Otis Warren (Plimouth) to Abigail Adams, 19 January 1774, in *Adams Family Correspondence*,

ed. L. H. Butterfield (Cambridge: Belknap Press of Harvard University Press, 1963), 1: 91; Burke, *On American Taxation*, 29–30. American Patriots did in fact explicitly accept the restrictions of the Navigation Acts: Lee, *Appeal to the Justice and Interests*, 39; John Adams, Diary, 2 September 1774, Smith, *Letters of Delegates to Congress*, 1: 8; Thomas Jefferson, *A Summary View of the Rights of British America* (Williamsburg, VA: Clementina Rind, 1774), 7; Resolves of Fairfax County, 18 July 1774, Scribner, *Revolutionary Virginia*, 1: 128; Declaration of the Causes and Necessity of Taking up Arms, 6 July 1775, in Oberg and Looney, *Digital Jefferson Papers*, Main Series, 1: 214; Jonathan Shipley (Bishop of St. Asaph), *The Whole of the Celebrated Speech* (Newport, RI: R. Southwick, 1774), 4–5; Caesar Rodney (Philadelphia) to Thomas Rodney, 12 September 1774, Smith, *Letters of Delegates to Congress*, 1: 66; John Adams (Philadelphia) to Abigail Adams, 18 September 1774, ibid., 1: 80; Resolves of Princess Anne County, 27 July 1774, Scribner, *Revolutionary Virginia*, 1: 155; Toasts of Westmoreland County, 22 June 1774, ibid., 1: 165. Shipley was a friend of Benjamin Franklin's: Benjamin Franklin (London) to Jonathan Shipley, 24 June 1771, *Franklin Papers Online*, vol. 18; Jonathan Shipley (Twyford) to Benjamin Franklin, 9 December 1773, ibid., vol. 20. Franklin relayed to Shipley that the speech was thought a "master-piece of eloquence and wisdom"; Benjamin Franklin (London) to Jonathan Shipley, 28 September 1774, ibid., vol. 21; Price, *Observations on the Nature of Civil Liberty*, 24; Samuel Adams (Boston) to John Wilkes, 28 December 1770, BL, Add 30871, f. 51.

19. Shipley, *Celebrated Speech*, 4; Burke, *On American Taxation*, 12; Price, *Observations on the Nature of Civil Liberty*, 39; George Dempster, 27 October 1775, Simmons and Thomas, *Proceedings and Debates*, 6: 140; Resolves of Dunmore County, 16 June 1774, Scribner, *Revolutionary Virginia*, 1: 123; John Norton (London) to Peyton Randolph, Robert Carter, Nicholas and Dudley Digges, 6 July 1773, ibid., 2: 37; Richard Henry Lee (Philadelphia) to Landon Carter, 1 April 1776, Smith, *Letters of Delegates to Congress*, 3: 470. The importance of India and the East India Company in North American thinking has been highlighted by Benjamin L. Carp, *Defiance of the Patriots* (New Haven: Yale University Press, 2010), 7–24; and Carla J. Mulford, *Benjamin Franklin and the Ends of Empire* (Oxford: Oxford University Press, 2015), 254–56.

20. Lee, *Appeal to the Justice and Interests*, 32. Christopher Gadsden and his friends in the South Carolina Association had advanced this argument in 1769: *Letters of Freeman* (London, 1771), 1–2, rpt. an advertisement from the *South Carolina Gazette*, 29 June 1769; Price, *Observations on the Nature of Civil Liberty*, 27.

21. Resolves of Fairfax County, 18 July 1774, Scribner, *Revolutionary Virginia*, 1: 130–31; Resolves of Prince George County, [June 1774], ibid., 1:

151; John Adams, Proposed Resolutions, 30 September 1774, Smith, *Letters of Delegates to Congress,* 1: 132; The Association, 20 October 1774, in Oberg and Looney, *Digital Jefferson Papers,* Main Series, 1: 151.

22. Ezra Stiles (Newport) to Dr. Richard Price, 10 April 1775, Beinecke, MS Vault Stiles, Correspondence Box 12; John Adams, Memorandum of Measures to be Pursued in Congress, 9–23 February 1776, Smith, *Letters of Delegates to Congress,* 3: 218; Robert Treat Paine (Philadelphia) to Joseph Palmer, 6 March 1776, ibid., 3: 344. For their activities, see Committee of Congress (Philadelphia) to the Maryland Convention, 28 March 1776, ibid., 3: 455; John Adams to William Tudor, 24 April 1776, ibid., 3: 578.

23. John Adams, Draft Resolutions for Encouraging Agriculture and Manufactures, 21 March 1776, Smith, *Letters of Delegates to Congress,* 3: 420; Elbridge Gerry (Philadelphia) to Benjamin Lincoln, 28 May 1776, ibid., 4: 89; Richard Henry Lee (Philadelphia) to Thomas Ludwell Lee, 28 May 1776, ibid., 4: 91; Elbridge Gerry (Philadelphia) to Joseph Palmer, 31 May 1776, ibid., 4: 107; John Adams (Philadelphia) to Henry Knox, 2 June 1776, ibid., 4: 115. Adams also proposed, but Congress rejected, a plan that all such improvements be coordinated by a congressional committee; Adams, *Thoughts on Government,* 23. Adams was here following Vattel: Emmerich de Vattel, *The Law of Nations* (London: J. Coote, 1759), 1: 48. At least one early reader of the Declaration thought creating public schools part of the agenda: Samuel Miller, *A Sermon Delivered in the New Presbyterian Church in New York July Fourth 1795* (New York: Thomas Greenleaf, 1795), 29; Samuel Chase (Montreal) to Richard Henry Lee, 17 May 1776, Smith, *Letters of Delegates to Congress,* 4: 22; John Hancock (Philadelphia) to George Washington, 14 June 1776, ibid., 4: 217 (creation of the War Office).

24. I owe this point to Don Herzog of Michigan Law School. Herzog himself makes the point with respect to the Federalist Papers: *Happy Slaves* (Chicago: University of Chicago Press, 1989), 117. This highlights the continuity of Patriot thought. George Johnstone, 26 October 1775, Simmons and Thomas, *Proceedings and Debates,* 6: 105; see also Price, *Observations on the Nature of Civil Liberty,* 15; Jonathan Shipley to Benjamin Franklin, June 1775, *Franklin Papers Online,* vol. 22; John Adams, Notes of Debates, 1 August 1776, Smith, *Letters of Delegates to Congress,* 4: 592; Benjamin Rush's Notes for a Speech in Congress, 1 August 1776, ibid., 4: 599.

25. Robert Morris (Philadelphia) to Horatio Gates, 6 April 1776, Smith, *Letters of Delegates to Congress,* 3: 495; John Adams to James Warren, 18 May 1776, ibid., 4: 32–33; Josiah Bartlett (Philadelphia) to John Langdon, 19 May 1776, ibid., 4: 38; John Adams (Philadelphia) to Samuel Cooper, 9 June 1776, ibid., 4: 176; John Penn (Philadelphia) to Thomas Person, 14 February 1776,

ibid., 3: 255; John Adams, Notes of Debates, 16 February 1776, ibid., 3: 261; John Adams, Notes on Foreign Alliances, 1 March 1776, ibid., 3: 312; John Adams to John Winthrop, 12 May 1776, ibid., 3: 662; Samuel Adams (Philadelphia) to Samuel Cooper, 3 April 1776, ibid., 3: 481; Richard Henry Lee (Philadelphia) to Patrick Henry, 20 April 1776, ibid., 3: 564; Richard Henry Lee (Philadelphia) to Edmund Pendleton, 12 May 1776, ibid., 3: 667. This same argument was advanced by George Wythe and John Adams: Thomas Jefferson, Notes of Proceedings in Congress, 8 June 1776, ibid., 4: 163; John Adams (Philadelphia) to William Cushing, 9 June 1776, ibid., 4: 178; Eliga H. Gould, *Among the Powers of the Earth* (Cambridge: Harvard University Press, 2012), 113–15; David M. Golove and Daniel J. Hulsebosch, "A Civilized Nation: The Early American Constitution, the Law of Nations, and the Pursuit of International Recognition," *New York University Law Review* 85, no. 4 (2010), 942–43; Peter S. Onuf, "A Declaration of Independence for Diplomatic Historians," *Diplomatic History* 22, no. 71 (1998), 82–83; Committee of Secret Correspondence (Philadelphia) to Silas Deane, 8 July 1776, Smith, *Letters of Delegates to Congress,* 4: 405. This was how Ethan Allen understood the significance of the *Declaration:* Ethan Allen (Halifax Jail) to Connecticut Assembly, 12 August 1776, in *Ethan Allen and His Kin,* ed. John J. Duffy (Hanover, NH: University Press of New England, 1998), 1: 60.

26. Paine, *Common Sense,* 31–32. Bernard Bailyn has called attention to this remarkable passage: *Faces of Revolution* (New York: Vintage, 1990), 75; Robert Morris (Philadelphia) to Silas Deane, 5 June 1776, Smith, *Letters of Delegates to Congress,* 4: 148; Elbridge Gerry (Philadelphia) to James Warren, 15 June 1776, ibid., 4: 220; John Adams to William Gordon, 23 June 1776, ibid., 4: 295. The Loan Office was created in October 1776.

27. This view is in tension with that advanced in Jeremy Black, *Crisis of Empire* (London: Continuum, 2008), 131.

28. Josiah Bartlett (Philadelphia) to John Landon, 13 January 1776, Smith, *Letters of Delegates to Congress,* 3: 88; John Hancock (Philadelphia) to Thomas Cushing, 17 January 1776, ibid., 3: 105–6; John Adams to Abigail Adams, 18 February 1776, ibid., 3: 271; Trish Loughran, *The Republic in Print* (New York: Columbia University Press, 2007), 40–49; Eric Foner, *Tom Paine and Revolutionary America,* updated ed. (New York: Oxford University Press, 2005), 79; Bailyn, *Faces of Revolution,* 67–71; Gordon S. Wood, *The American Revolution: A History* (New York: Modern Library, 2002), 55; Josiah Bartlett (Philadelphia) to John Langdon, 19 February 1776, Smith, *Letters of Delegates to Congress,* 3: 280; Benjamin Franklin (Philadelphia) to Charles Lee, 19 February 1776, ibid., 3: 281; Samuel Ward (Philadelphia) to Henry Ward, 19 February 1776, ibid., 3: 285; Samuel Ward (Philadelphia) to Henry Ward, 4 March 1776,

ibid., 3: 329–30; William Whipple (Philadelphia) to John Langdon, 2 April 1776, ibid., 3: 479; John Adams, Autobiography, in *The Adams Papers, Digital Edition,* ed. C. James Taylor (Charlottesville: University of Virginia Press, 2008–15), Diary and Autobiography of John Adams, 3: 331 (hereafter *Digital Adams Papers*); John Adams (Philadelphia) to Abigail Adams, 19 March 1776, Smith, *Letters of Delegates to Congress,* 3: 398–99.

29. Paine, *Common Sense,* 1; Lind, *Three Letters to Dr. Price,* 16. Lind coined the phrase "negative liberty," which he saw as the only proper function of government. The term has had a long and significant afterlife: see Isaiah Berlin, "Two Concepts of Liberty," in *Four Essays on Liberty* (Oxford: Oxford University Press, 1969); John Adams (Philadelphia) to Abigail Adams, 19 March 1776, Smith, *Letters of Delegates to Congress,* 3: 398–99.

30. John Adams to William Tudor, 12 April 1776, Smith, *Letters of Delegates to Congress,* 3: 513; John Adams to James Warren, 12 May 1776, ibid., 3: 661; Adams, Autobiography, in Taylor, *Digital Adams Papers,* Diary and Autobiography, 3: 331. John Adams was not unusual in this opinion: John Witherspoon, the president of New Jersey College in Princeton, denounced Paine as a man who flowed "with the tide of popularity," only recently abandoning his ministerial views: ibid., Diary and Autobiography, 3: 331, 334.

31. Thomas Jefferson (Monticello) to Henry Lee, 8 May 1825, *The Papers of Thomas Jefferson: Retirement Series,* Founders Online, National Archives; Thomas Jefferson, Notes on Proceedings in Congress, 8 June 1776, Smith, *Letters of Delegates to Congress,* 4: 163–64; Francis Lightfoot Lee (Philadelphia) to Richard Henry Lee, 1 July 1776, ibid., 4: 342–43; John Adams (Philadelphia) to Archibald Bulloch, 1 July 1776, ibid., 4: 345; John Adams (Philadelphia) to Samuel Chase, 1 July 1776, ibid., 4: 347; Josiah Bartlett (Philadelphia) to John Langdon, 1 July 1776, ibid., 4: 351; John Adams (Philadelphia) to Abigail Adams, 3 July 1776, ibid., 4: 376; Adams, Autobiography, in Taylor, *Digital Adams Papers,* Diary and Autobiography, 3: 336–37; Benjamin Rush, *Autobiography,* ed. George W. Corner (Princeton: Princeton University Press, 1948), 145–46, 151–52. My reading of the crafting of the document is similar to that of Pauline Maier, *American Scripture: Making the Declaration of Independence* (New York: Knopf, 1997), 97–105.

32. John Adams (Philadelphia) to Abigail Adams, 3 July 1776, Smith, *Letters of Delegates to Congress,* 4: 374. In this the Declaration sounded a great deal like the concluding sections of John Adams's *Thoughts on Government,* 26. This was also the passage that Alexander Hamilton later highlighted as providing the key to the document: Alexander Hamilton, Remarks on an Act Granting to Congress Certain Imposts and Duties, 15 February 1787, in *The Papers of Alexander Hamilton, Digital Edition,* ed. Harold C. Syrett

(Charlottesville: University of Virginia Press, 2011), 4: 77; John Lind, *An Answer to the Declaration of the American Congress*, 4th ed. (London: T. Cadell, J. Walter, and T. Sewell, 1776), 119; Thomas Hutchinson, *Strictures on the Declaration of Independence* (London, 1776), 20. On Hutchinson's remarkable career see Bernard Bailyn, *The Ordeal of Thomas Hutchinson* (Cambridge: Belknap Press of Harvard University Press, 1976). Lind likened Congress's activities to the state-making actions of the Long Parliament of the 1640s: Lind, *An Answer*, 65.

33. Lee, *Appeal to the Justice and Interests*, 33.

34. Burke, *On American Taxation*, 28–29; Lee, *Appeal to the Justice and Interests*, 42; Jefferson, *Summary View*, 11; William Petty 2nd Shelburne, 17 May 1775, Simmons and Thomas, *Proceedings and Debates*, 6: 53; Shelburne, 26 October 1765, ibid., 6: 86–87. Charles James Fox voiced similar views: Charles James Fox, 26 October 1775, ibid., 6: 118; George Dempster (Dunnichen) to Sir Adam Fergusson, 26 January 1775, in *Letters of George Dempster to Sir Adam Fergusson*, ed. James Fergusson (London: Macmillan, 1934), 85; Augustus Fitzroy, 3rd Duke of Grafton, 26 October 1775, Simmons and Thomas, *Proceedings and Debates*, 6: 78; Thomas Lyttelton, 2nd Baron Lyttelton, 26 October 1775, ibid., 6: 80; John Adams (Falmouth) to Abigail Adams, 6 July 1774, Butterfield, *Adams Family Correspondence*, 1: 125; The Association, 20 October 1774, in Oberg and Looney, *Digital Jefferson Papers*, Main Series, 1: 149–50; Pennsylvania Instruction to Delegates, 21 July 1774, Scribner, *Revolutionary Virginia*, 2: 148.

35. Maier has also noted the inclusion of longer-term complaints, and also pointed out that this document was therefore not about "the Americans' change of heart" but about why they plumped for independence: Maier, *American Scripture*, 115.

36. Frederick North, 26 October 1775, Simmons and Thomas, *Proceedings and Debates*, 6: 118. The British naval commander Richard Howe in fact claimed that disagreement over whether Americans should be allowed to trade with foreign countries was "the great ground" of the Revolutionary War: Benjamin Franklin (Philadelphia) to Lord Howe, 20 July 1776, Smith, *Letters of Delegates to Congress*, 4: 500; Gottfried Achenwall, "Some Observations on North America from Oral Information by Dr. Franklin," 1766, *Franklin Papers Online*, vol. 13; John Dickinson (Philadelphia) to William Pitt, 21 December 1765, NA, PRO 30/8/97/I, ff. 38–39; Petition of the Merchants of the City of New York, 28 November 1766, NA, PRO 30/8/97/I, f. 83r.

37. Robinson-Morris, *Considerations on the Measures*, 118; Benjamin Franklin, before 21 July 1775, printed in *Public Advertiser*, 18 July 1777, *Franklin Papers Online*, vol. 22; Jefferson, *Summary View*, 23. John Wilkes expressed similar sentiments in the House of Commons: John Wilkes, 26 October 1775, Simmons and Thomas, *Proceedings and Debates*, 6: 98.

38. Benjamin Franklin, contribution to pamphlet by George Whatley, March 1774, *Franklin Papers Online,* vol. 21; George Whatley, *Principles of Trade* (London: Brotherton and Sewell, 1774). This principle was central to the Model Commercial Treaty, "Plan of Treaties," 18 July 1776, in *Journals of the Continental Congress,* ed. Worthington Chauncey Ford (Washington, DC: Government Printing Office, 1906), 5: 576–77. A similar point has been made in the French imperial context as well: Jean-Pierre Hirsch, *Deux Rêves du Commerce* (Paris: Éditions de l'École des hautes études en sciences sociales, 1991); Jean-Pierre Hirsch and Philippe Minard, " 'Laissez-nous faire et protégez-nous beaucoup,' " in *La France, n'est-elle pas douée pour l'industrie,* ed. Louis Bergeron and Patrice Bordelais (Paris: Belin, 1998), 135–58; Tucker, *Four Tracts,* 163–64.

39. One of the Declaration's most bitter critics, Thomas Hutchinson, admitted that on immigration policy George III had reversed the course of imperial policy: Hutchinson, *Strictures upon the Declaration,* 16.

40. Arthur Young, *Observations on the Present State of the Waste Lands of Great Britain* (London: W. Nicoll, 1773), 5–6; Arthur Young, *Proposals to the Legislature for Numbering the People* (London: W. Nicoll, 1771), 5; Price, *Appeal to the Public,* 45; Tucker, *Four Tracts,* 201; Bernard Bailyn, *Voyagers to the West* (New York: Vintage, 1986), 26; Abigail Swingen, *Competing Visions of Empire: Labor, Slavery, and the Origins of the British Atlantic Empire* (New Haven: Yale University Press, 2015), 28–31; Bailyn, *Voyagers to the West,* 52; Eric Williams, *Capitalism and Slavery* (London: Andre Deutsch, 1964), 16–17; Richard Grosvenor, Lord Grosvenor, Hints Respecting the Settlement of our American Provinces, 25 February 1763, BL, Add 38335, f. 14v.

41. Stewart, *A Letter to the Rev. Dr. Price,* 47; Bailyn, *Voyagers to the West,* 55–56, 63–66.

42. Lee, *Appeal to the Justice and Interests,* 32; Jefferson, *Summary View,* 23; Peter Marshall, "Lord Hillsborough, Samuel Wharton and the Ohio Grant, 1769–1775," *English Historical Review* 80, no. 317 (1965), 738–39; Resolutions of the Darien Committee, 12 January 1775, in *The Revolutionary Records of the State of Georgia,* ed. Allen D. Candler (Atlanta: Franklin-Turner, 1908), 1: 40.

43. Mississippi Land Company's Petition to the King, December 1768, in Crackel, *Digital Washington Papers,* Colonial Series, 8: 150; A List of the Mississippi Company, NA, PRO 30/8/97/II, f. 2r; Benjamin Franklin, On a proposed act to prevent emigration, December 1773, *Franklin Papers Online,* vol. 20; *The Crisis,* 3 August 1776, p. 510.

44. Thomas Jefferson, Notes of Proceedings in Congress, 1–4 July 1776, Smith, *Letters of Delegates to Congress,* 4: 362.

45. Hutchinson, *Strictures upon the Declaration,* 9–10; "Thoughts on the Late Declaration of the American Congress," *Gentleman's Magazine* 46

(September 1776), 404; Lind, *Three Letters to Dr. Price,* 46; Lind, *An Answer to the Declaration,* p. 107; Johnson, *Taxation no Tyranny,* 89; Christopher Leslie Brown, *Moral Capital* (Chapel Hill: University of North Carolina Press, 2006), 127–30. This interpretative tradition has modern followers: Eric Slauter, "The Declaration of Independence and the New Nation," in *The Cambridge Companion to Thomas Jefferson,* ed. Frank Shuffleton (Cambridge: Cambridge University Press, 2009), 12–34.

46. James Otis Jr., *The Rights of the British Colonies Asserted and Proved,* 3rd ed. (London: J. Williams, 1766), 43–44; Pernille Roge, "The Question of Slavery in Physiocratic Political Economy," in *Governare Il Mondo,* ed. Manuela Albertone (Feltrinelli, 2009); T. H. Breen, "Subjecthood and Citizenship: The Context of James Otis's Radical Critique of John Locke," *New England Quarterly* 71, no. 3 (1998), 390–92; Granville Sharp, *A Representation of the Injustice and Dangerous Tendency of Tolerating Slavery* (London: Benjamin White and Robert Horsfield, 1769); Benjamin Franklin (London) to Anthony Benezet, 10 February 1773, *Franklin Papers Online,* vol. 20; Granville Sharp, *Memoirs of Granville Sharp,* ed. Prince Hoare (London: Henry Colburn, 1820), 81, 215. Sharp, though friendly with Quakers, was the grandson of the Anglican archbishop of York, John Sharp. Benjamin Rush (Philadelphia) to Barbeu Dubourg, 29 April 1773, in *Letters of Benjamin Rush,* ed. L. H. Butterfield (Princeton: Princeton University Press, 1951), 1: 76–77; Rush to Benjamin Franklin, 1 May 1773, ibid., 1: 79; Rush, *Autobiography,* 82–83; Benjamin Rush, *An Address to the Inhabitants of the British Settlements in America upon Slave-Keeping* (Philadelphia: John Dunlap, 1773); Benjamin Rush, *A Vindication of the Address* (Philadelphia: John Dunlap, 1773); Anthony Benezet, *Caution and Warning to Great Britain and her Colonies: in a short representation of the calamitous state of the enslaved Negroes in the British Dominions* (Philadelphia: Henry Miller, 1766); Anthony Benezet, *Potent Enemies of America Laid Open* (Philadelphia: Joseph Crukshank, 1774). For examples of other tracts and sermons condemning slavery published in this period: Samuel Copper, *A Mite cast into the Treasury* (Philadelphia: Joseph Crukshank, 1772); Levi Watson, *Liberty Described and Recommended in a Sermon Preached to the Corporation and Freemen in Farmington* (Hartford: Eben Watson, 1775); Ruth Bogin, ed., " 'Liberty further Extended': A 1776 Antislavery Manuscript by Lemuel Haynes," *William and Mary Quarterly* 40, no. 1 (1983), 85–105; Samuel Hopkins, *A Dialogue Concerning the Slavery of the Africans* (Norwich: Judah P. Spooner, 1776).

47. Edward Long, *Candid Reflections upon the Judgment Lately Awarded by the Court of King's Bench* (London: T. Lowndes, 1772); Richard Nisbet, *Slavery not Forbidden by Scripture* (Philadelphia: John Sparhawk, 1773); William

Knox, *Three Tracts* [1768]. These anticipated the pro-slavery sentiments that emerged in Virginia in the 1780s: Fredrika Teute Schmidt and Barbara Ripel Wilhelm, "Early Pro-Slavery Petitions in Virginia," *William and Mary Quarterly* 30, no. 1 (1973), 133–46; John Laurens (London) to Henry Laurens, 26 October 1776, in *The Papers of Henry Laurens*, ed. David Chesnutt and C. James Taylor (Columbia: University of South Carolina Press, 1988), 11: 276–77; Francis Kinloch (Geneva) to John Laurens, 28 April 1776, NYPL, Miscellaneous MSS (Francis Kinloch); Long, *Candid Reflections*, 18; *A Forensic Dispute On the Legality of Enslaving the Africans Held at the Public Commencement in Cambridge, New England* (Boston: John Boyle, 1773).

48. John Millar, *Observations Concerning the Distinction of Ranks in Society* (London: W. and J. Richardson, 1771), 200–205, 237. Victor de Riquetti, marquis de Mirabeau had earlier made similar arguments: *The Oeconomical Table* (London: W. Owen, 1766), 7; Edward Wigglesworth, *Calculations on American Population* (Boston: John Boyle, 1775), 12; Francis Hargrave, *An Argument in the Case of James Somersett* (Boston: E. Russell, 1774), 11–12, 42–43; Sharp, *Memoirs*, 71–75.

49. Christopher Gadsden (Charlestown) to William Samuel Johnson, 16 April 1766, in *The Writings of Christopher Gadsden*, ed. Richard Walsh (Columbia: University of South Carolina Press, 1966), 72; Christopher Gadsden (Charlestown) to Samuel Adams, 23 May 1774, ibid., 92–93. The wharf was in Charleston. *Letters of Freeman*, 13–14 (reporting on an August 1769 resolution); Henry Laurens (Charles Town) to John Laurens, 14 August 1776, Chesnutt and Taylor, *Papers of Henry Laurens*, 11: 224–25; Jack Rakove, *Revolutionaries* (New York: Mariner, 2010), 198–241; John Laurens to Francis Kinloch, March 1776, NYPL, Miscellaneous MSS (John Laurens). While I agree with Robert Olwell that South Carolinians, like most North Americans, were reluctant to break with the British Empire, the actions and statements of John and Henry Laurens and Christopher Gadsden, politically prominent South Carolinians, make it difficult for me to accept his suggestion that South Carolinians in general joined the revolutionary cause because of their fear of "a British-slave conspiracy." " 'Domestick Enemies': Slavery and Political Independence in South Carolina, May 1775–March 1776," *Journal of Southern History* 55, no. 1 (1989), 21–48; William Whipple (Philadelphia) to Josiah Bartlett, 28 March 1779, in *The Papers of Josiah Bartlett*, ed. Frank C. Mevers (Hanover, NH: University Press of New England, 1979), 250; Benjamin Franklin, *London Chronicle*, 18–20 June 1772, *Franklin Papers Online*, vol. 19; Benjamin Franklin, *The Public Advertiser*, 30 January 1770, ibid., vol. 17; Alan Houston, *Benjamin Franklin and the Politics of Improvement* (New Haven: Yale University Press, 2008), 200–216; John Witherspoon, Speech in Congress, 30 July 1776, Smith,

Letters of Delegates to Congress, 4: 585; Rush (Philadelphia) to Granville Sharp, 1 May 1773, Butterfield, *Letters of Benjamin Rush,* 1: 81; *New York Journal,* Supplement, 29 December 1774; Benjamin Franklin (London) to Richard Woodward, 10 April 1773, *Franklin Papers Online,* vol. 22.

50. Rush (Philadelphia) to Barbeu Dubourg, 29 April 1773, Butterfield, *Letters of Benjamin Rush,* 1: 76; Watson, *Liberty Described,* 20; *Newport Mercury,* Supplement, 13 June 1774; Charles Rappleye, *Sons of Providence* (New York: Simon and Schuster, 2006), 145–46; *New York Journal,* Supplement, 29 December 1774; Address of the House of Burgesses, 1 April 1772, Scribner, *Revolutionary Virginia,* 1: 87. The eight counties passing antislavery resolutions represented a little less than 20 percent of the counties of Virginia and covered a wide geographic range of the colony. Resolves of Caroline County, 14 July 1774; Resolves of Culpeper County, 7 July 1774; Resolves of Fairfax County, 18 July 1774; Resolves of Hanover County, 20 July 1774; Resolves of Nansemond County, 11 July 1774; Resolves of Prince George County, June 1774; Resolves of Princess Anne County, 27 July 1774; Resolves of Surry County, 16 July 1774, Scribner, *Revolutionary Virginia,* 1: 116, 119, 130–32, 140, 146, 151, 154, 162; Woody Holton, *Forced Founders* (Chapel Hill: University of North Carolina Press, 1999), 88–89. It is no coincidence that Benjamin Rush was also a strong advocate of diversifying the American economic base: Rush (Edinburgh) to Thomas Bradford, 15 April 1768, Butterfield, *Letters of Benjamin Rush,* 1: 54; Benjamin Rush (London) to ?Jacob Rush, 26 January 1769, ibid., 1: 74; Resolutions of the Darien Committee, 12 January 1775, in Candler, *Revolutionary Records of Georgia,* 1: 41–42; Resolutions of the Provincial Congress of Georgia, 23 January 1775, ibid., 1: 44; Kenneth Coleman, *The American Revolution in Georgia, 1763–1789* (Athens: University of Georgia Press, 1958), 45–46. I have found no textual evidence to support Holton's hypothesis that for wealthy gentlemen in the tidewater region of Virginia "raising the price of domestic slaves was one more reason to ban the Atlantic [slave] trade": *Forced Founders,* 90–91.

51. Brown, *Moral Capital,* 135–43; *Newport Mercury,* 13 June 1774; Resolution of the Continental Congress, 6 April 1776, Ford, *Journals of the Continental Congress,* 4: 258. I thus have a slightly different take from Brown, *Moral Capital,* 113. I disagree with Christopher Tomlins's account of the seamless continuity of "Anglo-American slave regimes" from the seventeenth through the nineteenth centuries: *Freedom Bound: Law, Labor, and Civic Identity in Colonizing English America, 1580–1865* (Cambridge: Cambridge University Press, 2010). In a brilliant dissertation John Blanton has demonstrated that there was significant legal contestation over slavery in Britain, Massachusetts, and Virginia: "This Species of Property: Slavery and Subjecthood in Anglo-

American Law, 1619–1783," Ph.D. diss., CUNY, 2015. Tomlins's legal narrative ends before the explosion of antislavery agitation that I have described. The growth of slavery in North America after the Revolution represents not continuity but the significant effects of the onset of cotton: Sven Beckert, *Empire of Cotton: A Global History* (New York: Knopf, 2015), 84–105.

52. Thomas Jefferson, Notes of Proceedings in Congress, 2 July 1776, Smith, *Letters of Delegates to Congress,* 4: 359. On unanimity: John Adams (Philadelphia) to Benjamin Hinchborn, 29 May 1776, ibid., 4: 96; Samuel Adams (Philadelphia) to James Warren, 6 June 1776, ibid., 4: 150. Here I dissent somewhat from David Brion Davis's brilliant and authoritative account. The clause was not the product of the mind of one man, however brilliant and ambiguous. Nor was it removed because he deferred to "older and more cautious men" but because of the political power of South Carolina: David Brion Davis, *The Problem of Slavery in the Age of Revolution, 1770–1823* (Oxford: Oxford University Press, 1999), 173; Edward Rutledge (Philadelphia) to John Jay, 29 June 1776, Smith, *Letters of Delegates to Congress,* 4: 337. Rutledge had earlier seen the Georgia delegation as opposed to his views on independence: Rutledge to John Jay, 8 June 1776, ibid., 4: 175. I thus agree with those who argue that defenders of commercialization could, at times, defend slavery. Capitalists equally criticized slavery. The debate was over what stage of cultural development British America had achieved. See Seth Rockman, "Liberty Is Land and Slaves: The Great Contradiction," *OAH Magazine of History* 19, no. 3 (2005), 8; Beckert, *Empire of Cotton,* 37–38; John Adams, Notes of Debates, 30 July 1776, Smith, *Letters of Delegates to Congress,* 4: 568–69; Francis Lightfoot Lee (Philadelphia) to Richard Henry Lee, 1 July 1776, ibid., 4: 342–43; Josiah Bartlett (Philadelphia) to John Landon, 1 July 1776, ibid., 4: 351.

53. Price, *Observations on the Nature of Civil Liberty,* 28; Benjamin Franklin, *The Public Advertiser,* 30 January 1770; Jefferson, *Summary View,* 16–17.

54. John Fabian Witt, *Lincoln's Code: The Laws of War in American History* (New York: Free Press, 2012), 15–19, 28–35; James Q. Whitman, *Verdict of Battle: The Law of Victory and the Making of Modern War* (Cambridge: Harvard University Press, 2012), 174; Vattel, *The Law of Nations,* 2: 51–52, 110. This was the language used among officers in the Continental Army; see Philip Schuyler (Albany) to Committee of the City and Country of Albany, 27 June 1776, NYPL, Philip Schuyler Papers, Box 18, pp. 218–19. I thus see these clauses as less about defining who counted as Americans than about announcing the Patriots to be the true civilized combatants in contrast to the barbarous George III. The sentiments of members of the Second Congress with respect to Indians were varied. Some called for their employment in the war as regular

troops: Philip Schuyler (Albany) to Timothy Edward, 22 February 1776, NYPL, Philip Schuyler Papers, Box 17, p. 372; John Hancock (Philadelphia) to George Washington, 10 June 1776, Smith, *Letters of Delegates to Congress*, 4: 183; John Hancock (Philadelphia) to George Washington, 18 June 1776, ibid., 4: 266; John Hancock (Philadelphia) to George Washington, 2 August 1776, ibid., 4: 606. Others wanted neutrality: Josiah Bartlett's and John Dickinson's Draft Articles of Confederation, 17 June–1 July 1776, ibid., 4: 239. Many insisted on strictly regulating the Indian trade to prevent colonists from abusing the Indians: John Adams, Notes of Debates, 26 July 1776, ibid., 4: 545–46. Still others sought to cultivate closer ties with Indians: Philip Schuyler (New York) to Colonel Benjamin Hinman, 28 June 1775, NYPL, Philip Schuyler Papers, Box 17, p. 4; Philip Schuyler (New York) to Committee of Albany, 28 June 1775, NYPL, Philip Schuyler Papers, Box 17, p. 5; Richard Henry Lee (Philadelphia) to Charles Lee, 27 May 1776, Smith, *Letters of Delegates to Congress*, 4: 87; Robert Morris (Philadelphia) to Silas Deane, 5 June 1776, ibid., 4: 148. For a different view, see Robert Parkinson, "The Declaration of Independence," in *A Companion to Thomas Jefferson*, 2nd ed., ed. Francis D. Cogliano (Oxford: Wiley-Blackwell, 2012), 54–56; Robert G. Parkinson, "Twenty-Seven Reasons for Independence," in *The American Revolution Reader*, ed. Denver Brunsman and David J. Silverman (New York: Routledge, 2014), 116–18; Peter Silver, *Our Savage Neighbors* (New York: Norton, 2008), 287–88. Silver's concern is much more, in this section, with anti-Indian sentiments after the war. Unlike Parkinson, he sees that the Declaration could be read in terms more friendly to the Indians.

55. John Wilkes, 26 October 1775, Simmons and Thomas, *Proceedings and Debates*, 6: 97; George Johnstone, 26 October 1775, ibid., 6: 101; William Bollan (Covent Garden) to John Erving, William Brattle, James Bowdoin, and James Pitts, 15 March 1774, Force and Clarke, *American Archives*, 1: 228 (referring to views of Lord Camden); Resolves of Caroline County, 14 July 1774, Scribner, *Revolutionary Virginia*, 1: 115; Resolves of York County, 18 July 1774, ibid., 1: 167.

56. Lord John Cavendish, 26 October 1775, Simmons and Thomas, *Proceedings and Debates*, 6: 96–97; John Adams (Falmouth) to Abigail Adams, 6 July 1774, Butterfield, *Adams Family Correspondence*, 1: 127; "To the Freeholders and Other Inhabitants of the Towns and Districts of Massachusetts Bay," 10 December 1774, *New York Journal*, Supplement, 29 December 1774; Hamilton, *Full Vindication*, 12, 25; *The Crisis*, 3 August 1776, p. 509; Resolves of Fairfax County, 18 July 1774, Scribner, *Revolutionary Virginia*, 1: 129; John Adams (Philadelphia) to John Penn, 19–27 March 1776, Smith, *Letters of Delegates to Congress*, 3: 402.

57. Ronald Hamowy, ed., *Cato's Letters* (Indianapolis: Liberty Fund, 1995), 1, no. 12, p. 67; Joseph Priestley, *An Essay on the First Principles of Government* (Dublin: James Williams, 1768), 64; Price, *Observations on the Nature of Civil Liberty*, 7; Charles Lennox 3rd duke of Richmond, 17 May 1775, Simmons and Thomas, *Proceedings and Debates*, 6: 44; Guillaume Thomas François Raynal, *A Philosophical and Political History of the Settlements and Trade of the Europeans in the East and West Indies* (London: T. Cadell, 1776), 4: 432. Raynal was at the time deeply influenced by the Patriots and a friend of the American cause, whatever his later views. Vattel, *The Law of Nations*, 1: 35.

58. Watson, *Liberty Described*, 11; Adams, *Thoughts on Government*, 4–5; John Adams (Philadelphia) to John Penn, 19–27 March 1776, Smith, *Letters of Delegates to Congress*, 3: 400; Declaration of the Causes and Necessity for Taking up Arms, 6 July 1775, in Oberg and Looney, *Digital Jefferson Papers*, Main Series, 1: 213.

59. John Adams (Philadelphia) to Mary Palmer, 5 July 1776, Smith, *Letters of Delegates to Congress*, 4: 389; Benjamin Rush (Philadelphia) to General Charles Lee, 23 July 1776, Butterfield, *Letters of Benjamin Rush*, 1: 103.

60. John Adams (Philadelphia) to John Winthrop, 23 June 1776, Smith, *Letters of Delegates to Congress*, 4: 299; John Adams (Philadelphia) to William Gordon, 23 June 1776, ibid., 4: 295.

Epilogue

1. George Washington, Undelivered First Inaugural Address, 30 April 1789, *The Papers of George Washington, Digital Edition*, ed. Theodore J. Crackel (Charlottesville: University of Virginia Press, 2008), Presidential Series, 2: 158–73. Thus while I share Max Edling's conviction that the supporters of the federal government sought "a strong national state in America," I dissent from his suggestion that they framed their aims narrowly in terms of the "fiscal military state"; Max Edling, *A Revolution in Favor of Government* (Oxford: Oxford University Press, 2003), 220.

2. The classic statement of this position is that advanced by Merrill Jensen, *Articles of Confederation* (Madison: University of Wisconsin Press, 1940), 240–41. More recent scholarship has modified and rejected many of Jensen's conjectures. Yet it still highlights the limits of the Articles: Gordon S. Wood, *The Creation of the American Republic* (Chapel Hill: University of North Carolina Press, 1969), 356; Jack N. Rakove, *The Beginnings of National Politics* (New York: Knopf, 1979), 190–91; Jack P. Greene, "The Background of the Articles of Confederation," *Publius* 12, no. 4 (1982), 16–17, 43–44. My

argument is focused less on the primacy of national or state governments than on the Patriots' commitment to creating a strong coordinated state. Alexander Hamilton, Unsubmitted Resolution Calling for a Convention to Amend the Articles of Confederation, July 1783, in *The Papers of Alexander Hamilton, Digital Edition,* ed. Harold C. Syrett (Charlottesville: University of Virginia Press, 2011), 3: 420; Thomas Jefferson (Boston) to James Madison, 1 July 1784, in *The Papers of Thomas Jefferson, Digital Edition,* ed. Barbara J. Oberg and J. Jefferson Looney (Charlottesville: University of Virginia Press, 2008–15), Main Series, 7: 356 (hereafter *Digital Jefferson Papers*); James Madison (Richmond) to Thomas Jefferson, 4 December 1786, *The Papers of James Madison, Digital Edition,* ed. J. C. A. Stagg (Charlottesville: University of Virginia Press, 2010), Congressional Series, 9: 189 (hereafter *Digital Madison Papers*).

3. Daniel Hulsebosch, "The Revolutionary Portfolio: Constitution-Making and the Wider World in the American Revolution," *Suffolk University Law Review* 47 (2014), 764; Worthington Chauncey Ford, ed., *Journals of the Continental Congress* (Washington, DC: Government Printing Office, 1906), 5: 576–89, 674–75; *Articles of Confederation* (Richmond: Dixon and Holt, 1785), [3]. The Articles were not ratified by all states until 1781; Ford, *Journals of the Continental Congress,* 9: 933–34.

4. That British Americans were the first to tackle such issues may perhaps be the erroneous impression given in Rakove, *Beginnings of National Politics,* 136. John Robertson, "Empire and Union: Two Concepts of the Early Modern European Political Order," in *A Union for Empire,* ed. John Robertson (Cambridge: Cambridge University Press, 1995), 5–6, 22–36; Steven C. A. Pincus, *Protestantism and Patriotism* (Cambridge: Cambridge University Press, 1996), 15–40; Charles-Irénée Castel, abbé de Saint-Pierre, *A Project for Settling an Everlasting Peace in Europe* (London: J. Watts, 1714), iv; Saint-Pierre, *Discourse of the Danger of Governing by One Minister* (London: T. Warner, 1728); Jean-Jacques Rousseau, *A Project for Perpetual Peace,* 2nd ed. (London: J. Johnson and T. Davenport, 1767); Richard Price, *Observations on the Nature of Civil Liberty, the Principles of Government, and the Justice and Policy of the War with America,* 9th ed. (London: Edward and Charles Dilly and Thomas Cadell, 1776), 7–8, 14; Adam Smith, *An Inquiry into the Nature and Causes of the Wealth of Nations,* ed. R. H. Campbell and A. S. Skinner (Indianapolis: Liberty Fund, 1981), 2: 621–23; John Witherspoon's Speech to Congress, 30 July 1776, *Letters of Delegates to Congress,* ed. Paul H. Smith (Washington: Library of Congress, 1979), 4: 586–87.

5. Samuel Langdon (Portsmouth, New Hampshire) to Ezra Stiles, 5 October 1761, Correspondence Box 3 1760–1763, Beinecke, MS Vault Stiles/Folder 347; Josiah Bartlett's Notes on the Plan of Confederation, 12 June–12

July 1776, Smith, *Letters of Delegates to Congress,* 4: 199; Jefferson, Notes of Proceedings in the Continental Congress, 30 July–1 August 1776, in Oberg and Looney, *Digital Jefferson Papers,* Main Series, 1: 325 (John Witherspoon), 326 (Benjamin Rush), 327 (James Wilson); John Adams, Notes of Debate, 30 July 1776, Smith, *Letters of Delegates to Congress,* 4: 568; James Madison, Weakness of the Confederation, 7 June 1788, in Stagg, *Digital Madison Papers,* Congressional Series, 11: 93. James Madison and Alexander Hamilton devoted the entirety of *Federalist* 20 to discussing the Dutch confederation: Terence Ball, ed., *The Federalist* (Cambridge: Cambridge University Press, 2003), 89–93.

6. On the Dutch economic miracle, see Jan de Vries and Ad van de Woude, *The First Modern Economy* (Cambridge: Cambridge University Press, 1997); Karel Davids and Jan Lucassen, eds., *A Miracle Mirrored* (Cambridge: Cambridge University Press, 1995). The Dutch struggle for independence remained as a model and parallel for Americans well into the nineteenth century: John Lothrop Motley, *History of the United Netherlands* (New York: Harper and Brothers, 1861–68).

7. Jonathan Israel, *The Dutch Republic* (Oxford: Oxford University Press, 1995), 276–77. Israel notes that the theory that sovereignty lay at the local level was often breached in practice. Abbé Raynal, *A Philosophical and Political History of the Settlements and Trade of the Europeans in the East and West Indies,* 2nd ed., trans. J. Justamond (London: T. Cadell, 1776). 5: 429–30; Jefferson, Notes of Proceedings in the Continental Congress, 30 July–1 August 1776, in Oberg and Looney, *Digital Jefferson Papers,* Main Series, 1: 325; Benjamin Rush's Notes for a Speech in Congress, 1 August 1776, Smith, *Letters of Delegates to Congress,* 4: 598–99.

8. William Williams (Philadelphia) to Joseph Trumbull, 7 August 1776, Smith, *Letters of Delegates to Congress,* 4: 637–38; Joseph Hewes (Philadelphia) to Samuel Johnson, 28 July 1776, ibid., 4: 555; John Adams, Notes of Debates, 26 July 1776, ibid., 4: 546; John Adams (Philadelphia) to Abigail Adams, 29 July 1776, ibid., 4: 556; Thomas Jefferson (Philadelphia) to Richard Henry Lee, 29 July 1776, ibid., 4: 561; Samuel Chase (Philadelphia) to Richard Henry Lee, 30 July 1776, ibid., 4: 570–71; Abraham Clark (Philadelphia) to James Caldwell, 1 August 1776, ibid., 4: 596–97; Josiah Bartlett (Philadelphia) to William Whipple, 27 August 1776, ibid., 5 (1979): 70; William Williams (Philadelphia) to Jabez Huntington, 30 September 1776, ibid., 5: 76; Thomas Burke (Philadelphia) to Richard Caswell, 11 May 1777, ibid., 7 (1981): 69; Samuel Adams (Philadelphia) to James Warren, 30 June 1777, ibid., 7: 271–72; William Williams (Philadelphia) to Jonathan Trumbull Sr., 5 July 1777, ibid., 7: 302.

9. In April 1777 Thomas Burke succeeded in amending the draft of the articles to assert "the principle that all sovereign power was in the States

separately." This amendment became Article 2 of the Articles of Confederation. However, the balance of the articles modified the sovereignty of the states in significant ways. Burke ultimately gave up on the Articles and became one of the fiercest critics of the document precisely because it gave so much power to the central government. Thomas Burke (Philadelphia) to Richard Caswell, 29 April 1777, Smith, *Letters of Delegates to Congress*, 6 (1979): 672; Thomas Burke (Tyaquin) to Richard Caswell, 4 November 1777, ibid., 8 (1981): 227; Cornelius Harnett (York) to Thomas Burke, 13 November 1777, ibid., 8: 254; Thomas Burke's Notes on the Articles of Confederation, 18 December 1777, ibid., 8: 434–35. Thomas Burke's position is perceptively described by Rakove, *Beginnings of National Politics*, 164–76. It should be clear that Burke's commitment to a decentralized state was not in fact typical "of an unreconstructed whig."

10. Edward Rutledge (Philadelphia) to Robert R. Livingston, 2 October 1776, Smith, *Letters of Delegates to Congress*, 5: 295; Daniel Roberdeau (York) to Thomas Wharton, 14 October 1777, ibid., 8: 122; William Williams (York) to Jabez Huntington, 22 October 1777, ibid., 8: 162; Samuel Adams (York) to James Warren, 29 October 1777, ibid., 8: 210; Cornelius Harnett (York) to Thomas Burke, 20 November 1777, ibid., 8: 290; James Duane (York) to George Clinton, 23 November 1777, ibid., 8: 308; Samuel Adams (York) to James Warren, 29 October 1777, ibid., 8: 210; Charles Carroll of Carrollton (Philadelphia) to Charles Carroll Sr., 26 June 1777, ibid., 7: 251. Carrollton's views were at odds with some in his own state.

11. Charles Carroll of Carrollton (Douharagen, Maryland) to Benjamin Franklin, 12 August 1777, Smith, *Letters of Delegates to Congress*, 7: 463; Richard Henry Lee (York) to Roger Sherman, 24 November 1777, ibid., 8: 319–20; Henry Laurens (York) to John Laurens, 10 October 1777, ibid., 8: 100–101; John Adams (Philadelphia) to James Warren, 7 July 1777, ibid., 7: 308. This despite the fact that Adams and his circle were profoundly opposed to slavery: Abigail Adams (Boston) to John Adams, 22 September 1774, in *The Adams Papers, Digital Edition*, ed. C. James Taylor (Charlottesville: University of Virginia Press, 2008–15), Adams Family Correspondence, 1: 162; Abigail Adams to John Adams, 25 October 1775, ibid., 1: 313;? (Fredricksburg) to John Adams, 9 June 1775, ibid., Papers of John Adams, 3: 19; Samuel Cooper to John Adams, 14 July 1776, ibid., 4: 458 (lamenting omission of antislavery clause); Woody Holton, *Abigail Adams* (New York: Free Press, 2009), 71, 102, 112; Nathaniel Folsom (York) to Meshech Ware, 27 October 1777, Smith, *Letters of Delegates to Congress*, 8: 198; Nathaniel Folsom (York) to Meshech Ware, 21 November 1777, ibid., 8: 299; Cornelius Harnett (York) to William Wilkinson, 30 November 1777, ibid., 8: 348–49. Benjamin Constant cited the failure to

eliminate slavery as evidence for the weakness of the United States confederation: Biancamaria Fontana, " 'A New Kind of Federalism': Benjamin Constant
and Modern Europe," in *Rethinking the Atlantic World*, ed. Manuela Albertone
and Antonino De Francesco (London: Palgrave Macmillan, 2009), 179.

12. Thomas Burke's Notes on the Articles of Confederation, 18 December 1777, Smith, *Letters of Delegates to Congress*, 8: 436–37. Burke's view of the
strength of the confederation has since been confirmed: John P. Kaminski and
Gaspare J. Saladino, Introduction, *The Documentary History of the Ratification
of the Constitution* (Madison: State Historical Society of Wisconsin, 1981), 13:
6–7. The historian David Ramsay also highlighted the extensive powers given
in the Articles: David Ramsay, *History of the American Revolution,* new ed.
(London: John Stockdale, 1793), 1: 356; *The Speech of the Hon. William Henry
Drayton* (Charlestown, SC: David Bruce, 1778), 4.

13. Charles Carroll of Carrollton (York) to Charles Carroll Sr.,
5 October 1777, Smith, *Letters of Delegates to Congress,* 8: 50; James Lovell
(York) to Horatio Gates, 5 October 1777, ibid., 8: 58; John Adams (York) to
Abigail Adams, 15 October 1777, ibid., 8: 123; Elbridge Gerry (York) to James
Warren, 28 October 1777, ibid., 8: 206; Richard Henry Lee (York) to Samuel
Adams, 15 November 1777, ibid., 8: 273; Cornelius Harnett (York) to Thomas
Burke, 20 November 1777, ibid., 8: 290.

14. Cornelius Harnett (York) to William Wilkinson, 30 November 1777,
ibid., 8: 348; James Duane (York) to George Clinton, 2 December 1777, ibid.,
8: 368; Ramsay, *History of the American Revolution,* 1: 357. Madison ascribed
the failure of the Dutch Confederation to similar causes; James Madison,
Weakness of the Confederation, 7 June 1788, Stagg, *Digital Madison Papers,*
Congressional Series, 11: 93; Thomas Jefferson, Answer to Démeunier's First
Queries, 24 January 1786, in Oberg and Looney, *Digital Jefferson Papers,* Main
Series, 10: 14; Thomas Jefferson (Paris) to John Adams, 28 September 1787,
ibid., 12: 189.

15. George Washington, Circular to the States, 8 June 1783, in *The
Writings of George Washington,* ed. John C. Fitzpatrick (Washington, DC:
Government Printing Office, 1938), 26: 483–96. For discussion of Washington's
perspective on government in this period, see Pauline Maier, *Ratification* (New
York: Simon and Schuster, 2010), 1–26.

16. To an underappreciated extent, that was what happened: J. Reuben
Clark Jr., *Emergency Legislation Passed Prior to December, 1917, Dealing with
the Control and Taking of Private Property for the Public Use, Benefit, or Welfare*
(Washington, DC: Government Printing Office, 1918). For some early examples
from Connecticut and Maryland, see "An Act to Encourage Fair Dealing, and
to Restrain and Punish Sharpers and Oppressors," *Acts and Laws of Connecticut*

(1777), 476; "An Act for the Regulation of the Prices of Labour, Produce, Manu-
factures, and Commodities within this State," *Acts and Laws of Connecticut*
(1778), 485; "An Act for Quartering Soldiers," *Laws of Maryland* (1777); "An
Act to Procure Cloathing for the Quota of this State of the American Army,
Laws of Maryland (1777); "A Supplementary Act to the Act, Entitled, An Act to
Regulate the Militia," *Laws of Maryland* (1777); "An Act to Procure a Supply of
Salt Meat for the Use of the Army," *Laws of Maryland* (1780); "An Act for the
Service of the United States," *Laws of Maryland* (1778). I owe this point to Bill
Novak. See our forthcoming cowritten piece, "Revolutionary State Formation:
The Origins of the Strong American State," in *State Formations: Histories and
Cultures of Global Statehood*, ed. John L. Brooke et al.

17. Here I disagree with the claims advanced by David Armitage, *The
Declaration of Independence: A Global History* (Cambridge: Harvard Univer-
sity Press, 2007). Washington, Circular, 8 June 1783, *Writings*, 26: 485; Ezra
Stiles (Newport) to Philip Furneaux, 12 April 1775, Beinecke, MS Vault Stiles,
Correspondence Box 12; William Hooper (Philadelphia) to James Iredell,
6 January 1776, Smith, *Letters of Delegates to Congress*, 3 (1978): 45.

18. Emmerich de Vattel, *The Law of Nations* (London: J. Coote, 1759),
1: 14, 36.

Index